Arsenal
THE OFFICIAL BIOGRAPHY

THE OFFICIAL BIOGRAPHY
The compelling story of an amazing club

STEVE STAMMERS

hamlyn

To my Mum and Dad Aimie and Arthur, my children Stephen and Melanie and my late uncle John Henry who was an Arsenal fanatic.

An **Hachette Livre UK Company**
www.hachettelivre.co.uk

First published in Great Britain in 2008 by
Hamlyn, a division of **Octopus Publishing Group Ltd**
2–4 Heron Quays, London E14 4JP
www.octopusbooks.co.uk

ISBN: 978-0-600-61892-8

A CIP catalogue record for this book is available from
the British Library

Printed and bound in Spain

10 9 8 7 6 5 4 3 2 1

'Arsenal' is a registered trademark of the
Arsenal Football Club PLC © 2008

Arsenal.com

Executive Editor **Trevor Davies**

Produced for Hamlyn by **Flanders Publishing**
Project Editor **Julian Flanders**
Designer **Craig Stevens**
Production **Nick Heal**

Contents

Foreword

When I arrived at Arsenal in 1996, I was aware of the respect in which the Club is held throughout the world and the success it had achieved. Everyone in world football had heard of players like Tony Adams, Ian Wright and Dennis Bergkamp and I felt very lucky to have inherited such a fantastic squad of talented players. But I did not fully understand the long history and tradition of Arsenal. However, it did not take me long to understand what the Club stood for and that success, secured in the right way, would be expected both on and off the pitch.

It is impossible to look back over the history of Arsenal Football Club without admiring Herbert Chapman's all-conquering team of the 1930s, that set the standard for the Club's tradition, innovation and success. I have always tried to follow these standards within my own teams and believe that with confidence you must also add humility and respect.

The Club's history, as this biography highlights, is full of colourful characters that have helped make it special. When I first arrived at Arsenal, I was lucky to have Pat Rice working alongside me, someone who had already been associated with the Club for three decades. His passion and love for Arsenal is infectious and can be seen in many other former players and staff who have remained here because of their fantastic loyalty. It is no surprise that former players such as Charlie George, Liam Brady, Steve Bould, and Gilles Grimandi returned to Arsenal after they retired from playing to help the Club build on its previous successes. This loyalty highlights just how special Arsenal is as a Club.

I have always been determined to build on this tradition and past successes whilst moving forward and continuing to develop the squad and Club to challenge for the highest honours. The players and staff here are proud of their club and I am determined to ensure that they can continue to be proud of our achievements and how these achievements are gained.

The *Biography* is the amazing story of a unique football club, much of it told through the characters that have helped make Arsenal one of the biggest clubs in world football. It gives me great pride to see my players continue the Arsenal tradition described in this book and take their place alongside the legends of this great football club.

Arsène Wenger
Manager, Arsenal Football Club

Chapter One

THEN AND NOW

Raise a glass to David Danskin
– without him there would be
no Arsenal Football Club

As the Arsenal players of today drive through the electronic gates at the Club's state-of-the-art training centre at London Colney and park their Porsches among the collection of Ferraris, Mercedes and BMWs, they might want to take a little time out and raise a glass of mineral water to David Danskin. Over their specially cooked meals prepared by a cordon bleu chef, it would do no harm to spare a thought for a man without whose determination, persuasive nature and sheer love of football, there would, quite simply, be no Arsenal Football Club and none of the luxury lifestyle that goes with the status of today's established professionals at one of world's top ten clubs. The comparison between the lifestyle of contemporary players and those who met on 1 December 1886 at the Royal Oak public house in Woolwich could not be more vivid.

'What a surprise, the club was formed in a pub,' exclaimed Arsène Wenger, the man who has taken the club to another level since his arrival from Japan in October 1996. 'I think everything in England is

somehow linked to a pub.' He has a point. But the birth of Arsenal is also heavily linked to a Scotsman forced south of the border by the lack of working opportunities in his native country.

On that December day in 1886, thanks largely to the enthusiasm of Danksin, Arsenal Football Club was formed. It was Danskin's Scottish accent that was heard above all others as the workers of the Woolwich Arsenal munitions factory in Dial Square met to discuss the formation of a football team to give themselves an escape from the dreary, drab and arduous work that was their lot on a daily basis. The weekly wage of the factory workers was around £1/10 shillings (£1.50). Danskin gave 3 shillings (15p) to bolster the 6 pence (2.5p) donated by the 15 other men who gathered at the pub that night, and they were able to buy a football.

Danskin had been born on 9 January 1863 in Back Street, Burntlisland. He was the second child of David Danskin and Janet Burton. He had an elder sister Magdalene and younger ones Christina, Janet and Betsy and two younger brothers Andrew and William. The family had lived in Burntisland for three years. Danskin's father worked in the railway workshops in what had become a ferry port and important railway terminus. But decent accommodation was, at best, at a premium – with narrow, grey streets and houses mostly filled with cold, damp rooms. Danskin senior left to go to Kirkcaldy where he continued his trade as an iron turner. By now the family had moved to Leslie a few miles away and David junior found the cramped living conditions less than tolerable. At the age of 18, he too found lodgings in Kirkcaldy. He was an apprentice engine fitter. But he wanted a better, more rewarding life and moved to London in 1885. At the age of 22, he started work at the Woolwich munitions factory.

He missed his family, of course. But he also missed his 'fitba'. Kent, the Garden of England and the home county of Woolwich, was a cricket and tennis area with rugby as the winter sport. None of these appealed to Danskin – but he eventually found two welcome allies in Fred Beardsley and Morris Bates who shared his passion for football. Both had played for Nottingham Forest but had moved to Woolwich in search of more financially rewarding work at the munitions factory. They had worked at an ordnance factory close to Trent Bridge and their arrival in London was just the incentive that Danskin needed. Between them there was no dream of glory, no fierce ambition to become the best in the country. What Danskin and his workmates wanted was a football team and, through that, a social club. Its first name was Dial Square, the location of the munitions factory.

With no home ground, the first match was staged a ferry ride from Woolwich on the Isle of Dogs on 11 December 1886. The kit was an assortment put together by the players and the match was against Eastern Wanderers on a pitch that bore no resemblance to the manicured lawn of a surface that graces Emirates Stadium today. There was an open sewer running across one-third of the playing surface, which was oblong in shape and had no markings. An extra match-fee was levied to have the mud cleaned from the dressing room after the game. Back gardens provided the boundaries to the rest of the pitch. As the secretary at the time, Elijah Watkins noted, 'I could not venture to say what shape the pitch was, because when the ball was not in the back gardens, it was in the ditch. Our players looked as though they had been clearing out the mud chute when they had done playing.' There were no pitch markings, no crossbars and no team colours. And there seems to have been some dispute about the score, though Dial Square claimed a 6–0 victory. Some start – but Danskin, the driving force behind the team, knew that progress had to be made and made quickly. They needed a name, colours and a permanent ground. All had to be sorted out. And so it was on Christmas Day 1886 back at the Royal Oak.

With the strong connection with Nottingham Forest – already an established and successful club – the colours were easily decided, red. Several players had already played for Forest and had kept their shirts. Next to come was a full kit, thanks to goalkeeper Beardsley. He spent a weekend off back at his old club and returned with a set of redcurrant shirts – the same as those replicated by the Club for their last season at Highbury – and another ball. Danskin could not disguise his delight. This was his dream coming true. He was captain, a more than decent player, and now the club was beginning to take shape. But there was still business to attend to, not least the name of the newly formed club. For the first game they had played as Dial Square and several players were keen to retain the name as it acknowledged what they were – a works team located in Dial Square. But the square was only one part of the munitions factory and others who worked in different parts of the facility objected. Enter one RB Thompson, who was speaking from a position of some strength after scoring the first-ever goal for the club in the match against Eastern Wanderers. The left winger was the only member of the team who was not employed at the munitions factory. He was a teacher and the youngest member of the team. With the debate becoming increasingly intense, Thompson offered his thoughts with a question that brought a moment's silence. 'Who,' he asked, 'outside of Woolwich, has heard of Dial Square? But who has NOT heard of the Royal Arsenal?' That was the end of the argument. Royal Arsenal it was.

A venue then had to be found for the club's first match under its new name and it was decided to play at Plumstead Common. A match against Erith was duly arranged for 8 January 1887. Because the Royal Artillery used the Common as a practice ground, it was again a less than ideal surface – stony and rutted as well as uneven. But they had managed to acquire a set of goalposts, which were kept in Beardsley's back garden. They came in useful that day as Royal Arsenal ran in another six goals, this time with one in reply. They finished the season with seven wins and two defeats in ten games.

The Danskin connection

The voice at the other end of the telephone had a distinct Australian twang. Matthew Danskin, a 23-year-old sales representative, could not disguise his pride at the strong family connection between him and Arsenal Football Club.

'When I think that someone from our family played such a big part in creating it, well, it is something to treasure,' said the midfield player with Perth Soccer Club who is the great, great, great nephew of David Danskin. But he was also remarkable candid. 'I have to be honest, though, it wasn't until just over a year ago that I became aware of the connection.

I had no idea that my relative from all those years ago had contributed so much to the formation of Arsenal.'

Matthew has inherited the football gene through the generations. He was headhunted by Werder Bremen and also had trials at Leeds, Rotherham and Sheffield Wednesday. Work permit problems prevented him from pursuing a career in Europe and he now plays for Perth on a part-time basis. His father – Andrew – played for Leeds before emigrating and the family are rightly proud of their new-found connection. 'I mean,' said Matthew, 'Arsenal are not just a football club are they? They are a worldwide organization. But I have to admit that I was totally unaware of the association until last year when a friend of mine's girlfriend went on to the Internet and discovered that my great, great, great uncle had been honoured in Scotland. I was gobsmacked. We are a kind of understated family, not one that goes bragging about things. So no one had said a word to me over the years. When I now look into the history of the Club, well, the way it has evolved is staggering. What did they play next to? A sewer? And now they play at a fantastic stadium like Emirates. The worst of the worst to the best of the best, I suppose. What I would love to do now is visit Emirates. It will mean just that little bit more.'

But Matthew did have an admission to make – because his father played for Leeds, it is at Elland Road where his allegiance lies. 'All these years, I have been supporting Leeds whenever they played Arsenal.'

Early characters

On 19 November 1887 the Club's first ever match against Tottenham took place on Tottenham Marshes. Royal Arsenal lost 2-1 despite taking an early lead. It was thanks to Beardsley in goal that Tottenham were restricted to just the two. But support was growing, not least from their co-workers at the munitions factory. In order to cope with the new interest in the Club, a permanent ground was needed and they opted to move to the Sportsman Ground on Plumstead Marshes. This was an old pig farm on the fringes of the marshes and the drainage was often found wanting. There had been heavy rain before their first match at the venue in February 1888 against Millwall. The pitch was, in a word, unplayable. However, there was some dry ground nearby at Manor Field not far from Plumstead Station. Jack Humble, one of the players, went to see the owner – Mr Walton – and he agreed to its being used as a football pitch. For the next two years Arsenal played there. Step by step, what David Danskin had thought of as a mere recreation outlet for the workers at a munitions factory, was becoming a Club to be reckoned with in London.

Danskin's connection with Arsenal ended in the 1893 season. He was still active in local football after that date, but in 1901 he left the munitions factory and set up a cycle business in Plumstead. He sold up six years later and moved to Coventry where he became an examiner at the newly formed Standard Motor company. But throughout a life that showed both stubbornness and courage he was always associated with Arsenal. When Arsenal won the FA Cup in 1936, his employers honoured him with a celebration dinner. But he had listened to a radio broadcast of the final, in which Arsenal beat Sheffield United 1–0, from his sickbed. His toils in combining work and football had begun to take their toll as he experienced serious problems with his legs and had to spend an increasing amount of time in hospital. However, he was one tough individual. During one stay in the Gulson Road Hospital in Coventry, he was advised that gangrene had been detected in one of his legs and that it should be amputated. Danskin gave the doctor a searing look. 'I have got two legs now,' he said, 'and if I am going to die, then it will be with two legs.' Needless to say, both legs survived intact, although he was in constant pain and was forced to retire.

And what the years of football and hard work in the factory had failed to do – kill the undaunted spirit of an exceptional man – the Luftwaffe also fell short. Danskin's house in North Street was severely damaged when the Germans blitzed the city in 1940 and the family had to evacuate without delay. Though Danskin survived the bombing, his treasured souvenirs did not. He kept all his jerseys, medals and valuables along with family photographs in a steel trunk. When he returned to the house to survey the damage the day after the bombing, that chest had been lost. He was devastated. With his failing health, Danskin needed daily hospital treatment and eventually, in 1942, he was admitted on a permanent basis. He died on 4 August 1948 aged 85 – a ripe old age for someone who had lived through the toughest of economic and social times. But his contribution to the life of Arsenal will never be forgotten. On 23 July 2007, Arsenal Scotland organized for a plaque to be placed in Burntisland to commemorate the birthplace of the man who founded and was the first captain of the Club. Guests at a special unveiling ceremony included former Arsenal goalkeeper and goalkeeping coach Bob Wilson, and Danskin's grandson, Richard Wyatt, who travelled over from Canada. The plaque is in the Kirkgate at the corner of Somerville Street close to where Danskin was born in 1863.

Another memorable player and colourful character who emerged in the early years was Andy Ducat – arguably Arsenal's first-pin-up boy in the days when glamour and grime were rarely entwined. Those were the days when the ability to excel in two sports was a godsend. Ducat swelled his income in the summer through playing cricket and indeed won one England cricket cap to go with the six that he earned playing for the England football team.

He was born in the year that the club was founded – 1886 – in Brixton, South London. He played for non-league Southend United before joining what had then become Woolwich Arsenal in 1905. He made his Arsenal debut on 11 February 1905 in a 2–0 win against Blackburn Rovers as a striker, and by all accounts made something of a favourable impression. Later Ducat himself was to recall that debut. 'I was nervous, very nervous and I didn't think I had played that well because of it. But I read one of the dailies, which gave me something of a surprise. They said I was, "A well set-up, clean-limbed player who was quite raw but had good potential".' He lost his place as a front man the following season but showed great tenacity and determination to force his way back into the first-team picture, this time as a midfielder. In the seasons 1907/08 and 1908/09 he established himself once again as a regular. During his time at Arsenal, he won three England caps – making his debut as a half back in February 1910 in Belfast against Ireland in a 1–1 draw. A month later, he scored the only goal in a 1–0 win against Wales at the Arms Park in Cardiff.

Arsenal had managed to emerge intact from a demanding era in English history. By definition, the hub of the Club was the munitions factory in Woolwich where most of the players worked and which also provided its fan base. The Boer War in South Africa created problems for both. The war effort meant more arms were needed on top of those already produced to keep the vast British Empire intact, and this obviously had a major impact on Arsenal. Between the start of the Boer conflict in 1899 and its finish three years later, there was an enormous drain on resources both on and off the field at Arsenal. Increased shifts were the major problem because they tapped into both the pool of players available to play and the support, the majority of which was made up of munitions workers. Indeed, the club's record win – a 12–0 thrashing of Loughborough Town on 12 March 1900 – was witnessed by less than 1,000 people.

But after winning promotion to the First Division in 1904, they were able to sign more quality players like Ducat. He became the star of the Arsenal team in those years, but the Club did not then enjoy the status they have now. Back then, when one of the more established clubs came knocking, Arsenal had to listen. As they did when Aston Villa wanted Ducat. In June 1912, Arsenal were experiencing a period of financial difficulties, and Ducat was sold to Villa for £1,000. Ducat went on to enjoy a remarkable career in football and cricket. He recovered from a broken leg to captain Villa to the club's sixth FA Cup win in 1920 and even regained his England place, winning three more caps to go with the trio he won at Arsenal, despite a ten-year gap. He fell out with his employers who wanted him to move nearer to Birmingham, and moved to Fulham in 1921. Three years later he retired from playing and took over as manager at Craven Cottage. But he was not management material and was sacked after two years in charge. He also finished playing cricket professionally when he left Surrey in 1931 after scoring 52 centuries. When he retired he filled the prestigious post of cricket coach at Eton College as well as becoming a sports reporter. Even in death, Ducat captured the headlines. In 1942, he was playing for the Surrey Home Guard against the Sussex Home Guard at Lord's and was not out at lunch. During the interval, he suffered a heart attack and died. He was 56. The match was abandoned and he remains to this day the only person in history to have died during a match at Lord's.

Training then and now

Just what training facilities were available to the likes of Danskin and Ducat is not clear – but they would probably have revolved around one football, a bumpy and arguably treacherous expanse of waste ground and unwieldy boots with a huge bar across the sole – more Dr Martens that Predator. The contrast today just could not be greater. Rather than the smokey, sulphurous air of the open space at Woolwich munitions yard, the Arsenal players of today enjoy a more healthy and secure environment – as the training centre at London Colney shows.

The first clue that the real world of the overcrowded M25 is left behind comes at the entrance to the complex. Huge electronic gates bar the way and access can only be gained when visitors are cleared through an intercom. The first impression is one of sheer space and tranquility – and a car park that would do credit to the Earls Court Motor Show. On the days when the first team squad is there, there must be close to £3 million worth of automobiles parked up. They make an impressive display and provide a true reflection of the wealth in the modern game. It's a far cry from the meeting in the Royal Oak public house all those years ago when Danskin had to fork out his own hard-earned cash to ensure that the team had a football. Inside the reception at the mightily impressive main building at the complex, close-circuit television allows the staff the monitor who is coming and going along the narrow strip of road that links the outside world to the training ground.

'Security,' stressed Sean O'Connor whose job it is to manage the centre, 'is paramount these days, so essential.' O'Connor used to oversee the running of the sports facilities for the University of Westminster before joining Arsenal when the complex was opened in 1999. A conducted tour of the facility is breathtaking. There is a story that goes back to the day that Barnet were the opposition in a closed-doors match at London Colney to help Tony Adams back to fitness. After the game, hospitality was laid on in the restaurant that takes up most of the first floor of the main building. 'My god' – or words to that effect – said one of the Barnet players when he looked at the food on offer and the panoramic view across the centre that the huge windows offered. 'How much is a weekend here, all-inclusive?' On a tour it is easy to see why the Barnet player was so impressed.

The first-team changing room is the first port of call. 'The dressing rooms at Emirates are designed on what we have here in terms of colours and styles. We have heated floors in the winter and you will see that the lockers don't have doors on them. That was Mr Wenger's idea,' explains O'Connor. 'Why?' 'Because if two people are having a conversation and someone comes and stands between them and opens his locker, end of conversation, because the door is in the way. He wants people to converse, to interact and to be able to speak to each other at all times.'

When Arsenal were planning the new training centre, Arsène Wenger flew with the chairman Peter Hill-Wood and directors Danny Fiszman and Ken Friar to the top training grounds in Europe – Bayern Munich, AC Milan, Auxerre. He took the best from them and put them into practice at London Colney. Everything is available to the players, and everything has its use. When boots are finished with, they are collected and sent to the Ivory Coast, the homeland of defender Kolo Toure, where they are much needed and most welcome.

The training ground has ten pitches, all up to the standard outlined by the FA. 'And whether they are for the first team or the under-18s, they are all of the same size and have the same quality of grass,' said O'Connor. 'They have all got undersoil drainage and two of the first team pitches have got undersoil heating. Snow, frost – not a problem. It makes no difference in terms of preparation.'

If there is a training complex that runs Arsenal a close second, it is perhaps the Chelsea facility at Cobham. That should come as no surprise because Chelsea's oligarch owner Roman Abramovich visited the London Colney site and was so impressed that he used it as a blueprint for his own club's centre. In total, London Colney covers 143 acres of land of which the playing surfaces take up 25 acres. The Club has also planted 45 acres of forestry – that is 28,000 trees. There are fourteen groundsmen, two gardeners and five staff who work in the kitchen. Five more staff service the building during the day and there are six cleaners and two security men. With the luxury, however, comes the criticism that the players are in their own enclave and totally out of touch with a public who, years ago, would come along to watch them train. Not now. 'They say we have become untouchable,' said O'Connor. 'I'm not being funny here, but if you have a million pounds in your house, would you lock it away or would you leave it sitting on the side. That is how you have to look at it, whether it is £3 million worth of cars in the cark park or whether it is the valuables in the dressing room. You can't leave your front door open like you used to be able to do.'

The facilities have been designed with the primary purpose of getting the players to fitness and complete readiness for matches. In the steam room eucalyptus has been added to the water so it keeps heads clear, and there are showers with three-bar pressure. In the treatment area is a swimming pool. But this is not just any swimming pool. 'It is for rehabilitation and it has a moveable floor,' said O'Connor. 'That means we can change the depth of the pool depending on the height of the player and the resistance we want. Whether they are swimming, running, recovering from a lower or upper body injury we can change the depth of the pool to suit the purpose. There are four windows at eye level with the bottom of the pool, two at each end. This means the physio can keep an eye on the player making sure they doing the right exercises. When Robert Pires was coming back from injury the physio could see that he was turning too much to the right to compensate for his injury, so the floor of the pool was adjusted. These kind of adjustments can help a player get back to fitness earlier.' There are also power baths that Wenger spotted when visiting Bayern Munich. Each bath does the work of a masseur, but costs a cool £18,000.

At the other end of the main building is the area where the youth players congregate. And decorating the walls are pictures of famous home-growns from the past to act as an inspiration for the youth players of today. Ray Parlour is there as, obviously, is Tony Adams. And Ashley Cole. 'Why not?' said O'Connor voicing the opinion of a

Club where they do not air-brush history just because it involves a player like Cole who, it must be said, did not leave Arsenal on the best of terms after his unseemly transfer to Chelsea. 'He stays on the wall,' said O'Connor. 'He was a successful product of our academy and whether the fans love him or hate him, while he was here he gave 100 per cent. He had been at Arsenal since he was seven years of age.'

It is not only a football education that the youngsters at Arsenal receive. Go back to the days of Danskin and company and maybe there was the occasional talented apprentice. The problem was he was an apprentice in metalwork, not football. These days, academic and sporting education go hand in hand and Arsenal have the facilities to cope. 'Their target when they come here is to get a two-year scholarship,' explained O'Connor. 'And they will enjoy facilities that many clubs would love to have in their main stadium, never mind the training ground.'

Next door is the gym – and a machine that looks as if it would not be out of place in a seaside arcade. 'It's called a batter machine and the idea is to punch out lights that come up as quickly as they appear. You have to get so many lights in 50 seconds but you know if you don't move your lower body, you don't get a good score. You remember when you used to see Patrick Vieira glide through the middle of the pitch and he'd clear every tackle? Well, these machines develop that body movement. That machine cost £7,000 but it is a great investment. The best ever at it has to have been Thierry Henry. He could hit 50 lights in 21 seconds.'

All this training is hungry work – and Arsenal have the perfect answer – their restaurant where the food is prepared by cordon bleu chef Rob Fagg and his four staff. There is also a lounge with a plasma television and a selection of newspapers. The walls are decorated with photographs of heroes of past and recent triumphs: Alan Smith with the European Cup-Winners' Cup, former captain and now assistant manager Pat Rice and Tony Adams with goalkeeper John Lukic after that famous 2–0 win at Anfield in 1989. And, as O'Connor is quick to point out, the whole place is decorated in light colours. 'You don't see a lot of fierce reds. These are all calming colours – colours that are easy-going. And there are big windows that let in lots of light and allow the players to look out over the training pitches. The boss likes natural light.' In fact, everything you see is down to the boss, one Arsène Wenger, even to the type of chairs at the tables. He said no to the wooden ones he was shown. 'Footballers are big guys – athletes,' he said. 'These chairs won't last six months. They will forever need to be repaired.' So they bought metal-framed chairs and went for some which had a degree of comfort. 'After all,' argued Wenger, 'we might have a team meeting for an hour and we are going to lose their attention if they are uncomfortable.'

Across from the main building is the education centre, used mainly by the youngsters, but which doubles as a media centre for press conferences. 'Originally, there was talk of it being a dormitory where the boys could stay, a bit like the one they have at Ajax. But the cost factor and the return of that investment didn't seem worth it,' said O'Connor. So the Club sticks to the tried and trusted system of using families to house the boys from outside London. 'There are eight classrooms, all kitted out with computers, and we have six tutors that come in. We can provide the players with two years' worth of education. Many get two A-levels in that period. Sebastian Larsson did that and so did Moritz Volz.'

Wenger's office in the main building has the look of a first-class lounge at an airport. 'We had to make it bigger than it was originally,' said O'Connor. 'I mean these days players turn up with agents and lawyers and we just had to make more room.' And from that room Wenger can see the latest addition to the training complex – the indoor centre. 'We don't play games in here,' said O'Connor, under what from the outside looks like half a giant hot air balloon. 'This is for fitness and conditioning work. Obviously, if the weather is really bad outside and it's snowing or it's really windy, the younger players can come here. It is, in fact, the same surface that England played on in Moscow in their European Championships qualifier in 2008 and the squad trained on it before they went out there. We also have a Community Programme which means the local authority can make use of it.' Just as birdwatchers – yes, birdwatchers – can make use of the training ground. 'We open up the whole site to birdwatchers twice a year. It is like 45 acres of wildlife sanctuary. You are sitting there and one minute there are bunny rabbits going past and the next there is the biggest pheasant you have ever seen. We also have lakes stocked with carp, about a hundred of them.'

This might seem strange, but on a walk down to the first-team training pitches the overriding impression is one of tranquility. 'Great isn't it,' said O'Connor who revealed that the immaculate playing surfaces – the same as at Emirates Stadium – are used for five days and then left for ten days to allow for growth and then trimming. The undersoil heating means no matter how severe the cold, the pitch will be playable. Again, this was at the insistence of Wenger whose eye for detail is evident throughout the centre. And what Arsenal have built has made a huge impact on the people that matter – the first-team players and other high profile visitors that use the facilities. 'I have got a letter in my office that I am very proud of on behalf of everyone who works here,' said O'Connor. 'The Brazilians trained here and they wrote to me saying the pitches were the best they had trained or played on anywhere in the world. That is some compliment. Countries like Ukraine, Scotland, Argentina and Germany have already trained here and England use it for preparation ahead of home games and before they travel abroad. It is because we can give these teams the perfect surface on which to prepare. There is never any mud in the goalmouths or anything like that. It doesn't matter what time of the year they come, the pitches will always be in top shape and never a problem.'

The investment, clearly, is playing off.

Chapter Two

FROM PLUMSTEAD TO HIGHBURY

Henry Norris – ruthless, ambitious – and chairman of Arsenal Football Club

I t is easy to think that football, with its universal appeal and its grip on the working classes, was always as it is now. But nothing could be further from the truth. Back in 1886, for example, there was no need for crossbars, players in the team were not required to wear the same shirts and, apart from a halfway line, there were no markings on the pitch. It was also the first year of professionalism in England – a development that met with fierce opposition from Scotland who went as far as to ban their players from having any connection with the clubs on the other side of Hadrian's Wall. Indeed, during an England v Scotland game in Glasgow that year, James Forrest, a professional with Blackburn Rovers, the dominant force of the time, who completed three successive FA Cup wins that year, was forced to wear a different colour shirt from the rest of the England players to make it clear he was not an amateur.

This was the definitive era of Victoriana with the Empire expanding and the Irish Question, which was to bedevil English governments for the next century, was nearing its peak. Woolwich was a key area for the military and the work on offer encouraged migration to south-east London from all round the country and, fatefully where Arsenal were concerned, from Scotland. But at the end of their first season Royal Arsenal had lost only two of ten matches. The fuse had been lit and progress was impressive. So impressive that within seven years, the Club had become members of the Football League. They had earned their status with some shrewd management off the pitch and relative success on it. They were semi-finalists in the London Senior Cup in 1889 (beaten 2–0 by Clapton) and the following season pulled off an impressive treble – the Kent Senior Cup, the Kent Junior Cup and the London Charity Cup. In what was still an all-amateur sport in London, Arsenal had the advantage of offering jobs at the munitions factory to players they wanted to add to their team. It was also not unknown for the management at the factory to buy footballing soldiers out of the army and install them in a job in the munitions works.

The arrival of professionalism

Success brought other problems, most notably that of finding a bigger ground. Manor Field had no proper facilities either for the supporters or the players. So in 1890 Royal Arsenal moved to the Invicta Ground on the other side of Plumstead High Street. The new ground had a stand, terraces and changing rooms. On Easter Monday 1891 more than 12,000 fans turned up to see them play Scottish champions Heart of Midlothian. But Arsenal's stay at the Invicta was short-lived. Following the Club's election to the Football League in 1893 the owner of the ground – George Weaver – sensing that there was more money to be made, asked for an increase in rent from £250 to £350 a year. But Arsenal wouldn't play ball. Instead, the Club and its supporters mustered enough money to repurchase their old ground (now renamed as the Manor Ground) and spent the summer of 1893 preparing for the start of the Second Division programme. And that is where they would stay for the next two decades.

Their progress into League Football was an important chapter in the Club's history. Two years earlier, the committee were becoming increasingly alarmed at the ease with which their best players were being headhunted by professional clubs. Royal Arsenal, of course, were still amateurs – give or take the regular expenses – and therefore players were not under any obligation to stay should one of the professional clubs in the fledgling league make them an offer. To compound this, defeats in a number of friendly matches against professional clubs, like Nottingham Forest and Hearts, during the 1890/91 season showed that the team was struggling to compete. It was a problem that exercised full back and committee member John Humble in particular. The London FA had a deep-seated suspicion of the 'northern' professional game and none of the clubs in and around London were prepared to challenge their stance against payments for players.

Humble, born in County Durham in 1862 and left without parents who died within months of each other in 1880, had decided to come south with his brother to look for work. While the Empire was expanding in Asia and Africa to bring untold wealth to a select few, the likes of Jack Humble had to do what they could to make ends meet. So, with no money for the train fare, they walked. The brothers found jobs as engine fitters at the munitions factory in Woolwich and Jack also became involved in the football club. His determination was again in evidence at the Club's momentous Annual General Meeting in 1891 held at the Windsor Castle Music Hall. Humble suggested that the Club turn professional, a plan that was accepted by a huge majority. The same meeting rejected a plan for the Club to become a limited company. Humble said at the time, 'The Club has been carried on by working men and it is my ambition to see it carried on by them.' He reasoned that such a step would wrest control of the Club from the people who had founded it and whose spirit was, to him, all-important.

The south of England's first professional club was to be known as Woolwich Arsenal, the 'Royal' tag thought to be somehow disrespectful for such an organization. Predictably, Arsenal's decision to embrace professionalism was met with horror and alarm by the strictly amateur London FA. They were immediately expelled from the London FA and banned from all competitions that came under its umbrella. This included the London Senior Cup, of which they were the holders. Effectively, this meant that Woolwich Arsenal had only one trophy to contest – the FA Cup – the rest of the fixture list would need to be made up of friendlies. And the FA Cup proved no early friend to the new professionals. They played their first tie in January 1892 and were hammered 5–1 by a club from the Midlands by the name of Small Heath – now better known as Birmingham City. Twelve months on and the Club missed out again on much-needed proceeds from the oldest cup competition in the world by losing 6–0 to Sunderland.

Election to the Football League

Enough was enough and Arsenal set about the search for other clubs in the south-east with which to form their own version of the Football League. Feedback was good with 12 clubs agreeing in principle to such an arrangement at a meeting on 24 February 1892 at Anderson's Hotel in Fleet Street (the same one used when the Football League was formed in 1888). The clubs were Chatham, Chiswick Park, Crouch End, Ilford, Luton, Marlow, Millwall, Old St Marks, Reading, Swindon, West Herts (now Watford) and Arsenal. Tottenham, however, were not elected as they mustered only one supporting vote. But the idea was met with unprecedented hostility by the London FA who threatened to do the same to the 11 other clubs as they had already done to Arsenal and throw them out. The threat worked and Arsenal were left with no local fixtures and very little income. They had no options left but to apply to join the Football League. Luck, for once, was on their side. For the 1892/93 season, the Football League decided to extend the Second Division from 12 to 15 clubs. And the three slots became five when two teams relegated from the First Division – Bootle and Accrington – considered it beneath them to play in a lower division. Five clubs joined the Football League that summer – Arsenal, Newcastle United, Rotherham, Liverpool and Middlesbrough. On reflection that was arguably the most significant close season in the history of League Football in this country. Arsenal, Liverpool and Newcastle were all brought into the fold – clubs that between them went on to win 20 of the next 80 league championships – a remarkable statistic.

Normally, such a huge influx of new clubs would not have been possible. Suddenly there were vacancies on a considerable scale. Maybe this was the origin of the 'Lucky Arsenal' tag that was to be the Club's burden for so many years. Also, they were based in the south and the League Management Committee could see the obvious benefits of having a club based in the capital. With transport now much easier, fixtures could be fulfilled in a way that could not have been contemplated some 20 years earlier. The League was also appreciative of the stand Arsenal had taken in turning professional. Indeed, by the summer of 1893, even the die-hard Scots were forced to admit that the tide of professionalism was one they could no longer resist.

For Arsenal, as for most of the fledgling football clubs, there was a continual need to raise money – for players, equipment and running costs on the Manor Ground. The decision was taken to form a limited liability company. There were objections from within because the players and supporters felt that the running of the club would be taken out of their hands. But in the close season of 1893, the company was formed with the issue of 4,000 shares at one pound each. A total of 860 people bought 1,552 shares with the remainder un-issued. One fear was allayed – the majority of the shares went to workers at the factory who obviously lived locally. Indeed there were only three individuals who had 20 or more shares and a local coffee house owner acquired the largest single allocation of 50. The first board of directors made impressive reading – a surgeon, a builder and six engineers from the munitions factory. But that, as it turned out, was the easy bit. For the next two decades there was almost anonymity as Woolwich Arsenal established themselves in the Football League. True, they did have Harry Storer in goal between 1894 and 1895 and he became the first Arsenal player to win representative honours when he played for the Football League against the Scottish League in April 1895.

However, Arsenal never threatened to reach the First Division as they enjoyed a mid-table existence in the second tier.

Promotion to the First Division

At one time Arsenal were the only professional club in London and their status in the metropolis did afford some advantages when players in the region opted to try their luck at the new professional game. Then there was the Boer War between 1899 and 1902. Arsenal, by definition, were a club with a fierce military tradition and background and such a vast commitment in South Africa was bound to have a substantial effect. The munitions factory, to cope with the demand of the war, brought in a Saturday afternoon shift. Already, players and supporters had been taken out of the area by the conflict. Now the traditional football afternoon was badly hit by the national cause. At that time – with away fans almost unheard of – it was an unwritten rule that workers finished early on a Saturday, went for a pint and on to the football. All that changed and the football club just had to cope. It goes some way to explaining why, in those early years of its existence, Arsenal could not develop into a major force. They did reasonably in the circumstances, however, and their remote location – still regarded as an outpost by the teams from the Midlands and the North – gave them an edge. They tasted defeat only 13 times at home in their first five seasons. But, by 1908, there were four others from London in the League – Clapton Orient, Fulham, Tottenham and Chelsea.

Woolwich Arsenal finished their first campaign in the newly formed Second Division with 28 points from 28 games, ending up in ninth place out of 15. It was an acceptable start. As well as Storer, there was another international player who came through in those early seasons – the improbably named Caesar Llewellyn Jenkyns. He had the honour of being the first Arsenal player to be an international when he was chosen to play for Wales against Scotland in 1896. But both he and Storer caught the eye of more glamorous clubs and left within a year – Storer to Liverpool and Jenkyns to

Newton Heath (later to be renamed Manchester United). Arsenal's lack of progress towards the top of the football tree was further highlighted when Arsenal were put out of the FA Cup by then non-league Millwall 4–2 in January 1896. The committee decided to appoint a secretary-manager, one TB Mitchell from Blackburn, though soon afterwards he was replaced by George Elcoat from Stockton. But it was his successor, Harry Bradshaw, who was to emerge as the first top-drawer manager of the Club.

Bradshaw acted fast and he acted firmly. He brought in Jimmy Ashcroft from Sheppey United – the first Arsenal player to be capped by England – to replace Storer. Another significant signing was an Australian full back Jimmy Jackson. Times were both changing and improving with crowds on the rise (the first four-figure gate receipts were collected at an FA Cup clash with Sheffield United in February 1903) and in 1904, under Bradshaw's shrewd guidance, the Club was promoted to the First Division after finishing second behind Preston North End. Tommy Shanks was the leading scorer with 25 league goals and the team included Percy Sands, a teacher from Woolwich, and Archie Cross from Dartford.

Arrival of Henry Norris

But this success was tempered rather during the summer of 1904 when Bradshaw left to become manager of Fulham. In fact, it was the start of a remarkable relationship between the two clubs. Fulham, a club with hard cash at the time, recruited nine of their first 14 managers from the playing or management staff at Arsenal. Five years after Bradshaw, his successor Phil Kelso also made the change from red to white. Kelso initially said he was quitting the Club to run a hotel back in his native Scotland but replaced Bradshaw at Craven Cottage within a month. Money troubles too appeared on the horizon at the Manor Ground. Despite two FA Cup semi-final appearances (losing to Newcastle in 1908 and to Sheffield Wednesday the following season) Arsenal were not financially buoyant and manager George

Morrell – who had taken over from Kelso – found himself in a no-win situation. The club needed money and the best players were sold. The inevitable result was a decline both in the success on the pitch and the gates. Among the players who left was a young inside forward called Charles Buchan who had a row with the Club over expenses. Buchan believed he was entitled to 11 shillings (55p) but the Club disagreed. Buchan left to join Sunderland, becoming the club's top scorer for seven successive seasons and becoming an England international before returning to Arsenal in 1925. By 1910 Arsenal was close to bankruptcy and was put up for sale. Enter Henry Norris, one of the most controversial figures in the Club's history and another man with strong Fulham connections.

Norris, from a working class background, was born in Kennington, south London in July 1865. He left school at 14 to join a firm of solicitors, leaving the company a year later to pursue – at the age of 15 – a career in property development. It was a stunning success story. To call Norris an opportunist would not be doing him justice; such was his rapid rise to wealth. He made his fortune in building, buying and selling houses in south and west London, and in Fulham in particular. He was commissioned into the 2nd Tower Hamlets Rifle Volunteers in 1896 but resigned the following year. He was elected Mayor of the Metropolitan Borough of Fulham for ten years between 1909 and 1919. He was also Conservative MP for Fulham East from 1918 to 1922. In 1917 he was knighted and given the honorary rank of Colonel for his services to his country in the Great War during which he had acted as a recruitment officer for the British Army. He was a prominent Freemason and rose to become the Grand Deacon of the United Grand Lodge of England. He was a well-known philanthropist and, with his close connections to the Church of England, became a personal friend of Randall Thomas Davidson, the Archbishop of Canterbury. He was a football fanatic and his first major involvement was as a director at Fulham. During his time at the club they were promoted from the Southern League to the Football League. He also played a significant part in the formation of Chelsea Football Club when he rejected an offer from local businessman Gus Mears to move Fulham to Stamford Bridge – and Mears then opted to found a club of his own.

When Arsenal's financial problems became all too obvious Norris spotted an opening too good to miss. His business acumen went into overdrive in 1910. His powers of persuasion had already been evident in the way that Fulham were elected to the Football League in 1907 when they secured by some distance the largest number of votes – 28 – and were chosen to replace Burton Albion. Through his business dealings, he mastered the art of making useful contacts, and one of them was John McKenna, president of the League Management Committee. Norris was a single-minded individual who stood for no kind of opposition in business or in the boardroom. As Leslie Knighton, Arsenal manager when Norris was chairman between 1919 and 1925, said in his autobiography, 'I soon found out that everyone was afraid of Sir Henry – and no wonder. I have never met his equal for logic, invective and ruthlessness. When I disagreed with him at board meetings and had to stand up for what I knew was best for the Club, he used to flay me with words until I was reduced to a fuming, helpless silence. Afterwards, Sir Henry would ask my advice, smile, wheedle and I was falling over myself to help him again. Those board meetings took years off my life.'

Fulham or Arsenal?

Norris, like many people with working class backgrounds, had long harboured a grudge against the Midlands and northern domination of the national winter sport. His plan was to form a club that would compete with the best that Birmingham, Manchester, Newcastle and Liverpool had to offer. He had tried Fulham but eventually came to the conclusion that the power, finances and fan base of that affluent area of south-west London would still not sustain a club with such lofty ambitions. For instance, by 1910, Fulham were in debt to the tune of £3,000, a significant sum in pre-First World War England. Arsenal were not in much better shape at the time, of course. But Norris had an idea – he would amalgamate the clubs. Arsenal were in a susceptible position after escaping relegation to the Second Division by a mere two points. His plan was to re-locate Arsenal to Craven Cottage and combine the resources of both clubs. That would mean First Division football in Fulham. The League, not surprisingly, rejected the proposal outright. But Norris came up with yet another proposal that would halve the costs and still give Craven Cottage top-flight football – Arsenal and Fulham could share the Cottage and play on alternate Saturdays. Opposition came immediately from the other London clubs and the scheme was abandoned. It had also occurred to the League that there was the prospect of a major conflict of interest – to have one man as chairman of two clubs. They told him he had to choose and, fatefully from Arsenal's point of view, he chose the club in Woolwich. He remained a director at Fulham and the Fulham chairman William Hall became a director of Arsenal. Their First Division status was no doubt a factor when Norris made his decision – although in 1913, Arsenal finished bottom of the First Division.

On the move again

Norris and Hall decided that it was time for action. And their plans were to have historic repercussions for the Club when they decided Arsenal would have to move. Plumstead, although close to London, was a nightmare journey for fans and visiting teams alike. 'Arsenal are a team that plays at the end of the earth,' reported one northern provincial newspaper. Norris wanted a location where the Club could tap into a more substantial population base and where a bigger stadium could generate much-needed revenue. After all, Arsenal had finished the 1913 season with the grand sum of £19 in the bank.

Norris had decreed that the new stadium had to be in the environs of London, that public transport provided easy access and that it needed to be in a heavily populated area to tap into a new fan base while not alienating the core support that had grown in Woolwich over the years. That support, co-incidentally, was regarded as among the most passionate and hard-nosed in the League. After all these were mainly munitions workers and soldiers who looked on their Saturday afternoons as the perfect release of the frustrations, hard work and military discipline that had been their lot all week. What better place to vent their emotions than the football ground? Too much so on more than one occasion. One match had to be abandoned because of the amount of swearing from the Manor Ground crowd and another had to be called off because the referee was beaten up by spectators.

Sites were inspected and rejected in both Battersea and Haringey. Norris finally identified Islington as the perfect site for the Club's new base. It could not have been more different in culture to the area of south-east London he wanted to leave behind. Norris had also seen the site he wanted – land owned by St John's College of Divinity – which housed a number of football and cricket pitches. When word leaked out that this was the preferred place of relocation, there was a furore. Many of the Woolwich-based supporters regarded such a move as a betrayal of the Club's origins and there were reports that Norris received death threats. His opponents went public with their disaffection accusing Norris of putting future financial gain ahead of the culture and history of the Club. The residents close to the college's grounds were also less than enamoured with the project while there were predictable objections from Clapton Orient and Tottenham who viewed the arrival of the new club as a threat to their own fans' catchment area.

In March 1913, a hastily arranged meeting of the League management mommittee was called to discuss the proposed move. By now Chelsea had become an ally of both Tottenham and Clapton Orient in opposition. The debate was lengthy and acrimonious and it dragged on into the early hours. However, Norris finally had things his own way. The League management mommittee had no option but to approve the plan because, they concluded, they had no right to block it. A few days later Norris did a deal with the Ecclesiastical Commissioners and negotiated a 21-year lease on the ground. Arsenal paid £20,000 for the lease and, as part of the deal, agreed not to play on the traditional football days of Good Friday and Christmas Day. However, this restriction was lifted in 1925 when, for £64,000 pounds, the Club bought the site outright. Once again Norris had overcome all objections to his scheme. When he set his heart on a project it invariably came to fruition, and so Arsenal moved to a new site called Highbury with plans to build what was to become one of the most famous football stadiums in the world.

Highbury opens for business

Woolwich Arsenal played their last game in south-east London in April 1913 when they drew 1–1 with Middlesbrough. Norris, who showed himself completely oblivious to local opposition to the Club's move, now began to invest big time. He raised £80,000, which included bank guarantees and loans, and far-reaching development work was carried out at the new ground. This included the levelling of the pitch, the partial erection of a new grandstand and terraces and the installation of turnstiles. Highbury Stadium opened for business. Cash was at a premium (the builder of the stand agreed to take a cut of the weekly gate receipts as payment) and when they played their first match – as a Second Division club simply called The Arsenal – on 6 September 1913, there were still no changing rooms. Indeed, one player, George Jobey, had to go off with an ankle injury and the trainer George Hardy borrowed a milk cart to take him back to his lodgings. But Arsenal won the match 2–1 against Leicester Fosse and the new era had a successful start.

The season as a whole was an adequate one. The team finished third and were only denied the First Division status that Norris craved on goal average by Bradford Park Avenue. However, there was a spectre on the horizon that was beyond even the influence of the all-powerful Norris. In September 1914 war was declared. As a club with strong military connections the effects of the war were keenly felt at Highbury. The Club lost both players and spectators who went to work in the munitions factory and other who joined the armed forces. The League went ahead during the 1914/15 season but it was played in a false and unreal atmosphere. In one case, the situation proved fatal. Bob Benson, a full back at the Club, went back to Woolwich to work in the munitions factory at the start of hostilities. In doing so he lost the fitness levels he had achieved through playing regularly. On a rare day free from working at the factory, Benson went to watch Arsenal play at Reading. His pal and fellow full back Joe Shaw was unable to get time off work for the game and Benson, fatefully, agreed to take his place. But he was palpably unfit to play and had to come off. He went to the dressing room and then collapsed into the arms of trainer George Hardy and died. He was buried in his Arsenal shirt.

It was a strange season with both teams and stadiums deprived of players and spectators because of the conflict in Europe. Still, the season was allowed to come to its conclusion and Arsenal finished fifth. Despite this success, the Club's finances were in a mess and the future looked grim. During the conflict football was still played but it was on a regional basis between teams made up of a mixture of players and guests. Attendances dwindled as the standard got lower and the war took its toll. At the end of the conflict, in 1918, Arsenal found themselves in an even worse state. The Club was a massive £60,000 in debt and was faced with the unattractive prospect of another season of Second Division football. The players returned after four years in the trenches just grateful and lucky to be alive but totally unprepared for professional sport. However, in another incident that may have earned the Club its 'lucky' tag, when League football resumed in September 1919 Arsenal were in the First Division – thanks, as usual, to Henry Norris and his wheeler-dealer character and powers of persuasion.

Norris's biggest coup

At the end of the last league season before the programme was abandoned in April 1915, Tottenham had been rock bottom of the First Division with Chelsea just one place ahead. Arsenal had finished fifth in the Second Division behind Derby, Preston, Barnsley and Wolverhampton Wanderers. It should have been a simple enough exercise to calculate who would be promoted and who would be relegated. It had been agreed before the start of the first season after hostilities that the First Division would be extended from 20 to 22 clubs. That should have meant that Tottenham and Chelsea were re-elected, while Derby and Preston – winners and runners-up in the Second Division – should be elevated to the top-flight. But the fiercely ambitious Henry Norris had other ideas.

Come the League Annual General Meeting in July 1919, Norris's campaign to persuade the Football League to allow Arsenal to take Tottenham's place in the top division hit top gear. In the run up to the meeting Norris, recently knighted, had used all his skills – especially on his close friend, League president and Liverpool owner John McKenna. At the meeting McKenna confirmed the promotion of Derby and Preston, but then insisted that the re-election of Tottenham and Chelsea should be decided by a vote. Chelsea were duly voted in – and then McKenna addressed the meeting on the subject of the north London rivals. He argued that Arsenal should take Tottenham's place because they had been members of the League 15 years longer. He did not even mention Wolverhampton Wanderers – a team who had finished ahead of Arsenal in the Second Division and been league members longer than the London club. Norris was like a dervish as he gathered support among the members for Arsenal's case. McKenna made it abundantly clear where he stood and it was enough to win the day as Arsenal secured 18 votes to Tottenham's eight.

It was a staggering decision and a triumph for the arch-politician Norris who had spent eight months on his canvassing. Tottenham chairman Charlie Roberts was dumfounded at the decision and, given the ill-feeling that already existed because of Arsenal's sudden appearance on Tottenham's north London 'patch', relationships between the two clubs were more strained than ever. Rumours abounded afterwards of money changing hands but nothing was ever proved – and Norris's long, angular features never betrayed a hint of his coup. He looked as laconic as ever and many just assumed that the approval of McKenna had been the key. 'If he thinks it is right, then it must be,' was the general opinion of the members of the committee.

Knighton takes over

The first manager to work for Norris at Highbury was Leslie Knighton. He had been successful with Manchester City and Huddersfield but at Arsenal Norris never really allowed him to manage in the truest meaning of the word. He was not allowed to sign players under 5 foot 8 inches tall, had a transfer limit of £1,000 for any single player and was expected to assemble a team made up of mainly local players – and all this following the dismantling of the scouting system as a cost-cutting exercise. To be fair, Knighton did reasonably well in the circumstances. He managed a ninth place finish in 1921 and he took the team to the FA Cup quarter-finals the following season where they were beaten by Preston.

Perhaps the most curious incident of the Knighton era concerned some 'energy pills' he was given to distribute to the players ahead of an FA Cup match at West Ham in January 1925. A Harley Street doctor and Arsenal fan gave Knighton the pills claiming they would do no harm and would improve the performance of the players. As bad luck would have it, the match was postponed because of fog. The players paced around the dressing room like a collection of 'lively lions' according to Knighton, many of them complaining about a raging thirst. They took the pills again the following Monday when the tie was re-arranged. But the game was postponed again, and the players noted the same after-effects. On the Thursday night, at the third attempt, the game finally took place. Having taken the pills before kick-off the players chased around almost supercharged – but there were no goals. Finally, the players rebelled, and for the replay at Highbury they refused to take any more pills. This time the match finished 2–2. There were more refusals for the second replay, which was at Stamford Bridge, and West Ham won 1–0. Nothing more was ever heard about the pills.

Though he toed the line most of the time Knighton fell foul of Norris when he signed 'Midget' Moffatt from Workington in the summer of 1925. Moffatt was only 5 feet tall, way below the minimum imposed by Norris, but Knighton had heard such glowing reports about him that he checked him out for himself – and was impressed.

So impressed, in fact, that he offered him a deal on the spot. The arrangement was for Moffatt to complete the deal the following day. But when Knighton arrived at Highbury next morning there was no sign of the player. A few hours later Knighton wasn stopped by the groundsman who told him there was a chap in the dressing room who said he had come to play for Arsenal. It was Moffatt – whose sense of direction on the pitch was better than off it. He had not noticed that Arsenal had dropped the 'Woolwich' from their name and had gone to the old ground in south-east London. A local road sweeper informed him that the Club had left that site before the war and in fact gave him a lift to Highbury. Moffatt duly signed and was a huge success on a pre-season tour to Scandinavia. A few days later Norris returned from his summer break in France. He saw the winger, noted his size, and within months he had been transferred to Luton and then on to Everton. He never mentioned it to Knighton – but the manager knew what had gone on.

It seems unlikely that the Moffatt incident was a factor in Norris's next move. But he was clearly unhappy with the team's performances on the pitch. They had finished in 19th place in 1923/24 and 20th place the following season and Norris was losing patience. Added to that, while his team was failing to make any kind of impact, their bitter enemies from Tottenham were emerging as the best-supported team in the area. Norris was frustrated. With his career in politics now at an end, he wanted to fulfil his ambition to see Arsenal become an established and successful club and he wasn't sure that Knighton was the right man for the job. Earlier in his career at Highbury, when things were going well, Knighton had been persuaded to stay at the Club despite an offer to move north, on the promise of a lucrative benefit game, against Tottenham and the use of a London apartment. Co-incidentally, the first game of the 1925/26 season was against Tottenham and in an even stranger coincidence Knighton was sacked shortly beforehand. 'I believe he sacked me to get round offering the benefit money,' Knighton later claimed. Norris just shrugged his shoulders and offered him a one-off £500 payment.

Knighton went on to have success with Chelsea and Birmingham. For his part Norris had one more major contribution to make to

Arsenal Football Club. Shortly before sacking Knighton he had approached Herbert Chapman, then the very successful manager of Huddersfield Town, with a view to his taking over in the hot seat at Highbury. It was a brilliant move and one that would have the exact effect that he wanted on the Club. However, Norris had begun to make mistakes in his business dealings, mistakes that would cost him dearly. In 1927, he was the subject of an FA investigation into illegal payments and breaching the rules concerning club funds. These included the sale of the team bus and pocketing the proceeds of £125 and also using club funds for his own use. The *Daily Mail* reported the findings of the FA inquiry and suggested that Norris had also made illegal payments to Charlie Buchan to bring the striker back to Arsenal from Sunderland. Norris had a litigious nature and sued the FA for leaking the details. But on this occasion, it was a battle he lost. In February 1929, the Lord Chief Justice found in favour of the authorities and Norris was banned from football for life. Although his link with Arsenal was severed in such controversial circumstances, Henry Norris's influence on the future through the appointment of Chapman can never be denied. And thanks to his admittedly underhand methods, Arsenal secured a place in the top flight that they were never to lose.

Chapter Three

THE VISIONARY

Herbert Chapman –
innovator, master-tactician
and motivator supreme

Today no one doubts the contributions made to Arsenal's success by the likes of Bertie Mee, George Graham and Arsène Wenger. But there is one man missing from that list – a portly man from the South Yorkshire town of Kiveton Park near Rotherham, Herbert Chapman. Born on 19 January 1878, by the time he died cruelly and prematurely from pneumonia on 6 January 1934, he had transformed a football club with potential and promise a-plenty into the most dominant one in English football.

He revolutionized training methods, introduced numbered shirts and brought a tactical nous and know-how into the game that had not been evident before. He even persuaded London Transport to rename Gillespie Road Underground station as Arsenal – a staggering achievement worth untold millions in free publicity. Every resident in London and every visitor to the capital who used the city's underground system became aware of the existence of the Club. To this day Arsenal is the only football club to have a station named after it. Chapman was a marketing man's dream and his ideas and ability to capitalize on any situation would have made him a stunning success in the 21st century.

Not that his life in football was plain sailing, far from it. His upbringing was tough. He was one of 11 children born to a coalminer and, like many of that era, he assumed his life was to be down the dreaded pit. But the young Herbert refused to contemplate that prospect and used his natural intelligence to win a place at Sheffield Technical College where he studied mining engineering. But sport was his first love, a trait that was also evident in other members of his family. Two of his brothers – Harry and Tom – played professional football. Harry, his younger brother, played for the Sheffield Wednesday team of the early 1900s that won two league titles and an FA Cup. His older brother Tom played for Grimsby. While another brother, Matthew, later became a director at the Lincolnshire club.

Chapman's playing career

If you consider the great managers in football, few of them were exceptional as players – Arsène Wenger and Bertie Mee at Arsenal would be prime examples. But both had the ability to absorb the finer, tactical points of the game and used that knowledge to mould highly successful teams. Chapman was of this ilk. In the jargon of that era, he was a robust inside right who compensated for his lack of individual talent with application, determination and natural strength. For most of his playing career he remained an amateur, which meant where he played was governed by what work he could find. For instance, while at Grimsby in 1898 (at the same time as his brother Tom), he took a job in a local solicitor's office. But he was not a great success at Grimsby. A 7–0 hammering in the FA Cup by powerful Preston North End went hand-in-hand with a mediocre league season and the club finished tenth at the end of the 1898/99 season. They tried him as a striker the following season, but that didn't work and he left the club soon afterwards. He then tried his luck at non-league Swindon Town but was unable to find a job to finance his football. After three games and two goals he left and his league football career came to an abrupt halt.

However, motivated by his love of the game and his determination to play it, Chapman signed for Sheppey United. Unfortunately, they finished bottom of the Southern League, despite his contribution as top scorer, and once again he failed to find work. So he returned to his Rotherham roots and played for Worksop Town in the Midland League in the 1900/01 season, also resuming his studies at the Technical College in Sheffield. Because of his studies, Chapman played mainly for the reserves and only occasionally for the first team. On one of those rare appearances, however, he played against Northampton Town who were suitably impressed by his tough and gritty approach. He was offered a contract and in 1901 he signed on as a professional. He was regular during the 1901/02 season and ended the campaign as top scorer – 14 goals from 22 matches.

Things were now very much on the up for Chapman. Sheffield United had seen him play in the FA Cup and liked what they saw. They offered Chapman a contract at the end of the season. He accepted – but as an amateur because he wanted to make use of the engineering qualifications that he had worked so hard to acquire. Things were different at Sheffield United where he was suddenly surrounded by internationals. He played 22 games and scored twice during the 1902/03 season, but found it increasingly hard to hold on to his place in the team. He moved again in 1903, this time to Notts County for £300. He found life there just as hard. In two seasons, he made only seven appearances and scored just once. The following year County opted to lend him to Northampton, and a year later came a permanent move – ironically to a Southern League team by the name of Tottenham Hotspur. He cost Tottenham £75 and repaid their faith in him by scoring 11 goals in the 1905/06 Southern League. But the following season was not so successful. He found his appearances had become sporadic and he scored just three times. In 1907, Chapman had experienced enough of a player's life and decided to leave professional football for good, or so he thought.

Moving into management

Then came management, and like many managers his career started with a massive stroke of luck. There is no evidence that Chapman had even flirted with the idea of becoming a manager. Indeed, just before he left Tottenham he heard that Northampton were looking for a new manager and recommended his White Hart Lane team-mate Walter Bull for the job. Bull agreed – and then had a change of heart that was to be immensely significant in the life of Herbert Chapman. Bull rejected the chance to manage Northampton, and suggested that Chapman take the job. He agreed – and became player-manager in April 1907. The two years prior to Chapman's arrival, Northampton had finished bottom of the Southern League. Chapman's arrival was to have a big impact.

The deep-thinking Yorkshireman began by introducing some revolutionary new tactics. He started by asking his wing halves (midfielders in modern parlance) to drop deeper to give his front players more space. Defenders were encouraged to pass rather than hoof their way out of trouble. He was also in the ears of the directors, asking for more hard cash to strengthen his team, and Welsh international Edwin Lloyd-Davies was one of the first to arrive. The effect was immediate as Northampton were transformed from perennial strugglers to a respectable eighth place in the Southern League table. But Chapman was ambitious and wanted more – both on the pitch and off it. Striker Albert Lewis arrived from Coventry and David McCartney was signed as a midfield playmaker. And to the delight of the club and surprise of its supporters, Chapman brought the Southern League title to Northampton in 1909 with Lewis proving the judgement of his manager to be spot-on as he finished the season as top scorer.

Chapman had arrived on the managerial scene with a vengeance. He had hung up his boots that season, playing his last match against Watford early in 1909, and this allowed him more time to devote to tactics and strategies. Northampton took on Newcastle in the Charity Shield and lost 2–0, but Chapman's reputation was growing. There were to be no more titles, though they achieved top-four finishes in the Southern League over the next three seasons, but Chapman was successful in putting Northampton on the national map with their exploits in the FA Cup. Mighty Sheffield Wednesday were beaten and both Nottingham Forest and Newcastle United were taken to replays, though Northampton lost 1-0 on both occasions. These were truly heroic efforts. And Chapman's abilities did not go unnoticed.

He was keen to get Northampton into the Football League where more stern and demanding tests would be faced on a weekly basis. There was, however, no automatic promotion into the league in those days and Chapman had to devise a way to break into the closed shop. Visionary that he was, he suggested a two-division Football Alliance underneath the League with automatic promotion and relegation – but this was rejected. Chapman was left a frustrated man but a chance to further his ambitions was to come in 1912. Leeds City of the Second Division wanted him as their manager and Northampton did not stand in his way.

The Leeds City scandal

The season before Chapman took over, Leeds had finished second to bottom and his first job was to see them re-elected. He then set about bringing in new faces and introducing a new approach to the game. The new signings included Billy Scott from Everton, and Evelyn Lintott and Jimmy Spiers from Bradford City. He demanded that his team entertain and there was no shortage of action on the pitch. In February 1913 they beat both Leicester Fosse and Preston North End 5-1, with a 6-0 defeat at Stockport County squeezed in between. But there was no danger of re-election in 1913 as the club finished in sixth place. Chapman had been bullish about the prospects of Leeds once he had sized things up. 'Promotion in two years,' was his bold pledge. He failed... but only just. City duly improved the next season and finished fourth – just two points away from promotion. There was a real feel-good factor within the club and attendances were increasing along with income. The fans and directors were happy – a rare occurrence in any era.

But the First World War was to interrupt the Chapman plan for Leeds City. Attendances went down as men signed up to fight the Germans. Chapman had assembled a formidable squad but the absence of so many of the players who signed up for military duty made team selection difficult. Confronted by such disruption, Leeds finished the 1914/15 season in 15th place. League football was then suspended for the rest of the hostilities and Leeds were restricted to playing in regional competitions. The war effort led to the defection of more players because of a drop in wages, and that meant that Leeds had to use guest players for many of the matches. Bored and frustrated by this unfortunate turn of events Chapman, a fierce patriot, decided to make his own contribution to his country in a time of need. He took his administrative skills away from football and took over as manager of a munitions factory at Barnbow in 1916. For three years, his assistant manager at Leeds, George Cripps, stood in to fulfil an administrative role at the club while chairman Joseph Connor and another director took charge of the team.

The end of the war saw the resumption of League Football and a scandal at Leeds that resonated around the game. It was revealed that Leeds City had been involved in what were termed 'financial irregularities' – making illegal payments to guest players during the wartime matches. The sanctions were fearsome. Leeds City were expelled from the Football League in October 1919, eight games into the new season. By the end of the year, the club had been dissolved and five officials at the club – including Chapman – were banned from football for life. The players were auctioned off and the Elland Road ground was taken over by the newly formed Leeds United.

Chapman was stunned, hurt and bitter. But, ever the pragmatist, he took a job as superintendent at an oil and coke works in Selby. Continuing bad luck saw him laid off by Christmas the following year. But 1921 brought renewed hope. The hierarchy at Division One side Huddersfield Town had been impressed with Chapman's work at nearby Leeds and wanted him back in football. They offered him the chance to be assistant manager to Ambrose Langley, an old friend of Chapman's brother Harry, and offered to back him in his appeal against the lifetime ban. The argument had more than a ring of logic.

At the time when the payments were made, Chapman was doing his duty for King and Country at the munitions factory. He was not involved at Leeds at the time. Their argument won the day, the ban was overturned and on 1 February 1921 Chapman was appointed as the assistant to Langley.

Chapman's luck changes

Chapman had another stroke of luck the following month. Langley quit Huddersfield and Chapman took over as secretary-manager. At last Chapman had the stage he craved to put his ideas into action and make his mark as a manager. He spent little time dithering about what to do at his new club and signed England international Clem Stephenson from Aston Villa and an 18-year-old by the name of George Brown. In his first full season, Huddersfield won the first major trophy in their history. They beat Preston North End 1–0 at Stamford Bridge to win the FA Cup. Their cup run came as a welcome relief from the more demanding world of the league in which Huddersfield had spent most of the season involved in a battle against relegation. They finished the 1921/22 season in 14th place and Chapman decided to spend the close season adding to his squad.

He was also able to start introducing his favoured tactics. These were based on a strong, resolute defence and fast counter-attacking. He liked short, accurate passing and had a great belief in the influence of wingers. Now that he was in total control, he could ensure that this pattern of play was extended to all teams connected with the club, including the reserves and the third team. All of them would play in the same way, as the Chapman philosophy became the philosophy of Huddersfield Town. That meant that if anyone was needed from the back-up teams or were playing well enough to be promoted to the first team, they would immediately know what was required. Chapman also introduced a scouting system that was arguably the best and best organized in the country. The scouts had one remit – find players who would suit Huddersfield and their strategy. There was cash available to Chapman after the FA Cup success and he used this to bring in new players like goalkeeper Ted Taylor and strikers Charlie Wilson and George Cook. Huddersfield were transformed, a fact reflected in the 1922/23 season in the toughest test of all, the First Division, when they finished third.

The force in English football

But the following season came the prize that Chapman wanted most – the league title. It was a close run affair, however, very close. Huddersfield finished level on points with Cardiff City but the Yorkshire club had a marginally better goal average – 0.024 of a goal to be exact. And on the final day of the season, the signing of George Brown proved inspirational. Huddersfield beat Nottingham Forest 3–0 and Brown scored the vital third goal. Huddersfield's resolute defence had been their lynchpin for most of the season but it was Brown's goal that made the difference between being champions and runners-up.

Under the guidance of Chapman, Huddersfield Town had arrived as *the* force in English football. Chapman brought in winger Joey Williams and goalkeeper Billy Mercer for the defence of their title in 1924/25. It was a campaign that tested Chapman and his men to the full. After an impressive start, Huddersfield had slipped to ninth in the table during the late autumn and early winter and an injury to star goalkeeper Taylor did not help their cause. Mercer came in and did well and the defence stayed strong – going through the season without conceding more than two goals in any match. By February, they were back on top with a 5–0 win over Arsenal. After that they didn't look back, eventually retaining the championship, winning by two points from West Bromwich Albion.

Chapman went into the close season of 1925 plotting to win a third successive title – a feat that had previously been beyond everyone. That same summer, Arsenal chairman, Sir Henry Norris, set about looking for a replacement for Leslie Knighton who had just been sacked as manager and Norris placed an advertisement in the much-read and highly-respected *Athletic News*.

ARSENAL FOOTBALL CLUB

is open to receive applications
for the position of
TEAM MANAGER.

He must be experienced and possess the highest qualifications for the post, both as to ability and personal character. Gentlemen whose sole ability to build up a good side depends on the payment of heavy and exorbitant transfer fees need not apply.

Chapman saw the advertisement and decided to apply. It was a huge decision. For all their size and growing reputation, Arsenal were consistently mid-table fodder in the First Division. But what attracted Chapman was the club's potential, which he thought was enormous. Chapman also 'liked a pound note', as they say – and Norris was willing to double his salary from £1,000 to £2,000 a year. He also wanted fame and was confident that he could find that status in London. He agreed to become Arsenal manager in the summer of 1925 and the Club never looked back.

The start of something big

Despite his pursuit of money and fame, there was a warm and caring side to Chapman and that was illustrated in one of his first appointments. One of the Club's players, midfielder Tom Whittaker, had been to Australia that summer on a Football Association tour and had badly injured a knee during a match in Wollongong. The FA seemed unwilling to do anything about it. On meeting his player and hearing the story, Chapman immediately contacted the FA and ensured that they paid his wages of £6 a week until his playing career was decided one way or the other. Whittaker then said that the surgeon Sir Robert Jones had been recommended to him. Although it seemed unlikely that the FA would sanction surgery, Chapman arranged for Whittaker to see the surgeon anyway. The news from Sir Robert was not good. He could ensure that Whittaker could have full use of his right leg in the future, no problem, but the limb would not be sturdy enough for Whittaker to play football again. The operation was carried out and, after immense haggling by Arsenal and Chapman in particular, the FA also paid £450 to Whittaker as compensation.

Despite successful surgery and the compensatory payment Whittaker, naturally, was down having had a promising career taken away from him so cruelly. But, just when he was at his lowest ebb, Chapman lifted his spirits in spectacular fashion. He took him to the highest point on the East Stand at Highbury and asked him to survey the scene. He said, 'I am going to make this the greatest club ground in the world and I am going to make you the greatest trainer in the game. What do you say to that?' Whittaker was aghast. Aghast and happy – and the words from Chapman were to prove prophetic because not only did Whittaker indeed become a respected and knowledgeable trainer, he went on to be a successful Arsenal manager.

Chapman meant what he said and sent Whittaker to spend a year of study with Sir Robert Jones where he would learn about physiology, massage, the use of electrics in therapy and how gymnastics could be used for medical purposes. Ever professional, that was Chapman. Whittaker turned out to be a natural in physiotherapy. Not only could he absorb the knowledge he needed, he also had what they call 'magic hands' – players trusted him and his methods. It explains the great fitness record of Arsenal players in the years to come.

Getting down to business

'It will take us five years to win a trophy but we will get there,' said Chapman to Norris after his appointment. And while he did have to operate under restrictions in the transfer market, he was not slow to make it clear that he first wanted to bring Charlie Buchan back to the Club from Sunderland, where he had enjoyed a magnificent career. In Buchan, Chapman spotted a leader. Norris queried the wisdom of signing a 33-year-old but Chapman eventually persuaded him that the team needed a striker still in prime form and who could benefit from the change in the offside law that had been modified that summer to help teams become more attack-minded. Chapman was so keen to sign Buchan that he went in person to see him at his thriving sports shop on Wearside.

Sunderland wanted £4,000 for the player, arguing that despite his age, Buchan was still capable of scoring 20 goals a season. Norris rejected that demand and instead came up with another formula of a £2,000 down payment and a further £100 for every goal Buchan scored. As a sweetener to persuade Plumstead-born Buchan to leave Sunderland, Norris also paid him £125 under the counter. Chapman, of course, always denied all knowledge of the payment. Sunderland eventually caved in and Buchan was on his way back to London.

Once he arrived at Highbury, Buchan – no mean tactician himself – and his new manager talked long and hard about how to capitalize on the new offside law. Instead of three players (including the goalkeeper) between a player and the opposition goal, there now had to be only two. Buchan suggested that the traditional 2-3-5 formation should be changed to a 3-4-3, giving the centre half – who used to be more of a roaming midfield player – the role of stopper at the back. That, in turn, meant that the inside forwards could come back into the midfield area. In the football jargon of the day, this became known as the W-M formation – so named because of the shape produced when the players' names were written down on the team-sheet. Offside was now the responsibility of the centre half, with the full backs filling a wider berth.

Norris's tight hold on the Club's finances had clearly frustrated Chapman's predecessor Leslie Knighton. But Chapman was more persuasive and after Buchan, he secured the services of another key player, goalkeeper Bill Harper for £5,000. The 1925/26 season began brightly for Arsenal with four wins and three draws in the first eight games. But on 3 October Chapman found out that he was not the only man to see the profit that could be made from a revision of tactics encouraged by the new offside law. On a trip to Newcastle, for instance, who used Charlie Spencer in the stopper role, Arsenal were beaten 7-0. Queens Park Rangers and Tottenham also adopted the W-M formation that season. But Chapman was both wily and shrewd. He worked on refining the system to give Arsenal the ability to counter-attack with venom when an opposition attack broke down. He told his players, 'The most opportune time for scoring is immediately after repelling an attack because opponents are then strung out in the wrong half of the field.'

Arsenal finished the season as runners-up. Ironically, it was the club he left – Huddersfield – who won the title and in doing so became the first club to win three championships in a row. Chapman had left a mighty legacy in West Yorkshire. The following season was something of an anti-climax at Highbury as Chapman searched for the players who would fit into the system he wanted to play. Gradually, he started to recruit the players he needed. In February 1926, he signed the lightning-quick winger Joe Hulme from Blackburn and in the close season he was joined by striker Jack Lambert and full back Tom Parker, who would later succeed Buchan as captain.

A slip away from glory

Arsenal still lingered in mid-table while Chapman did his fine-tuning although there was a glimpse of glory in the 1926/27 campaign. It was an important season in many ways: the last at Arsenal for Sir Henry Norris, whose financial misdeeds have already been documented, and the Club had dropped 'The' from their name because, as Chapman said, 'We will be first in the list of clubs.' On the pitch, things took a turn for the better, not in the league but in the FA Cup, a competition in which the Club had a poor record. Indeed, only four times had they progressed further than the last 32 – or the fourth round as it is now known. Suddenly Arsenal fans had a reason to cheer while Chapman's ideas were waiting to bear fruit in the league.

In the third round Arsenal beat a powerful Sheffield United 3–2 on their own patch. They then despatched Port Vale in a fourth-round replay at Highbury. Vale proved stubborn opponents and the match was not the cakewalk that many Arsenal fans had anticipated. Exasperated, trainer George Hardy took it on himself to leave his seat and go pitch-side to order one of the Arsenal front players to push further forward. Chapman was annoyed. This was not in the trainer's remit and after the match Chapman showed his ruthless side by sacking him. For the fifth round, Arsenal were drawn at home to Liverpool and won 2–0 with goals from striker Jimmy Brain and skipper Buchan. In the quarter-finals, Jack Butler headed the winner in a 2–1 win over Wolverhampton Wanderers. Incredibly Arsenal were within touching distance of Wembley with only mid-table Second Division side Southampton standing in their way in the semi-final at Stamford Bridge. Arsenal went 2–0 up courtesy of strikes from Charlie Buchan and Joe Hulme before Southampton caused some anxious moments with a late goal of their own. But Arsenal held on. Wembley beckoned for the Club's first ever FA Cup final.

Many believed that the final that Arsenal would prove victorious for Buchan and his team and make history for the North London Club. But there was some doubt about team selection for the match. Following Hardy's dismissal Tom Whittaker, who had been under his wing, had been appointed first-team trainer. The final gave him an early opportunity to show that he was blessed with the 'magic hands' that are the hallmark of all great physiotherapists. Midfielder Alf Baker, a vital component in the Chapman tactics, was a serious doubt for Wembley with a bad knee injury. Whittaker worked round the clock after pledging to get Baker fit – and he was as good as his word.

Arsenal duly made history – but not the kind that was predicted – as Cardiff became the first club to take the FA Cup out of England. To add to the irony, it was Arsenal's Welsh goalkeeper Dan Lewis – who had ousted Bill Harper from the team – who was at fault. It was the first time the FA Cup final had live radio commentary but it was not the contest that the broadcasters had hoped would launch their innovation. The game was dull with Arsenal emerging as the team most likely to make a breakthrough. However, with just 15 minutes left, came the moment that Lewis wanted to forget as he let a tame 25-yard effort from Cardiff's Hugh Ferguson squirm from his grasp and roll towards the goal. As Lewis turned and attempted to make amends for his error, his arm hit the ball over the line. Moments later the Cardiff keeper failed to catch a long, floated centre from Sid Hoar. The ball bounced in front of him and over his head to leave Buchan and Jimmy Brain with the chance to equalize. There was a huge misunderstanding, however, as both players left it to each other and the chance had gone. One goal was enough, and Cardiff City won the cup.

After the match Lewis was inconsolable. He even threw away his runners-up medal because it would, in his mind, be forever associated with his dreadful error, although team-mate and compatriot Bob John scoured Wembley to retrieve it. Then it was down to Buchan to play a real captain's role by restoring spirits. After the team bus dropped the players at Marylebone Station, Buchan led the invasion of a nearby pub and ordered drinks all round. What had happened, however, was not lost on Whittaker. Because of the lush surface, Wembley left the ball slippery. 'It polishes the ball,' explained Whittaker. That combined with a new goalkeeper's jersey worn by Lewis to mark the day played a crucial part in the goal. 'The sweater was shiny,' said Whittaker. 'The ball was polished – and that explains why Lewis was unable to hold it.' When Arsenal reached finals in the future, Whittaker ensured there would be no repeat of the 1927 catastrophe by insisting his goalkeeper wore a used shirt. It is a tradition that continues to this day.

Chapman's team takes shape

Though defeat was not easy for Chapman to take, he regarded the FA Cup final appearance as the ignition for his work at Arsenal, not the end. He wanted to build on the achievement and set about strengthening his squad. He wanted a left-sided defender, preferably a full back, and he showed his talent for unearthing diamonds with the recruitment of Eddie Hapgood. Most First Division clubs gave little attention to non-league clubs when looking for players that would be first-team calibre. Chapman, though, remembered his non-league days with Northampton Town and how much talent there was, ready to be tapped, outside the league. He had been alerted to a promising, Bristol-born youngster who was working as a milkman and playing for Kettering Town. He had only played a dozen first-team games and at first sight seemed to lack the strength and stature of a defender. His fitness was never in doubt – he worked tirelessly to stay in peak condition – but his strength was open to question, especially when he was actually knocked-out on more than one occasion by the heavy leather footballs of the time. But Chapman liked what he saw and persuaded Arsenal to invest £750 in the player.

Tom Whittaker was determined to add bulk to Hapgood's slight frame and insisted that the player abandon his vegetarian diet for one of hearty steaks to develop weight and strength. But in Hapgood Arsenal had signed a player with that priceless gift – character – well illustrated in 1930 when the full back was badly burned in a domestic accident but demanded to play the Saturday afterwards. Whittaker duly made a harness that Hapgood could wear to stop the burns rubbing.

Chapman also had his eyes on a more established name and he was to pull of one of the great transfer coups of the time by bringing David Jack to Arsenal. Jack was a star of the time, a cultured attacking midfielder – or shadow striker as Dennis Bergkamp was later to describe the role. His fame was assured as early as 1923 when, as a Bolton player, he scored the first-ever goal in an FA Cup final at Wembley as West Ham were beaten 2–0. Bolton, one of the elite clubs of the time, won the Cup again three years later. But in the summer of 1928, they made it known they would listen to offers for any of their players – except Jack. Chapman and director George Allison decided to pay a personal visit to speak with the Bolton board. They asked about the chances of signing Jack and were told, in no uncertain fashion, that he was not for sale. Undeterred, they asked what would it take to get Jack and Bolton came back with a response that was clearly designed to be a deterrent and send Chapman and Allison back to London without Bolton and England's prize asset. Bolton wanted £13,000 at a time when the record transfer fee was £6,750.

But Chapman wanted Jack and wanted him badly. May 1928 had marked the end of Charlie Buchan's career as an Arsenal player when the team drew 3–3 at Everton (for whom Dixie Dean scored a hat-trick to make it 60 goals in a single season – still a top-flight record) and Chapman wanted Jack to replace him. He eventually got his man – courtesy of an insight into human nature. A dinner was arranged at the Midland Hotel in Manchester, at which the finer points of the deal were to be discussed. Bob Wall, who had recently been appointed as secretary-assistant to Chapman, later recounted what happened during the evening. 'We arrived at the hotel half an hour early. Chapman immediately went into the lounge bar and called over the waiter. He put two £1 notes in his hand and said, "George, this is Mr Wall, my assistant. He will drink whiskey and dry ginger. I will drink gin and tonic. We shall be joined by guests. They will drink whatever they like. See to it that our guests are given double of everything but that Mr Wall's whiskey and dry ginger will contain no whiskey and my gin and tonic will contain no gin."' Wall recalled later how the ambience was immensely relaxed and there was no hard bargaining needed over what was then a record transfer deal of £11,500.

But there was more to come. Jack could provide the goals, but could not replace the authority on the field previously provided by the legendary Buchan. Chapman needed to look elsewhere for that, a fact well illustrated during Jack's first week at Arsenal. His failure to turn up for work on the Thursday alarmed Tom Whittaker whose severe fitness regime was unbreakable. Whitaker was concerned that he was injured and went round to his house. He was astonished to find him with his feet on the mantelpiece and a cigarette in his mouth – one of 25 that Jack would have in a day. Jack's explanation? 'I always had Thursday off at Bolton,' he said. 'There is nothing wrong with me.' Suffice to say that the traditional day of rest for Jack came to an end.

Next on Chapman's list was 'an inside forward with vision, nous and awareness' as the jargon of the day would have it. He found his man in Alex James. He had the kind of football brain that Chapman admired and the ability to inspire his team as he had illustrated when he drove the 'Wembley Wizards' on to their famous 5–1 win over the Auld Enemy in 1928. James had started his career with Raith before moving on to Second Division Preston where, in four seasons essentially as a midfielder, he had scored 60 goals. In the summer of 1929, Preston put him up for sale and, unsurprisingly, there was no shortage of interested parties – Liverpool, Aston Villa and Manchester City among them. But Chapman was at the head of the queue. He had been impressed by James's remarkable ball control and ability to read the game. James was the quick-thinker that Chapman needed and Arsenal got their man for the relatively modest fee of £8,750. Cue an inquiry from the Football League. There were eyebrows raised about how, in view of the competition for the player, the fee was lower than that paid for David Jack. However, Chapman had been clever. James had already secretly signed for Arsenal and had been promised a job at the prestigious London store of Selfridges to supplement his income. Chapman knew there would be talk of illegal financial offers and it was *he* who approached the League asking for the inquiry and told them that until the investigations were completed, he would not sign James. The deal went through, it was mission accomplished for Chapman.

Chapman knew that in James he had not signed just an ordinary player – or man. The Scot was a complex individual who needed special handling and Chapman had the gift to bring out the best in him. But James was to tax Chapman's management skills like no one else. He was a one-off and Chapman recognized that he needed the sort of leeway that he would not afford to a less-gifted player. As an example, Chapman used to insist that his players were together from mid-morning onwards on match-days. James? He could stay in bed until midday if he wanted. Success always comes at price and Chapman certainly indulged James, no question. But Chapman also showed a more stern side to his character when the occasion demanded. In the summer of 1931, for instance, James was being belligerent and was at odds with the Club over a new contract. The Club had arranged a holiday for him. Just before he was due to leave Chapman contacted him and said there had been a change of plan and that he would be going on a cruise instead. It would do him good, said Chapman. James duly went down to the Port of London only to find that a berth had been arranged for him on a working cargo ship. At first James refused to go but was talked round by John Peters, the Club's assistant secretary at the time. He stayed on board until the boat reached the South West of France – then he came back to sign his new deal. His return to training brought the inevitable banter from his team-mates.

But James was not the only new arrival in 1929. There was Cliff 'Boy' Bastin as well. His was a real precocious talent with an intelligence and a maturity far in advance of his years. He was born in Devon and by the age of 15 was playing for Exeter City Reserves. Reserve football was not for him, though, and he preferred to play for local teams in the Bible Class League. At 17, he was offered a contract by Exeter – on £4 a week in the first team and £3 in the reserves. Bastin rejected the offer and insisted on being paid the £5 a week – the maximum wage at the time. Chapman swooped again. Just as he had recruited Hapgood from the relative backwater of Kettering, so he went down to Devon to make left winger Bastin an Arsenal player.

There were a few teething problems. Firstly, Bastin kept the Arsenal manager waiting while he finished a tennis match. Then he had to ask for his mother's blessing before making a decision on a move across the country from the homely south west to the capital. His mother made it clear she would not stand in his way and Bastin duly signed. Then, when he reported for training at the start of the season, he was to be met with a greeting that was to be echoed many years down the line by one Tony Adams, whose Arsenal career was nearly over before it started because he turned up at Highbury to find no one expected him and he was told to leave. Only the intervention of Terry Burton, a youth coach at Arsenal at the time, enabled Adams to get his trial at the age of 14. Bastin was three years older and a player under contract. But his boyish looks fooled the commissionaire who asked him what he wanted when he arrived at the ground. 'I want to join the rest of the Arsenal players,' said Bastin who later recounted, 'He then patted me on the back and edged me towards the door. He said, "Well, sonny, you are a bit young at the moment but never mind. One day you may be good enough to play for Arsenal."'

Another trip to Wembley

To help him adjust to his spectacular change in lifestyle from Exeter to London, Chapman decided that Bastin should begin his Arsenal career in the reserves. He also wanted him to get used to the style of play he could expect when he got into the first team. He had arrived at Highbury soon after Alex James and the Scotsman's accent was an immediate source of bewilderment to the youngster who had led such a comparatively sheltered existence in Devon. After James had introduced himself, Bastin later said, 'It was an accent I have never heard rivalled before or since.' The pair were to form an immensely effective and almost telepathic understanding on the field, but Bastin would always struggle to understand what James was saying. Young as he was, Bastin recognized class and he saw that quality in abundance in James. 'Nobody had greater faith in the qualities of Alex James than Alex James himself,' said Bastin, 'not even Herbert Chapman.'

In contrast to James, Bastin needed that confidence to help him settle down at Arsenal because he did not find it easy. However, a first-team opportunity for Bastin came much quicker than expected. A poor start to the 1929/30 season was brought to a head by a defeat against Bolton at Highbury and, in a bold move, Bastin was called up to the first team for the next match, a 1–1 draw at Everton. Chapman started with Bastin as a right-sided attacking midfielder, Charlie Jones, a signing from Nottingham Forest, on the left wing and David Jack in a more central role. But the upheaval in his life probably caught up with Bastin at that point and towards the end of November and most of December he was left out. Then came Boxing Day 1929 – and more evidence of the supreme man management skills of Chapman. Chapman saw Bastin as an outside left, a role he had not filled since he turned ten years of age. Before the game, against Portsmouth, Chapman turned on his best persuasive charm and by the end of the conversation, Bastin was convinced he was born to play there. Such was the manner of Chapman. Despite a 2–1 defeat Bastin played well and kept his place for an FA Cup third-round clash with Chelsea at Highbury.

It was a game with an edge but Chapman – a man that Bastin was to believe in without question during his career – decided that the youngster was equipped to handle the occasion ahead of regular first choice Charlie Jones. The act of faith was repaid in comprehensive fashion as Bastin scored the second goal in a 2–0 win. But the selection of Bastin was not the only shock decision that day – Chapman also dropped Alex James, who had been troubled by ankle problems. Indeed within a fortnight, Chapman confined James to bed because he felt he was in need of a complete break. No football and, difficult as it was for James to accept, no golf – the Scot's favourite pastime. Bastin stayed in for the fourth round and scored in a 2–2 draw against Birmingham City at Highbury to take the tie to a replay. St Andrews was a tough enough place anyway, but there was the extra incentive for Birmingham because their manager was Leslie Knighton who had been so unceremoniously dumped by former chairman Sir Henry Norris to make way for Chapman. The Arsenal manager knew it would be hard and there would be no place for faint hearts – and there was the added pressure that an FA Cup run would salvage Arsenal's poor league season.

The day after the draw at Highbury Chapman decided to recall James. He went to James's home and brought him to training. Big games need big players, argued Chapman and he gambled on James re-discovering that golden touch. Although he was not at his best, the move paid off – Arsenal won 1–0. The winner came from a penalty, converted by Alf Baker. A win was a win and a place in the fifth round had been secured. The character and resilience of the team was to be tested again in the fifth and sixth rounds. First Arsenal had to go to Ayresome Park, Middlesbrough, where they won 2–0 and there followed an even more impressive victory in the sixth, 3–0 at Upton Park against West Ham.

In the semi-final, Arsenal were drawn against Second Division Hull City in a match to be played at Elland Road. And Dan Lewis, the villain against Cardiff in the final three years before, was again badly at fault as Hull – who would be relegated from the Second Division at the end of the season – took the lead. Lewis's poor clearance went straight to Hull midfielder Howieson who promptly volleyed it into the net. Worse was to come before half-time as Hapgood made a vain attempt to block a shot from Duncan and succeeded only in diverting the ball into his own net. There were less than 20 minutes left when Arsenal's incessant attempts to retrieve the situation paid off. The architect of the first goal was Joe Hulme, who crossed for David Jack to reduce the deficit. Then James fed Bastin with a shrewd pass and the youngster's mazy run ended with a stunning shot into the net. To the massive relief of Chapman and his men, the game ended 2–2. The replay, in midweek at Villa Park, was a feisty affair. Hull clearly brought a grievance from the first match, which they thought they should have won, and when they had a man sent off during the replay – centre back Arthur Childs – for a wild kick at Jack Lambert, they started to dish it out. However, with the Second Division team down to ten men there was an inevitability about the result, and the winning goal came when David Jack converted a cross from Joey Williams.

The final was to be a showdown between Chapman's new club and his old one, Huddersfield Town, who had beaten Sheffield Wednesday 2–1 in their semi-final at Old Trafford. It was a showdown that would test his managerial ability to the limit and something that Chapman had waited for since his arrival five years earlier. True, he had been to Wembley before, in 1927, but that came almost too soon. By 1930, however, he had assembled the squad he felt could fulfil the ambitions he harboured for Arsenal, and they did not let him down. The captain was Tom Parker, the leader on whom Chapman relied heavily. There were setbacks ahead of the match for Chapman. Regular centre half Herbert Roberts was injured, and Bill Seddon took his place, while the unpredictable Charlie Preedy was in goal in place of another injury victim, Dan Lewis. However, Chapman had faith in both. Think Preedy and then Bruce Grobbelaar, the eccentric Zimbabwean who starred in goal for Liverpool many years later. 'He never hesitates to leave his goal if the occasion demands,' said the Wembley programme of Preedy. This was something of an understatement. He was either brilliant or guilty of a horrendous error.

Thankfully for Arsenal, this was a good day. In many ways it was to be a perfect day. The reigning monarch, King George V, made a surprise appearance after it was feared he would miss the match through an illness that had bothered him for more than a year. There was even the sight 20 minutes into the game of the enormous *Graf Zeppelin* airship over the national stadium. And the weather was fine... as was Chapman's team.

They had the boost of a goal from a pre-arranged move between Cliff Bastin and Alex James. The wily Scot scored after 17 minutes when he played a quick free-kick to Bastin and then took the return and slotted the ball home. It would have been better had Joe Hulme and Jack Lambert taken chances that came their way before half-time. Chapman was an uncomfortable figure watching the action, knowing that a second was needed to kill off Huddersfield. However, in the 83rd minute, James played an accurate through-ball down the middle and Lambert controlled it to fire home and clinch the first major honour in the Club's history. The goal had relieved a spell during which Preedy's goal had been under siege and there is an enduring image of Lambert turning after he had scored only to find himself alone in the Huddersfield half. He contented himself with several moments of self-applause.

That night both teams enjoyed each other's company with an FA Cup final dinner at the Café Royal. For Huddersfield it was the end of an era because they were never to win another major honour. For Arsenal and Chapman it was the opposite. They may have had a mediocre league season – they finished 14th – but this was more than adequate compensation. This was just the start.

Chapter Four

THE FABULOUS THIRTIES

Five League titles in seven years – and the 'Lucky Arsenal' tag

There is no doubt that Chapman was a football visionary, well ahead of his time in tactics and how best to use the abilities of his team. All-out attack was not for him. 'You can attack too long,' he once said. 'I am not suggesting Arsenal go defensive for tactical reasons but some of the best scoring chances have come when Arsenal have been driven back and then broken away to strike suddenly and swiftly.' This was a philosophy that was to make Arsenal the best supported club in world football during the 1930s.

Supporters were important to Chapman. The thirties was a time of social deprivation and hardship for the working classes in Britain with unemployment rising. With his working-class roots, Chapman sympathized with the working men who were the backbone of support for the national game. He was also a committed family man and had a settled and contented family life away from football. His wife – Annie Poxon from Annesly, Nottinghamshire – was a schoolteacher and they had two sons, Ken (born in 1908) and Bruce (born 1911), and two daughters, Molly (born 1915) and Joyce (born 1919). Ken was more interested in rugby union than football and went on to play for Harlequins. He also served as the president of the RFU. When Herbert was asked to nominate the proudest moment of his life, he chose the time when his son Ken qualified as a solicitor rather than any football-related glory.

He indeed loved his family but he also cherished Arsenal Football Club and was determined to build on the Wembley success. He may have believed in counter-attacking football but he also liked goals and recruited players to suit his thinking. He had a simple theory – attack as a team and defend as a team. He was not ultra-defensive, as some critics claim, he merely used common sense to exploit what he felt had become a defensive game for many teams. He must have done something right because Bastin was later to say that the Arsenal team of which he was part, 'played the best football I have ever seen' – and he included international matches in that assertion. That is some compliment from a player who had won every honour in the game before his 21st birthday.

But, as they say, reputations are easy to get and hard to lose. Because of their set-up, it was claimed by many observers that the team was based on defence – and played with the idea that if you start with a point and keep a clean sheet then you finish with a point. To outsiders it looked as though Arsenal's game-plan was to frustrate the opposition by absorbing pressure, then strike forward and score. This ability to win or draw matches that they had not dictated is actually the origin of the 'Lucky Arsenal' tag – one the Club has never been able to lose. But nothing could be further from the truth as far as Chapman was concerned. Yes, he wanted a strong and resolute defence, but he also wanted the speed, guile and goalscoring abilities of the likes of Cliff Bastin, Joe Hulme, Alex James and David Jack.

The innovator

Chapman made sure that the set-up at Arsenal was exactly as he wanted it. During his highly successful time at Huddersfield he insisted that all the club's teams played in the same tactical manner. The benefits were obvious. If a player from the third team was put in the reserves or a reserve came into the first team, he would know exactly what was required. He would not need to familiarize himself with what was happening around him. He put the same system in place at Arsenal. This was also an era when many club directors were all-powerful – even having a say in team selection. Chapman would have none of it. He would not be satisfied with a decent FA Cup run and a respectable league position. He was a winner – a disciplinarian and a winner. Yes, he could be a warm and sometimes genial person but he was also not shy of imposing his will to make a point as Joe Hulme was to find out after a match at Bolton. Arsenal had won, he had scored two goals and he was from Bolton. He assumed he would be allowed to spend the rest of the weekend with his family in the area. He was forced to think again by Chapman who did not think he had contributed enough to the game and insisted he travelled back to London with the rest of the players.

But first and foremost, Chapman was an innovator. It was he who introduced weekly meetings with the players during which their input was both encouraged and welcomed. He was also the bane of the FA's life. He wanted to introduce numbers on the back of players' shirts. The authorities said no – as much, it would appear, to spite the innovative Chapman rather than give the idea any serious thought. He wanted a 45-minute clock at Highbury. Again, an idea based on common sense, and again rejected by the FA. (Despite this rejection the famous clock at the Highbury Clock End was installed anyway, though with a full 60-minute compass.) He agued that floodlit matches should be staged in midweek to boost attendances that were badly hit by the afternoon kick-offs. Predictably, the idea was met with another negative response. And just to show that Chapman was indeed ahead of his time, he suggested that two further officials be used solely as judges as to whether the ball had crossed the line. 'No', said the FA

– and more than 75 years on that debate is still raging, albeit with many now advocating the use of video technology.

Chapman's views extended beyond the confines of Highbury and his foresight was even respected at the FA. He was not a supporter of the fact that the England team was selected by committee, a practice that would continue into the 1950s. He also felt that squad get-togethers were at least as valuable as meaningless friendlies – another debate that continues to rage today. 'I would like the England selectors to bring together 20 of the most promising young players for a week under a selector, trainer and coach,' he said. 'They would practise and then, at the end of the time together, views could be frankly exchanged. These players could be kept together during the season and I believe the result would be astonishing. But I don't think I have a hope of this policy being adopted.' And Chapman was also the arch-realist. Here are excerpts from a piece he wrote for the *Sunday Express* in 1934. Modern fans are always hankering after 'the good old days' and insist that Charlie George is better than Robin van Persie, that George Best is better than Cristiano Ronaldo. Chapman was not of that way of thinking.

It is sometimes said that if the old players were to come back, they would show up the limitations of today. But there is no coming back. I know how boldly and confidently the old-timers speak of their prowess and how they are inclined to belittle present players. To support their arguments, they point to the difficulty of the selectors in trying to build up a stable national side. England teams come and go. From one season to another they can scarcely be recognized. They have unfortunately to be altered from match to match. Men good one day fail the next. They do not even play consistently in their club form. This is one tell-tale piece of evidence of how football has changed. In the old days, the right of six or seven men to be picked was not questioned and they never let the side down. Because of this team selection was a comparatively easy matter.

I am not prepared to depreciate the men of today being fully conscious of the many matters, which have added to their difficulties. Competition has heightened enormously and it is no longer possible for men or teams to play as they like. Thirty years ago, men went out with the fullest licence to display their arts and crafts. Today, they have to make their contribution to a system. Individuality has to be subordinated to teamwork. Players have to take part in many more matches and the strain on their physical resources has greatly increased. The strain, too, has been intensified by the demands of the public. This is a point which I am afraid is only slightly appreciated.

For Chapman, read, in any particular order, Winterbottom, Ramsey, Revie, Greenwood, Robson, Taylor, Venables, Hoddle, Keegan, Eriksson, McClaren and Capello.

Chapman was even allowed to dabble in the preparation of the England team. The FA allowed him to travel with an England squad that visited Switzerland and Italy in 1933 and was even – despite opposition from some FA 'blazers' on the selection committee who saw his presence as an erosion of their power and influence – allowed to act as team manager. He gave the pre-match talks and was permitted to devise the strategy of the team. Actually, the FA showed rare common sense. There were several Arsenal players in the squad and they were, of course, familiar with Chapman's way of thinking. The tour was a resounding success. England drew 1–1 with future World Cup winners Italy in Rome and then thrashed Switzerland 4–0. The one-manager idea, however, was not repeated until 1947 when Walter Winterbottom was appointed to the post.

Another of Chapman's significant contributions to the Arsenal cause was persuading the railway authorities to change the name of Gillespie Road Underground station to Arsenal. Chapman was not slow to spot an opportunity and to have the club name on travel maps for London was a chance he did not want to miss. Initially the idea met with considerable opposition. The London Electric Railway threw their arms up in horror at the prospect of altering maps and train tickets, and there was the prospect of other clubs in London wanting a similar facility if they gave in on this one. But Chapman was persistent. He had noted as far back as 1913 when he was in charge of Leeds City how close the station was to the stadium. He argued that the change might well encourage more passengers to use the railway and the LER finally gave in. On 5 November 1932, Arsenal station became a reality and the team celebrated in appropriate fashion with a 7–1 hammering of Wolverhampton Wanderers.

Earlier that year, Chapman the innovator was in evidence yet again when he gave instructions for floodlights to be installed in the new West Stand at Highbury. He had visited Belgium two years earlier where he had seen his first floodlit match and was suitably impressed. Because there was no official sanction for the use of floodlights in competitive matches until the 1950s, Chapman's men could only use the facility for training. He was an advocate of white balls and he also insisted that his team wear hooped socks. 'It makes it easier for the players to pick each other out,' he explained. And another legacy survives until this day – with the exception of the last season at Highbury when the original redcurrant coloured shirts were used to commemorate their first season at the old ground – and that is the kit of red shirts with white sleeves. The colour was changed to a more vivid red and the white sleeves, Chapman felt, gave the kit a more distinguished look.

Chapman was also ahead of his time when it came to the game in continental Europe. He was not afflicted with the closed-mind of many of his British contemporaries and believed there was much to learn from foreign teams. Among his friends was Hugo Neisl, coach of the Austrian 'Wunderbar' team of the 1930s. And he went as far as to propose a European club competition – an idea that was not adopted until some 20 years later when Matt Busby took Manchester United into the European Cup. Again, he was ahead of his time and at every opportunity took his Arsenal team abroad to play friendlies. He also blazed the trail in the recruitment of black and foreign players. As well as signing Walter Tull, one of the first black professionals in English football, he attempted to bring Austrian international goalkeeper Rudy Hiden to Arsenal in 1930. But the Players Union and the Football League objected to the idea and the Ministry of Labour blocked the move. Again, Chapman eventually got his way when he signed Dutch goalkeeper Gerard Keyser for Arsenal as an amateur – the first man from his country to play in England. His influence even spread to the FA Cup final. As he had managed both finalists – Arsenal and Huddersfield – the two teams came out together as a mark of respect. That ritual has continued ever since.

Arsenal on the rise

Herbert Chapman had begun to fashion a team that would dominate English football for a decade and make the name Arsenal famous worldwide. Using the FA Cup final victory as a springboard, the Club went on to a magnificent season in 1930/31. The football provided true entertainment for the fans from the start in late summer to the end in the spring. They lost only four games throughout the campaign despite an exacting start to the programme with away games at Bolton and Blackpool. They won both matches 4–1, and it was not until the tenth game, away at Derby County, that they first tasted defeat.

Their main rivals were Aston Villa, who were beaten 5–2 at Highbury but then exacted revenge with a 5–1 win at Villa Park. Rivalry between the two sides was intense but never bitter, despite Arsenal knocking Villa out of the FA Cup in a fourth-round replay at Villa Park. Indeed, Villa were present at the end-of-season Arsenal banquet. But there was to be no walk down Wembley Way for the Arsenal fans that season. In the fourth round, they were beaten 2–1 by Chelsea at Stamford Bridge. But it could have been a blessing as it allowed Arsenal to concentrate on the league – and the focus was evident at Highbury in the next game when Grimsby were hammered 9–1, Arsenal's biggest-ever First Divison win, and they followed up with a 7–2 win against Leicester at Filbert Street (a ground where they had been involved in a 6–6 draw the previous season).

Arsenal clinched the title two weeks before the end of the season when Villa's persistent challenge was finally ended with a 3–1 defeat at Liverpool. They set a points record (for the two-points-for-a-win system) of 66, a record not broken until Leeds United won 67 points in 1969. And as for 'boring' Arsenal – that was seen to be a totally unwarranted tag as the team scored a remarkable 127 goals, one less than runners-up Aston Villa. Arsenal ended the campaign with identical records at home and away, a true mark of consistency and a triumph for the tactics of Chapman – winning 14 games, drawing five and losing two. The line-up that season – which usually included Preedy, Parker, Hapgood, Baker, Seddon, John, Hulme, Jack, Lambert, James and Bastin – is generally reckoned to be one of the most formidable in the history of the Club.

The following season, 1931/32, promised much but delivered little. The season began with optimistic talk around Highbury that the first League and FA Cup double of the 20th century was a possibility. Aston Villa had become the first team to achieve it in 1897 and Arsenal were now thought to have a chance of emulating them. In the end, they won nothing. In the opening game of the campaign Arsenal lost to 1–0 at home to West Bromwich Albion, a result that set the tone for the opening month. Their first win, over Sunderland, did not come until September. Over Christmas, Arsenal lost all three of their holiday games and it was only in the New Year that the team started to gain any real momentum as they chased league leaders Everton. The chase was in vain, however, and Arsenal finished runners-up, two points behind the Merseysiders.

Things looked better in the FA Cup, however, as Darwen were beaten 11–1 at Highbury and victories over Plymouth, Portsmouth and Huddersfield followed to set up a semi-final against Manchester City at Villa Park. An even contest was decided in the last minute when Cliff Bastin scored to take the Londoners to Wembley for the second time in three years. Their opponents in the final were Newcastle United.

There was something of a furore in the build-up to the match concerning the fitness of Alex James and Joe Hulme. Tom Whittaker had told Chapman that neither would be fit enough to play and neither was included in the squad that Chapman took to Brighton to prepare for Wembley. Indeed, three days before the match, Chapman announced his line-up with youngster Pat Beasley and Bob John on the flanks. To Chapman's anger, the *Daily Sketch* arranged for James and Hulme to undergo a fitness test for the paper's cameras at Highbury and published photos under the headline, 'The Two Fittest Men in Football are out of the Cup final'. Chapman was furious and demanded sackings for those who had allowed the stunt to take place. He called both players down to the south coast for more fitness tests that were witnessed by some 40 photographers. Hulme came through and was added to the line-up in place of Beasley. But one last tackle by Whittaker to test James for the benefit of a latecomer photographer left the Scot writhing in agony and he was ruled out. Bastin was moved infield to take on the role normally filled by James.

Chapman's team selection appeared to be an inspired one after John put Arsenal ahead in the 14th minute. But Newcastle equalized through one of Wembley's most controversial goals. Jimmy Richardson accelerated down the right and looked to everyone but the linesman to have run the ball out of play. But the ball came over as Arsenal waited for the whistle to award them a goal kick and Jack Allen headed Newcastle level. 'Everyone except the referee knew the ball was over the line,' said Bastin. Arsenal now had to re-focus after feeling so badly done by while Newcastle were given an unexpected lift. The effects were evident in the second half and a rejuvenated Newcastle secured the win through another goal by Allen. After all the promise, the season ended with no silverware.

There were encouraging aspects of the season, however, particularly in defence. Chapman had been alerted to a promising young goalkeeper called Frank Moss playing for Oldham reserves. His arrival at Highbury was another example of Chapman's cunning. Initially, Chapman approached Oldham to ask whether their first choice keeper, Jack Hacking, was available. His enquiry was quickly and abruptly rejected. Chapman then, almost as an afterthought, asked about Moss and was told yes. Chapman duly achieved his primary aim and in November 1931, Moss signed. Moss was a natural, combining bravery with tremendous reflexes and went on to play for Arsenal for the next five years until his career was cut short by a shoulder injury. There were changes too at full back. With captain Tom Parker coming to the end of his career Chapman needed a partner for Eddie Hapgood. He signed wing half George Male from Clapton, and as usual, called the youngster into his office for one of his legendary 'chats'. Male comment said afterwards, 'I came out after we had spoken, and not only did I believe that I could play right back. I was also convinced that I was the best right back in England.' The partnership with Hapgood flourished at Highbury and on the international stage as the pair were selected for England – the lively Hapgood, never short of a word of encouragement, always lifting the players around him with his advice. In contrast, Male was more of a quiet assassin – hard in the tackle, quick on his feet and with a retiring personality.

The new season, 1932/33, began well with a 1-0 win away at Birmingham, and got better. Alex James was back from injury and the goals were raining in from Bastin, new centre forward Ernie Coleman, Hulme, Jack and Lambert. They went unbeaten for 12 games between September and November and were at the top of the table for Sheffield United's visit to Highbury on Christmas Eve. Arsenal looked invincible as they won 9–2 to delight those packed into the new West Stand which had been opened by the Prince of Wales earlier in the month. Challengers Aston Villa and Sheffield Wednesday both visited Highbury in April and both were sent packing, leaving Arsenal in pole position. A 3–1 win against Chelsea at Stamford Bridge on 22 April and the title was clinched.

Humiliation

Ironically, however, the season will also be remembered for one of the most humiliating defeats in the history of the Club. As it still is today, early January sees the third round of the FA Cup. Arsenal were drawn away at West Midlands club Walsall. The match came just a matter of weeks after the win over Sheffield United and the country already knew that despite the efforts of the likes of Aston Villa and Sheffield Wednesday, the title was coming to Arsenal.

Illness had claimed Bob John, Jack Lambert and Tim Coleman. Injuries had left Chapman without a fully fit Eddie Hapgood and Joe Hulme and the manager was left with a simple choice. Should he include players who had only just recovered from a debilitating illness or a nasty injury or should he go into combat with fresh and fully fit reserves. Chapman, anticipating a difficult and demanding match, opted for the reserves who would be able to last the 90 minutes. True, Chapman drafted in second-string names like Tommy Black, Norman Sidey and Charlie Walsh, but he could still call on a wealth of experience in the likes of Moss, Male, Roberts, Jack and Bastin. It was hardly a team of nobodies. Though Walsh had been gnawing away at Chapman for a chance in the first team, the nerves clearly got to him. Before they left the dressing room, Chapman told him, 'I am expecting a big game from you today, lad.' Walsh said he was ready to which

Chapman said, 'Good – well go put your stockings on or you will be a laughing stock when you go out.' In the heat of the moment, Walsh had forgotten to put on his socks. An omen if ever there was one. The country were watching in anticipation not least because Arsenal had been built up as the aristocrats who owned, '£87 worth of football boots' while little Walsall existed on, 'fish and chips and beer,' and £75 a season. The contrast could not have been greater.

Walsall set about their apparently impossible task in the manner expected of a minnow against the big fish. They tackled hard and often to unsettle Chapman's men and the ploy worked. Walsh in particular had a nightmare. He missed one open goal and then took the ball off David Jack's toe just as he was shaping to shoot. Alex James, the heartbeat of the Arsenal team, was singled out for special treatment. The mud was thick and Arsenal just could not get any momentum into their game. On the hour disaster struck on a fateful afternoon for Scot Tommy Black who went missing as Walsall sent over a corner. He was supposed to be marking Gilbert Alsop but was nowhere to be seen as Alsop rose to head the Third Division side into the lead. Walsall smelt blood – and the intensity of their tackling increased, much to the annoyance and disgust of Arsenal. 'They could not have complained if five of their men had been sent off in the first hour,' said Bastin afterwards. Black's day was about to get worse, if that was possible. A wicked and possibly vengeful tackle on Alsop five minutes after the goal brought a penalty that was converted by Billy Sheppard. That was to prove to be enough and the celebrations went on long and hard after the game. Chapman was appalled at what he had seen. It is still not known if it was down to his tackle or his awful defending but Black was not even allowed back at Highbury and was transferred to Plymouth within days. Come the end of the following January and Walsh was on his way to Brentford.

It has been labelled as the most stunning giant-killing in FA Cup history. And it was a result that was to be the cause of immense joy countrywide. Mighty Arsenal had been humbled by little Walsall and the embarrassed players headed back to London in disgrace.

During the expected post-mortem the newspapers accused Chapman of underestimating his opponents and leaving out several big name players on the assumption that victory was Arsenal's by right. But this is an insult both to Walsall and to Chapman's professionalism. In fact, he had them watched for the four games before Arsenal played them and the fact that a fair sprinkling of his names were absent from his starting line-up was down to a flu epidemic and a lengthy injury list rather than any arrogance. Indeed the team that Chapman put out at Fellows Park that fateful day owed more to his gut instinct about how the tie could be won rather than any misplaced superiority complex.

The man who raised the cup

For most of Chapman's time at Highbury his chosen captain was Tom Parker. One of the new manager's first signings in 1926, he took over the captaincy from Charlie Buchan in 1928. A solid defender, he had a cool head and a marvellous positional sense to go with his deadly accurate penalty taking. If Tom Parker had one problem it was that he was born into the wrong generation of footballers. If fate had dictated that he saw the light of day some 40 years after his actual date of birth on 19 November 1897, he would surely have collected international caps that went into double figures at a time when England games were few and far between. In fact he played only once for his country.

Parker was born in Woolston near Southampton and started his career with local amateur sides Sholing Rangers and then Sholing Athletic. His potential was noted by Southampton, then in the Southern League, and he joined them in 1918, just before the end of the First World War. When professional football re-started after the conflict, Parker took his place at right back. League football came his way in the 1920/21 season when Southampton became founder members of the Third Division, and the following season they were promoted to the Second Division. He caught the eye in 1925 when he was an integral part of the team that reached the semi-finals of the FA Cup, losing to a powerful Sheffield United team at Stamford Bridge. Unfortunately, Parker, who had done so well in the competition up until then, had a bad day. He scored an own-goal and then missed a penalty.

To compound his misery, there was a mix-up between him and goalkeeper Tommy Allen that gave United their second.

But he had done enough that season to warrant a call-up for his one and only England cap against France in May 1925 when England won 3–2. His performances had also been noted by Herbert Chapman. Inquiries were made but rejected by Southampton. However, the south-coast club were forced to adopt a more pragmatic approach to Arsenal's overtures when the need arose for a cash injection to buy their ground. They eventually accepted an offer from Arsenal of £3,250 for the player. On 3 April Parker made his debut for Arsenal against Blackburn and it was match that was to start a remarkable sequence. Parker was to go on to make 172 consecutive first-team appearances for the Club – a record that still stands today. In Parker, Chapman saw a natural leader. True, he was not the quickest defender in the country but he had the air of quiet authority about him and he was made captain and led the club to their first FA Cup final in 1927 when they lost to Cardiff.

But he was not to be denied his moment of glory at Wembley, and in 1930 he became the first Arsenal captain to pick up the famous old trophy as Arsenal beat Huddersfield. Parker went on to earn more honours as Arsenal won the league title in 1930/31 and followed that with another FA Cup final appearance the following year in the defeat against Newcastle. The original Mr Consistency, Parker missed just six league games in his seven seasons with the Club. By 1932, he was approaching his 35th birthday and the game began to take its toll on his body. At the start of the 1932/33 season he was replaced by George Male. His last game for Arsenal was in October 1932 against Derby, after which he left the Club to become manager of Norwich. His record with Arsenal was remarkable. He played a total of 294 matches and scored 17 goals – mainly from penalties. Despite his miss in that semi-final in 1925, Chapman had no hesitation in nominating the man with the ice-cool demeanor to take the spot-kicks.

At Norwich, Parker enjoyed initial success. They won the Third Division South Championship in 1933/34 and were promoted to the Second Division. Then he went back to his Hampshire roots and took over at Southampton where he began fashioning a side of real quality. His target was promotion from the Second Division and he was ready to invest in players to achieve that aim. He spent £9,000 pounds on the likes of Billy Bevis, Sam Warhurst and Bill Dodgin. But arguably his most memorable signing proved that he shared his former manager Chapman's eye for talent. He went back to Norwich and signed Ted Bates – a man who was later to become manager at the Dell himself. The outbreak of the Second World War interrupted his work but anyway he had a furious row with the Southampton board in 1943 and walked out. He took a job as a ship's surveyor in Southampton docks. He was tempted back into the game a dozen years later when Norwich asked him to return, but a bottom-place finish led Parker to the decision that he had had enough and he went back to his work at Southampton docks. He retired in 1962. Bates, who by then was in the hot seat at Southampton, had never forgotten how Parker had a knack of unearthing talent. He asked Parker to take on the role of part-time scout and later chief scout. Parker gave the role up in 1975 and enjoyed a happy retirement until he died in 1987 at the age of 89.

Chapman's tragic death

At Christmas 1933 Arsenal were four points clear at the top of the table and looked odds-on to defend their league title. But there was a massive shock just around the corner. Herbert Chapman had spent New Year's Day 1934 in London before travelling north to see Arsenal's next opponents, Sheffield Wednesday, play on 2 January. He spent the final night of his trip in his hometown of Kiveton Park. He had a cold on his return to London and, against the advice of his doctor, went to watch the Arsenal third team play against Guildford City to see what young talent was coming through the ranks. It was a wet night and his cold got worse. Soon, it turned to pneumonia, an illness from which he was never to recover. He was cremated four days later at St Mary's parish church in Hendon.

The Club later recognized his contribution with a bust and commissioned the famous sculptor Jacob Epstein to make it. It held pride of place in the famous Marble Halls of the East Stand and has since been re-located to Emirates Stadium.

Bastin spoke for the rest of the players who had last seen him at the away match in Birmingham just before the New Year when he had looked in perfect health. 'Near the ground, the newspaper sellers were shouting out the news about his death. It seemed just too bad to be true. In the dressing room, no one spoke and yet everyone knew what the others were thinking. Herbert Chapman had been loved by us all.' Before the Sheffield Wednesday game, which kicked off on the afternoon of his death, there was a silence observed by both teams. It was difficult for the players to play in those circumstances and as Bastin later described, 'The 90 minutes seemed to last 90 years.' The match finished 1–1 but the damage to Arsenal's morale was severe. They lost three matches in succession including home defeats against Everton and Tottenham. After the funeral, director George Allison became acting manager while the day-to-day running of the team was left to Tom Whittaker and Joe Shaw. At a difficult and emotional time at least this meant there was no disruption to the pattern that had been established under Chapman. That did not stop interested parties applying for the job, however, and there were hundreds of letters from men hopeful of becoming Chapman's successor. Allison rejected them all. The players were aware of Allison's limitations and a handful resented him taking the job. But Allison knew what he was doing in terms of administration and shared Chapman's faith in Whittaker and Shaw.

The transition was not always a seamless one but it worked. The team returned to winning ways, helped by new signing Ted Drake who scored on his debut against Wolves in March and again to secure a fine away win at second-placed Huddersfield Town in April. They secured their second league championship in a row by picking up seven of the last ten points available, and finishing three points ahead of Huddersfield. They hadn't scored too many goals, Bastin top scoring with 13, but their defence was the meanest in the league. There was, however, to be no double as Aston Villa had ended Arsenal interest in the FA Cup quarter-final.

Allison gets the top job

At the end of the 1933/34 season Allison took over as manager on a permanent basis. The board had no hesitation in offering him the job – after all the Club had just won its second league title in a row. For all his faults Allison was regarded as just as shrewd an operator in the transfer marked as his predecessor. His first signing, in March 1934 when he signed striker Ted Drake from Southampton was already deemed a success. He looked lethal from day one and seven goals in ten games had already helped Arsenal to the title.

During the summer of 1934 Allison had a clearout of some of the older players including Jack Lambert and David Jack, and brought in wing halves Jack Crayston and Wilf Copping to refresh what Chapman had already thought was a ageing team.

The season started in an avalanche of goals: eight against Liverpool, five against Spurs, four against Blackburn and West Bromwich Albion, with Drake almost unstoppable. At the other end of the pitch, the defence got meaner and in January the team went five games without conceding. There was progress too in the FA Cup as Brighton, Leicester and Reading were brushed aside. March saw a wobble as Sheffield Wednesday brought the cup run to an end and then Sunderland, one point behind leaders Arsenal, got a point from a 0–0 draw at Highbury. But they soon hit their goalscoring stride once more. Away at Everton keeper Moss dislocated his shoulder. He returned to the pitch a little later and played on the left wing with Hapgood taking over between the posts. Incredibly, playing through the pain, Moss scored in a 2–0 win, part of an eight-match unbeaten run, including another 8–0 thrashing, this time against Middlesbrough, which saw Arsenal to a third title in succession.

The 'Battle of Highbury'

Highbury has staged many memorable matches over the years – and such was the status and facilities at the stadium, that England used the ground on four occasions to stage international matches. But none came near the controversy generated by the infamous Battle of Highbury in November 1934. It was a clash between England and the newly crowned World Champions Italy, who were playing their first match since winning the tournament – one, incidentally, that England did not enter. They were not to appear on the world stage until 1950 as the insular thinking within the Football Association took a grip on the policy towards international football. It was felt there was nothing to be either gained or learned from such a participation. Indeed, such was their arrogance that they even billed this match as 'The Real World Cup final'.

It was a game, however, that Italy desperately wanted to win – so much so that Italian dictator Benito Mussolini offered each player an Alfa Romeo car and a modern day equivalent of £6,000 a man if they beat England. England won the game 3–2 but it is not remembered for footballing reasons.

As arguably the dominant club in the country and also because the match was staged at their home ground, five Arsenal players were included in the initial selection. This became seven in the actual line-up after a series of injuries. George Male was drafted in when Tom Cooper had to drop out, and two days before the game Manchester City striker Frank Tilson was forced to withdraw. George Hunt was called up as replacement, but he too had to cry off – and in came Ted Drake. It remains a record to this day for a club to have such a formidable representation in the England team. Tragically, Herbert Chapman had passed away ten months before and did not get the opportunity to see the team he fashioned provide such a cornerstone for the England team. But he was also spared the sight of the atrocious happenings on that Wednesday in late autumn.

Italy, managed by Chapman's close friend Vittorio Pozzo, played with a completely different system to England. Luisito Monti was the focal point of their defence – a creator rather than a stopper – but he was to have close to no impact on the game. Up against him was Drake and in the first minute the Arsenal front man tackled Monti heavily. The Italian had to go off with a broken bone in his foot and protested afterwards that the tackle was deliberately designed to injure him.

Drake, naturally, protested his innocence but the tone of the match had been set. Take no prisoners. England's aggressive style clearly unsettled the Italians who went 3–0 down with goals from Brook, who scored twice, and Drake.

The Italians, seeing that the match was drifting away from them and that they were on the verge of defeat against a country who had not even entered the World Cup competition they had won, started to hit back. The tackles got more and more fierce. Victim number one was Eddie Hapgood who got an elbow in the face from midfielder Serantoni and suffered a broken nose. Ray Bowden picked up a bad ankle injury and Manchester City's Eric Brook fractured his arm. Captain Jack Barker was forced to have his hand strapped. And it wasn't half-time yet. But after treatment he went back on just to make his point.

Italy launched a comeback and scored twice through star front man Giuseppe Meazza who almost scored an equalizer but hit the bar instead. Victory went to England but with the Italians playing for most of the match with only ten men they claimed a moral victory. Back home they were feted as the 'Lions of London'.

A key factor for England was the togetherness of the team that was forged through the Club connection and which came to the fore. Italy bombarded the England goal but they could not salvage an equalizer thanks largely to the acrobatics of Frank Moss in goal and the tough tackling of no-nonsense defender Wilf Copping. Such was the contribution of Copping that Arsenal midfielder Jack Crayston went in to see his manager George Allison the following day and made his unforgettable comment concerning the Yorkshireman. 'If we played Italy again tomorrow,' said Crayston, 'there could be only one half back line – Copping, Copping and Copping.' And a young Stanley Matthews was to say, 'That was the most violent match I have ever played in. Ever.' The ramifications were severe. The FA seriously considered pulling out of any future matches against teams from the European mainland because of the events of Highbury. They relented – but it reflects the cocooned thinking of the authorities at the time.

David Danskin: Scottish, right back, team captain and tough as teak. After relocating to Woolwich from Burntisland in Fife to work at the Royal Arsenal munitions factory Danskin got together with some like-minded colleagues to play football. A year later the set up a team and so the history of Arsenal Football Club began.

Workers around the gates of the Arsenal munitions works during the early years of the 20th century. The Club's first name was Dial Square, so-named after one of the workshops in the factory complex. As well as providing most of the players in the early days, many of the team's early fans worked at the complex.

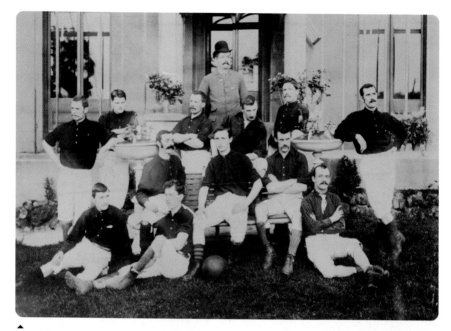

A meeting in the Royal Oak pub in Plumstead at Christmas 1886 agreed that the Club's name should be changed. They became Royal Arsenal, a name that seemed in keeping with their ambitions. The players were also presented with their own matching shirts and a ball, courtesy of Nottingham Forest.

Action from the Manor Ground in Plumstead in April 1905, a First Division match which saw visitors Notts County leave with the points in a 2-1 victory.

Henry Norris, who oversaw the Club's move from south to north London and built a stadium suitable for top-quality football.

This is the Woolwich Arsenal team that took on Leicester Fosse in its first match at Highbury on 6 September 1913. Arsenal won 2-1.
▼

Perhaps the most iconic image of Highbury stadium is the Art Deco frontage of the East Stand, opened in 1936.

Arsenal manager Leslie Knighton (left), captain Bill Blyth and goalkeeper Steve Dunn make their way to the FA enquiry into the controversial match between Arsenal and Tottenham Hotspur in September 1922.

Manager Herbert Chapman (centre) chats with Alex James (right) ahead of the 1932 FA Cup Final against Newcastle.

Arsenal players training with manager Tom Whittaker (left) at Highbury during the late 1930s, including Jack Crayston, George Male, Ted Drake, Cliff Bastin, Wilf Copping and George Swindin.

Eddie Hapgood clears during a rare Blackburn attack during a league match in February 1933. The Gunners won 8-0.

Skipper Charlie Buchan leads the team out for the FA Cup semi-final against Blackburn Rovers at Leicester in March 1928. Blackburn won 1-0.

◀ **Ted Drake** holds the Club record for most goals in a season after scoring 42 goals in 41 appearances during the 1934/35 campaign.

Cliff Bastin, a star of the Gunners first team at the age of 17, will always be remembered for his goalscoring even though he was a winger. His total of 178 goals for the club, set when he retired in 1946, was only bettered in 1997 by Ian Wright.
▼

Crowds outside Islington Town Hall in Upper Street greet the victorious Gunners after beating Huddersfield to win their first FA Cup in April 1930.

More silverware at Highbury

Ted Drake had been a major part of the Club's record-equaling three-in-a-row, which emulated Huddersfield's exploits between 1923 and 1926. He top-scored during his first full season with the Club, netting 42 league goals, a record that still stands today. However, it was not the last record he would break. On 14 December 1935 he performed a feat that would remain as part of Arsenal folklore. Arsenal were playing Aston Villa at Villa Park in front of a near 70,000 crowd. Because of their simultaneous success, the rivalry between the two clubs was immense and the clashes were regularly eventful. But this was a season of problems for Villa who started the game bottom of the First Division while Arsenal were trailing in fourth place behind Sunderland. But still the fixture had a lure of its own.

Villa had spent hard cash to rescue a desperate situation and could boast six internationals in their line-up. Injuries had deprived Arsenal of two key men in Alex James and Joe Hulme. Drake, with a knee heavily strapped, played despite his handicap. Villa were dominant but Drake was at his lethal best. He had a first-half hat-trick of goals that were classic examples of the Arsenal philosophy – quick counter-attack, accurate passing and a striker at the end of the move. Drake was the beneficiary. By the time 60 minutes had passed, Drake had scored three more and Arsenal were 6–0 up. His scored his seventh in the last minute and before that one had hit the bar and one was saved. It was clinical finishing at its best – Drake had scored seven goals with nine shots. The match ended 7–1.

It was not good enough, however, to win the title for Arsenal. That went to Sunderland who beat Arsenal 5–4 at Roker Park in what many thought was the title decider despite being played in December. Allison's team had to be content with sixth place. But considerable consolation was to come in the FA Cup with impressive away wins against Bristol Rovers and Liverpool. 'One of the most glorious in Arsenal history,' said the Arsenal programme. The draw was not kind for the fifth round, however, sending Arsenal to St James' Park to play Newcastle. Key men like Moss, Roberts and Drake were missing through injury and Arsenal came away with a 3–3 draw. Two penalties from Bastin helped Arsenal to a 3–0 win in the replay. The sixth round brought relief from their travels as Barnsley came to Highbury and were soundly beaten 4–1. A semi-final pairing with Grimsby was treated with some trepidation as Grimsby had already beaten Arsenal in the league earlier in the season. But Arsenal showed resilience and a Cliff Bastin goal was enough to ensure a fourth final in ten years.

Indifferent form in the league had made the FA Cup Allison's primary target for the season and he showed the same kind of common sense as Chapman, making sure he would have as strong as possible a team for the meeting at Wembley with Second Division Sheffield United by fielding weakened teams for several league games beforehand. Arsenal were fined £250 for this by the FA, but Allison felt it was a price worth paying. Despite this there were doubts about the fitness of Drake, Roberts, James and Hapgood, who had all fallen ill in the week before the game. Drake was not in good shape anyway having just had cartilage operations and one comeback game. Allison knew that James would be a necessary gamble and to accommodate him Bastin was switched to the left wing, and he also took a risk on the others.

As has so often been the case in FA Cup finals over the years, it was the team with nothing to lose that looked the more relaxed at the start of the game. Think Sunderland against Leeds, West Ham against Arsenal and Wimbledon against Liverpool. However, despite their more impressive opening to the game – United hit the bar with a Jack Dodds header on the half-hour – they could not find a way past Alex Wilson in the Arsenal goal. And the sting in the tail came with 15 minutes left when Bastin set up Drake and the prolific scorer added another to his list. He injured himself in the process but always maintained that the pain was worthwhile. Despite a last minute shock when Dodds hit the bar with a header, the cup was back at Highbury.

End of an era

The following season was a real anti-climax as the team originally assembled by Chapman and taken on by Allison began to age and lose its venom. Indeed, by early autumn of 1936 they were 17th in the table and players like the mercurial James were losing the edge that had helped make Arsenal such a force in English football. In fact, it was his last season – he retired on 1 May 1937. There was no question that he was a genius in the true sense of the word. He always looked unkempt but his control, touch and vision were truly remarkable. Chapman had indulged him because of his talent and even made allowances for the times when James went missing. When he retired he worked for a football pools company and later became a journalist. He did go back to Arsenal as a coach but died prematurely at the age of 51 in 1953.

In the league that last season, James contributed immensely to an Arsenal revival in the second half of the campaign that at one stage took them to top of the table. But a late surge by Manchester City proved to be irresistible and when City beat Arsenal 2-0 at Maine Road in April, the title was clinched. Arsenal's defence of the FA Cup ended at the sixth round stage against West Bromwich Albion, so the season ended with no silverware. Allison also lost the hugely experienced Bob John and Herbie Roberts at the end of the season and the need to re-build was paramount – and Allison knew it.

The last campaign had seen Arsenal's grip on English football loosened. They were not the force they once were and in 1937/38 trips to Highbury, where they dropped points regularly, were not as daunting for the away teams as they had been. Allison had already brought in players like Alf Kirchen and Bobby Davidson, though he was to leave in the middle of the season. Others arrived too: forwards Reg Lewis and Eddie Carr, Leslie Jones from Coventry and George Drury from Sheffield United. Others, like Bernard Joy and George Swindin, were breaking into the first team.

Arsenal were inconsistent for much of the campaign, but somehow they kept up with the leaders. Though unfashionable Brentford led the table into the New Year, it was widely reckoned that the title race was between the more powerful outfits of Wolves and Arsenal. The Midlanders appeared to have established a psychological advantage by beating the Londoners 3-1 in the league in January. Arsenal took revenge in the FA Cup a week later, but their interest was to end in the next round when they were knocked out by Preston

North End. Despite Brentford's two wins over Arsenal at Easter they fell away to leave the championship as a straight two-horse race. However, Arsenal also dropped a point against Birmingham and left Wolves in the driving seat with five games left. Preston emerged as a sudden threat after an impressive sequence of results in the run-up to their FA Cup final meeting – and eventual victory – over Huddersfield. There was even talk of the elusive league and FA Cup double at Deepdale. Arsenal went to the north west and won 3–1. However, on the final day of the season the destiny of the championship was out of their hands because if Wolves won at Sunderland then they would finish top. All Arsenal could do was beat Bolton at Highbury and hope that a Sunderland team motivated by nothing but professional pride would at least give Wolves a game. They did that and more. Arsenal did their bit, hammering Bolton 5–0. But the shock came at Roker Park where Sunderland showed commitment above and beyond the call of duty as they beat Wolves 1–0, despite having ten men for much of the second half.

It was the Club's fifth championship in eight years. Yes, they won the league by one point, and with the joint lowest points total of 52 for a 42-match season, but they remained the best team in the country.

There was, however, a spectre on the horizon and one that is not unknown in the more modern game – massive debt. Highbury had been developed into one of the most impressive stadiums in the world in the 1930s but it was progress at a price. By 1937, the outlay meant that the Club's debt had escalated to £200,000 – massive by the standards of the day – and Arsenal needed gates of 40,000 just to break even. By the outbreak of the Second World War in September 1939, Arsenal had a mere £4 in the bank – that was a reflection of the size of the problem. But Allison had persistently argued, going into that last season before the outbreak of hostilities, that, first Chapman, and then he himself had not been the outrageous spenders that they had been portrayed. And he was insistent on strengthening his squad to build on the success of the previous season.

His target was Bryn Jones of Wolverhampton Wanderers. Arsenal had already set the record fee when they splashed out £11,500 for David Jack a decade earlier. Wolves were determined to force Arsenal to exceed that figure and refused to back down after refusing a lower offer. Eventually agreement was reached at £14,000 and Jones was to find that fee a burden as he struggled to live up to the billing. His nephew was Cliff Jones, of the Tottenham double-winning side of 1961, so talent ran in the family, no question. But much was expected of Arsenal's Jones – perhaps too much. A bright start was followed by a spell of indifferent form and, after a heart-to-heart talk with Allison, it was decided he would benefit from a spell in the reserves. But the pressure was unrelenting under the microscope of a club of the status of Arsenal as Jones was to find out when a staggering 33,000 people turned up to see him play for the second string. He asked never to be put under that kind of spotlight again. Allison persistently and stubbornly defended the signing – 'I never, for one moment, considered him a bad buy,' he said. Given time, Jones may have flourished for Arsenal as Allison had hoped. The manager pointed to the problems that Alex James had settling in before producing his best a year into his Arsenal career and, to be fair, Jones had only one season before football was suspended at the outbreak of the Second World War. Cliff Bastin was never convinced by Jones and maintained that he should never have left Wolves. 'He would have been happier if he had stayed there,' said Bastin who had played for England against Welsh international Jones.

In all, the season was another anti-climax after the drama of the campaign that preceded it. Arsenal could manage no higher than fifth in the league behind champions Everton while their FA Cup quest came to an abrupt end in the third round when they lost at Chelsea. The following season was only three games old when football was stopped because of the war. But there was one distraction for Arsenal in what was a year of concern for everyone in Europe following the Nazi invasion of Czechoslovakia and Hitler's annexation of Austria. For their final league game of the 1938/39 season, Highbury was the setting for a film called *The Arsenal Stadium Mystery*. The match was against Brentford (referred to as Trojans for the purposes of the film), whose players were also to appear as extras in the film. The plot centres on a footballer who died of poisoning during a game at Highbury. Scotland Yard are called in to investigate and all the players become suspects. Brentford – to help the cameras in a film made in black and white – wore white shirts and black shorts. Arsenal won the match 2–0 with goals from Alf Kirchen and Ted Drake.

Chapter Five

THE WAR YEARS AND BEYOND

George Allison, Tom Whittaker and the setting up of the Arsenal Dynasty

Both Arsenal and Highbury contributed massively to the war effort and a total of 42 from Arsenal's 44 professional players went into the services. Nine were never to return – the highest loss of life suffered by any single club. The nine who perished were Henry Cook, Bobby Daniel, William Dean, Hugh Glass, Leslie Lack, William Parr, Sidney Pugh, Herbie Roberts and Cyril Tooze.

Highbury Stadium was used as a base for the Air Raid Precautions (ARP) unit and the Club moved to White Hart Lane for its wartime matches. There was a similar scenario in Manchester where Manchester United had to play at City's Maine Road ground because of bomb damage to Old Trafford. Highbury was hit several times because of its proximity to Kings Cross station, and people who lived near the stadium took shelter in the Arsenal Underground station during the raids. The ground was also used for other purposes, like providing rooms where air raid wardens could sleep while off duty and for the storage of gas masks and other equipment. Among the more serious hits on Highbury were a 1000-pound bomb, which fell on a practice area next to the ground and killed two RAF personnel, and the damage caused when five incendiary bombs hit the roof of the North Bank. In the fire that followed, the roof at that end of the ground collapsed.

It was only natural that supporters would fear for the welfare of the players who had joined the armed forces. Some were exempt, like Cliff Bastin. He was plagued with hearing difficulties that made him unfit for the call-up – although that information clearly did not find its way to Italy. Knowing how revered Bastin was in England as a footballer, Italian radio, as an ill-judged exercise in propaganda, declared that he had been taken prisoner. In fact, he never left London where he spent the war working as an ARP officer. Other Arsenal men who joined up included Tom Whittaker, who joined the RAF along with Eddie Hapgood, Ted Drake, Bernard Joy, Jack Crayston, Alf Kirchen, George Marks and Laurie Scott. Denis and Leslie Compton joined the army along with George Swindin, Bryn Jones and Reg Lewis.

Wartime success

During the Great War, football had been seen as an unnecessary luxury by the government who wanted the population's focus and all their energy on the war effort. But this time around, attitudes had changed and the game was actively encouraged. Indeed, the thinking was that such games kept spirits high in what was a desperate time for the country. A number of the Arsenal players in the forces contributed as fitness instructors and those who were not posted abroad played in re-shaped competitions. It also became accepted that clubs could use guest players. It was a logical step that meant that players could feature for the club nearest to the camp where they were based. In this way, for example, Stan Mortensen of Blackpool, Stanley Matthews of Stoke and Preston's Bill Shankly all pulled on the red shirt of Arsenal.

With Allison still managing the team, Arsenal's pre-war success was matched in the new competitions. In the 1939/40 season, they won the South A League and a year later they reached the final of the Football League War Cup. The match, against Preston, was played at Wembley. Leslie Compton missed a penalty and then Arsenal fell behind to a goal from Andy McLaren. But Denis Compton salvaged family pride by scoring an equalizer. The replay was at Blackburn but Arsenal's fate was sealed when Ted Drake was injured early in the game to effectively leave Arsenal with ten men. It was a handicap they could not handle as they lost 2–1. But more success was not far away. They won the London League in 1941/42 and the Football League South in 1943/43. They also reached the final of the Football League Cup South that year, which turned out to be a personal triumph for Reg Lewis. Their opponents, Charlton Athletic, were without their first-choice and popular goalkeeper Sam Bartram and were hammered 7–1 in front of 75,000 fans. Lewis scored four of the goals. The others came from Ted Drake, who scored twice, and Denis Compton. But it wasn't all glory for the Gunners that year. They played the winners of the League North Cup, Blackpool, at Stamford Bridge in a winner-takes-all play-off and were undone by the wing play of one Stanley Matthews.

Then, however, the military duties of several key players began to make an impact and deprived the Club of a number of top players: George Male (who went to the Middle East), Bryn Jones (to Italy) Leslie Compton and Reg Lewis (part of the invasion force to mainland Europe) and Denis Compton (who went to India). Ted Drake's career, too, came to a premature end after he suffered a slipped disc. But come the end of the war, the Club's problems had only just begun. As was becoming clear in the last season before the war, they had money problems. The Club had debts of £150,000 as football resumed post-war on a regional league basis during 1945/46 despite the ending of hostilities. The FA Cup, however, was revived though Arsenal had little joy in the competition, losing 6–1 to West Ham in the first of a two-legged tie. A 1–0 win at their adopted home of White Hart Lane in the second leg was little more than a consolation.

The Dynamos burn brightly

That season was also to produce one of the most remarkable matches ever seen in this country. In November 1945, Moscow Dynamo came to England to play a few friendly matches. They had already looked impressive in a 3–3 draw against Chelsea and they had annihilated Cardiff 10–1. Dynamo had also insisted on having a match against Arsenal on their tour itinerary.

As it transpired they played an Arsenal team in name only. The Club was still badly affected by military commitments and George Allison set about recruiting a team made up of several guest players in dervish-like fashion. He wanted to provide the standard of opposition that the Russians would have expected from an Arsenal side and the team he eventually assembled was a formidable one. There were six guests for the match played at White Hart Lane – goalkeeper Bill Griffiths from Cardiff, Joe Bacuzzi from Fulham, Reg Halton from Bury and three outstanding forwards... Stanley Matthews, Stan Mortensen and Ronnie Rooke. Allison rated Rooke highly and indeed would sign him from Fulham the following season. The match, which attracted 54,000 fans, was a strange affair to say the least. The day was thick with fog and for a time it seemed that the match might be postponed. However, the match got underway and, despite some extraordinary decisions from the Russian referee and his two linesmen Arsenal took a 3–2 lead with two goals from Mortensen and another from Rooke.

During the second half word reached Allison that if the Russians fell further behind the officials would abandon the match. At another point the Russians were thought to have had 12 players on the pitch. In the event, the Dynamos scored twice to take a 4–3 lead. Towards the end of the 90 minutes, with Arsenal desperate to equalize, a number of illegal incidents in the Dynamo penalty area went unpunished. The match ended with the visitors' honour satisfied.

Post-war rebuilding

It is worth describing here just what life was like in the years that followed the Second World War. The bombing of London had been ferocious and Highbury and its surroundings had not escaped the attentions of the Luftwaffe. Times were hard – very hard. It is difficult to appreciate what awaited the homecoming servicemen and women. The first problem they had to contend with was rationing. It is a concept that would be lost in these affluent days but what the homecoming heroes had to endure was incredible. The war had taken its toll in all walks of life but a shortage of food was the most difficult to accept for those who had put their lives on the line for freedom only to find that so little awaited them when hostilities ceased. Indeed, food rationing did not end until 1953 – some eight years after the war had ended.

Each person's weekly entitlement amounted to 4 ounces of meat, 2 ounces each of cheese and butter. Eggs? 'You were lucky if you saw one a week,' and bread was hard to come by. Jobs were also scarce. Many of the country's factories had been adapted for war work and were out of action. Fords at Dagenham, for example, a massive pre-war source of employment, had closed its gates for redevelopment. Others were left without work because their offices or factories had been destroyed during air raids and the jobs they left when called up just did not exist any more. It came as no surprise therefore that, despite the suffering and danger of the previous six years, many men and women re-enlisted to make sure of regular work and a square meal every day. However, around four million people had volunteered or been enlisted to take up arms against Germany and Japan, and many of those now struggled to feed their families.

By 1950, the average wage was about £9 a week. Some of those disenchanted with post-war life in Great Britain turned instead to emigration in search of a more promising future. What, after all, were they leaving behind? Those in jobs often worked a three-day week because of the shortage of fuel to allow their employers to operate. Power cuts were a regular occurrence. There were glimmers of hope under the new Labour government that had been voted in and ousted the heroic wartime leader Winston Churchill. The most welcome of all the reforms was the establishment of the National Health Service – used as a model throughout the world. The trains were also nationalized and were both economic to use and efficient.

But in this austere environment entertainment outlets were at a premium. There was the cinema, where Saturday morning shows for children were introduced to help ease the harsh monotony of their lives. Television? Forget it. Financially, that medium was a luxury way beyond the means of the vast majority of the population who, instead, listened avidly to the radio. And, of course, there was always football. 'Such a welcome release and escape,' said one pensioner who lived through those years. Massive crowds were drawn to all the London stadiums. Stamford Bridge, White Hart Lane and, when it was repaired after the war damage, Highbury, all attracted huge attendances of men who were anxious to forget the drudgery of their everyday lives and the hardships they had endured during the war. Despite the vast crowds there very little sign of hooliganism. 'We were used to discipline, to depending on each other in battle just a few years before,' was how it was explained to me. 'And football was a relief, not a reason to fight again. We had had enough of that.' Despite all that had happened there was still a general respect for authority among the population, people were tired of conflict and were searching for a more peaceful period in their lives. Football was an outlet for their frustration and provided a few hours of escapism. A pint before the game, a sandwich and Bovril at half-time then straight home – it was a grand day out!

Return to Highbury

In time Highbury was ready to stage football once again and Arsenal's first home match came in September 1946 against Blackburn. There was a feeling of anticipation in the ground before the game, and the fans were desperate to see their returning heroes in action again. Football was the perfect release from the grim years of conflict. However, the match did not provide the dream start that Arsenal wanted, with the Gunners losing 3–1. This on top of the 6–1 hammering they had received against Wolves at Molineux in the first match of the season did not bode well.

Only Bernard Joy, George Male, Reg Lewis and Cliff Bastin remained from the pre-war team and there were weaknesses all over the pitch. Things went pretty badly during the autumn and winter, with the team sitting second from bottom in December. Allison changed the team around regularly. Icelander Albert Gudmonssen was one of 31 players used in the league that season, a list that also included the flamboyant Irish doctor Kevin O'Flanagan who famously played for his country at football and rugby union. The only good thing was the goals of Reg Lewis, who scored 11 goals in the first ten games of the season.

In November Allison started planning for the New Year. The young Welsh full back Walley Barnes returned from injury and Allison made some crucial signings intended to get the Club out of trouble. The manager was made aware of a dispute between England wing half Joe Mercer and Everton. So disillusioned was Mercer that he seemed intent on retiring from the game altogether and running his grocery business in Wallasey. Allison made his interest known and Mercer duly signed – provided he could live and train in Merseyside. Allison saw no risk in paying out £7,000 for the bow-legged midfielder as, aged 32, he brought the experience that was needed to steady the ship. He also signed 35-year-old Ronnie Rooke from Fulham for £1,000. Both players were to prove inspired acquisitions.

Results improved in January and February, thanks mainly to the continuing flow of goals from Reg Lewis who ended the season with a total of 29, though Rooke chipped in with a highly respectable 21 in 24 games. The team ended the season in 13th place, their lowest finish since 1929/30. Interest in the FA Cup ended at the third round stage – although Arsenal were involved in a mammoth tussle with Chelsea that went to a second replay at White Hart Lane. The Pensioners eventually went through, courtesy of two goals from Tommy Lawton.

'Magic Hands' takes over

The end of the season also signaled the end of two distinguished Arsenal careers. The winter of 1947 had been particularly harsh and the Football League had been forced to extend the season into June. The hassle, the aggravation, the extra administration generated by the extension was too much for George Allison who, after some 40 years, decided to sever his ties with the Club. He made it clear that the match against Everton at the end of May would be his last. He said, 'Now I feel the need for a less strenuous life and I leave the future of Arsenal in other hands.' And Cliff Bastin, who had been hampered by injury and increasing deafness and whose last appearance had come the previous September, also announced his retirement.

It was a summer of takeovers in key roles at the Club. With Allison gone the board had to find a successor. The players petitioned them to appoint Tom Whittaker to the post. He had been a squadron leader during the war and was in fact awarded the MBE for his heroics. As trainer-come-physiotherapist, he had the trust and confidence of the players, who nicknamed him 'Magic Hands'. The board also liked what they saw in Whittaker who had been at the club for some 28 years as a player and then in the backroom staff that Herbert Chapman had assembled in such painstaking fashion. Chairman Samuel Hill-Wood asked Whittaker to join him in the boardroom. Whittaker had reservations. He liked the role of trainer, which had a low profile and enabled him to carry on his job effectively and anonymously. Whittaker was less outgoing and more reserved than Allison and baulked at any publicity and detested the limelight. But he accepted the job of secretary-manager.

One of Whittaker's first appointments was Joe Shaw, who had played for the Club with such distinction before the war, and who was now assistant-manager at Chelsea. He jumped at the chance to be Whittaker's right-hand man. On the playing side Allison had left the Club with the ingredients of a side capable of challenging for honours. As well as Rooke, Mercer and Barnes, a gifted inside forward by the name of Jimmy Logie was beginning to make his mark. He had been signed a few months ahead of the outbreak of the war from Lochcore

Juniors and when the conflict started he joined the navy and served his time on trawlers. Whittaker added Archie Macauley from Brentford and Don Roper from Southampton. He had planned to make Leslie Compton his captain but, just before the season started, discovered that Compton still had some County Championship games to play for Middlesex, so the responsibility was handed to Joe Mercer.

Expectations were high for the first game of the season against Sunderland. Things went well, with Ian McPherson, Logie and Rooke putting Arsenal 3–0 up at half-time and, although Sunderland pulled one back, the result was never in doubt. Neither was the outcome of the following game as Arsenal won 4–2 at FA Cup holders Charlton. Another win followed, against Sheffield United, beaten 2–1 with goals from Rooke and Roper. Then Charlton were beaten again, this time 6–0, with Lewis claiming four and Rooke another two. Sheffield United were lulled into a full sense of security when they went a goal up but Rooke snatched the equalizer and Roper scored the winner from 35 yards. Next up were Charlton again and they fared little better – indeed a lot worse – than in the previous encounter as they were thrashed 6–0 with Lewis scoring four with Rooke claiming the other two.

On 6 September Arsenal welcomed Manchester United to Highbury. Even back then, this clash had a lure of its own. United had a decent team that season, one that would go on to win the FA Cup the following May. But such was the interest in the game and there were 10,000 fans locked out when the match started. It was a titanic affair and fully lived up to its pre-match billing as Matt Busby's talented team went down 2–1 to goals from Rooke and Lewis. Bolton were next to try their luck at Highbury but they too went home with their tails between their legs after McPherson and Rooke, with a penalty, struck with no reply. But the Club's resources were now being strained and Arsenal finished the game with only seven fit men following injuries to Lewis, Alf Fields, Rooke and McPherson. Leslie Compton was still unavailable because of his cricket commitments and Whittaker gave serious thought to breaking their agreement with Middlesex to allow Compton to continue playing for them as he struggled to find enough quality players to maintain what had been a blistering start to the season.

But Compton was back for the next game, against Preston at Deepdale. Moments before the team went out to play Compton, who had been named captain that morning, made the most magnanimous of gestures. He threw the ball at Joe Mercer and said, 'Lead us out, Joe. You haven't been doing too badly in the job so far.' The match ended goalless as Arsenal badly missed the strike power of the injured Lewis, but the unbeaten run was extended. Further good results followed as Arsenal put together a sequence of 17 matches unbeaten and went six points clear at the top of the table. Suddenly the goals dried up and the run ended at the end of November at Derby's Baseball Ground where the Rams' Reg Harrison scored the only goal of the game. Defeat against Manchester City at Highbury seven days later was only avoided thanks to an 85th minute penalty from Rooke.

Champions again

Then the fixture list smiled on Arsenal. After a tough and exacting run of games came a visit to Blundell Park on 13 December to play bottom club Grimsby, and the scoring touch duly returned. The prolific Rooke scored two and Jimmy Logie and Don Roper scored one each in an emphatic victory. A hard-earned point at Roker Park against Sunderland, thanks to a late equalizer from Bryn Jones, left Whittaker impressed by the resilience of his team. A superb 3–1 win at Anfield on Christmas Day was matched by defeat at home to the same team two days later. But Arsenal's quality that season was to respond in exactly the right way whenever there was a setback, and they duly beat Bolton at Burnden Park, which marked the start of another unbeaten run.

Then came another of the FA Cup upsets that were to haunt Arsenal intermittently during their history. On the face of it, the home draw against Second Division Bradford Park Avenue looked a formality. A fourth-round place beckoned, though Whittaker cannot be accused of taking the task lightly. Indeed, he took his players down to Brighton to prepare for the match. However, the break was to no avail as Bradford won a famous victory, winning 1–0 with a goal from future England international winger Billy Elliott. Centre back for Bradford that day was one Ron Greenwood, and the future manager of West Ham and England was outstanding as Arsenal were kept at bay. The Arsenal players were despondent but Whittaker made it clear to them that self-pity was not an option.

There were two massive league games ahead against fellow title-challengers Manchester United and Preston. With Old Trafford still in the rebuilding stage after the damage inflicted during the war, Maine Road provided the setting for what was to prove a thrilling clash. United, in truth, had to win. But they fell behind to a strike by Lewis and hard as they tried, United could not add to an equalizer from Jack Rowley. The match was played in front of 83,260 spectators – still a record attendance for a Football League match. The result enabled Arsenal to recover their self-assurance after the Bradford humiliation and by the time Preston came to Highbury, they were back at their best. Two goals from Lewis and another from Rooke were enough to make sure of the points. Goalkeeper George Swindin was in inspired form for the following match at Stoke that finished goalless, and for the home game with Burnley Whittaker was able to call on fit-again Denis Compton. Burnley still considered themselves as contenders for the title but they were put in their place in no uncertain manner as Roper and Rooke – with two goals – ensured a vital victory.

A new player, Alex Forbes, made his debut against his former team Wolves at Highbury on 6 March. He scored in a 5–2 win, a game in which Denis Compton was outstanding. Compton scored twice himself in a 2–0 win over Everton the following week. A 7–0 mauling was handed out to Middlesbrough, but that was sandwiched between defeats at home to Chelsea and away at Blackpool. However, a 2–0 home win against Blackburn meant that victory at Huddersfield would secure the title. A 1–1 draw meant frayed nerves amongst the players travelling back to London on the train. But when the party reached Doncaster, Denis Compton was able to buy a paper with the classified results, and it emerged that Manchester United, Derby and Burnley had all lost and Arsenal were champions again. They celebrated in style at Highbury on the last day of the season as hapless Grimsby were thrashed 8–0. It was a significant match because it was the last for George Male – the last remaining link with the Herbert Chapman era.

The defence had proved mean all season, with Mercer and Macaulay outstanding. In midfield Jimmy Logie's scheming had unlocked many defences and Roonie Rooke's goalscoring prowess saw him hit the mark 33 times during the campaign. All aspects of the team's play had contributed to Arsenal's sixth league title.

Mercer's clump of turf

The following season was pretty average for the Club, a fifth-place finish in the league and defeat by Derby in the fourth round of the FA Cup. One good aspect of the season was the arrival of Doug Lishman from Walsall. A talented forward and former commando Lishman was as tough as they come. Ronnie Rooke left Highbury at the end of the season, despite scoring 14 goals at the age of 37, and moved on to Crystal Palace as player-manager. But the hub of the team remained Joe Mercer. At the start of the 1949/50 season Mercer was 35 and many people expected him to quit. But he was having none of it. As an Everton reserve before the war, his dream had been to play in the FA Cup final. In 1933, Everton reached the final and won the cup. Albert Geldard, who had played in the match, was aware of the young Mercer's burning ambition and offered him a clump of the Wembley turf that he had brought back to Merseyside as a treasured souvenir. Mercer declined. 'No thanks,' he said. 'I will get my own one day.'

That day was a long time coming – but come it did. The league season was launched in disappointing fashion. Indeed, Arsenal lost four of their first five games and the only victory came at Chelsea courtesy of goals from Lishman and Peter Goring. Though the Club recovered sufficiently to finish in sixth place the season's best was reserved for the FA Cup. A last-minute goal from the ageless Reg Lewis ensured victory over Sheffield Wednesday in the third round. In the fourth round the draw was kind again and the Gunners met Second Division Swansea at Highbury. Again, Arsenal made heavy weather of things and needed a penalty from Walley Barnes to see them through on a bone-hard January pitch. The fifth round brought another home tie, this time against Burnley. Once again Lewis put the Gunners ahead and Denis Compton added another with no reply. When the quarter-final draw brought another lower division side, in the shape of Leeds United, to Highbury, Arsenal supporters began to think, 'Our name is on the cup.' The Yorkshire outfit defended stoutly but their bravery came to nothing as, once again, that man Lewis ended their resistance.

Home advantage was finally surrendered for the semi-final, which as always, was played on a neutral ground. Even then, Arsenal emerged with good fortune. They were paired with Chelsea in a match to be staged at White Hart Lane – then Arsenal's second home as they had played there when Highbury was out of action through bomb damage. It may not have been a massive advantage but every psychological edge is welcome in what is traditionally a tense match like an FA Cup semi-final. Except it was Chelsea who looked far more at home than Arsenal as they went into a two-goal lead in the first 25 minutes. Chelsea were on fire, both goals coming from Roy Bentley, and Arsenal were struggling. Arsenal needed a boost and it came on the stroke of half-time. Winger Freddie Cox, who had signed from Tottenham the previous September, took a corner in the 44th minute. He curled the ball with the outside of his right foot. Harry Medhurst in the Chelsea goal was anticipating a cross. He realized too late that the ball was curling goalwards and it crossed the line to give Arsenal some hope at the break.

With 15 minutes left Arsenal, for all their improvement, were still trailing. Their incessant pressure earned another corner and as Denis Compton shaped to take it he beckoned his brother Leslie forward from defence to bolster the numbers already in the Chelsea area. Mercer attempted to stop the manoeuvre but the elder Compton would not listen. He duly went forward... and duly headed the equalizer. In the replay, again at White Hart Lane four days later, goals were at a premium. It was 0–0 after 90 minutes. The match was settled by another Freddie Cox strike, late in the first half of extra-time. Arsenal – at last – were back at Wembley.

Ironically, the five-mile trip from Highbury to Wembley was the longest journey Arsenal had needed to make en route to the final. They were due to meet Liverpool, a pairing that caused a number of problems for Joe Mercer. He still lived in the north-west and trained with the Liverpool players during the week. 'You can still train but only in the afternoons,' was the message to Mercer from Liverpool who feared he might just pass on their tactical plan to Arsenal. The build-up was all about Mercer. He was one of those figures whose personality had generated popularity among all the football-loving public, no matter what their club allegiance. Two days before the match, Mercer picked up the Football Writers' Footballer of the Year trophy. But he really wanted the one honour that had been missing from his impressive collection – an FA Cup winner's medal.

Liverpool, though, would be formidable opponents. They had a strong team, made up mainly of homegrown players, and led by powerful striker Billy Liddell. They also had a man with experience of the first Wembley final in manager George Kay who had played for West Ham against Bolton in 1923. The Liverpool team was confident having recorded two league victories against Arsenal that season – 2–1 at Highbury and 2–0 at Anfield.

The job of marking Liddell was given to Alex Forbes. But the major decision for manager Whittaker concerned Lewis. He was unsure whether to risk playing him as, despite his regular goalscoring, he tended to drift in and out of matches. Mercer, as captain, made the point politely yet forcibly to Whittaker that Lewis should be included. 'He is a match-winner,' was Mercer's argument. Whittaker finally agreed to play him. It was a decision vindicated after just 17 minutes of the match. The architect of Arsenal's first goal was the gifted Jimmy Logie who released Lewis with a perfectly weighted through-ball. The inside left then scored with a low shot. In the 63rd minute Harry Goring crossed from the left, Cox backheeled the ball and Lewis did the rest with a shot from 15 yards. Joe Mercer duly lifted the cup, received his coveted medal... and went home with his piece of Wembley turf.

Nearly the elusive Double

The league season, however, had not finished – and two wins, over eventual champions Portsmouth and Stoke City, ended the season on a high. That summer marked the end of Denis Compton's football career. He felt it was no longer practical to combine football and cricket at the top level, but he also had a recurrent knee injury to contend with. The 1950/51 season was another transitional year as new blood was brought into the line-up although it was the other Compton brother who could look back on a particularly memorable season. At the ripe old age of 38, Leslie Compton was given his England debut in November 1950 against Wales at Roker Park. A week later, Compton won his second – and last cap – against Yugoslavia and, fittingly, the 2–2 draw was staged at Highbury. Whittaker had introduced new faces into his line-up in a season that never reached the heights of the previous campaign even though Arsenal led the table at the halfway point of the season. The watershed game came against Stoke at Highbury on Christmas Day when two major players picked up bad injuries. Doug Lishman, who had already notched up 16 goals for the season, broke a leg, and keeper George Swindin suffered a bad knee injury. They were big losses.

Lewis was back for the second half of the season and the inexperienced Cliff Holton was drafted in but Arsenal had lost their rhythm and momentum. They finished fifth behind Tottenham who claimed their first title. The FA Cup defence ended at Old Trafford in the fifth round. The luck of the draw that had been so apparent the previous season was absent this time round. Arsenal had to go to Carlisle for a third-round replay and although Northampton were beaten in the fourth round, a Stan Pearson goal at Old Trafford was enough to ensure there would be no open-top bus parade around the streets of Islington in May 1951. Fifth in the league, fifth round of the FA Cup – it was a symmetry of disappointment.

The following season saw a marked improvement. With George Swindin back in goal and Ray Daniel installed at centre back instead of Leslie Compton, Joe Mercer was as indefatigable as ever and the defence remained solid. Cliff Holton and Doug Lishman looked a potent threat up front. The league was a close-run thing that season with a cluster of clubs staying in contention throughout the campaign; Arsenal among them.

The season was punctuated with a number of 'prestige friendlies', which were played under newly installed floodlights. The first – after a novelty encounter between famous boxers and jockeys of that era – was a clash with Hapoel Tel Aviv. Predictably, Arsenal won easily by 6–1 with Holton hitting three, Lewis two with one from Arthur Milton. The attendance was 44,000, the idea clearly one with merit. There was also a stage-managed christening for the lights from manager Whittaker. With the crowd already in the stadium and only minimal lighting to brighten the dark sky there was a sudden and uniform gasp as the floodlights were switched on. It had a massive impact on all who were there.

But Arsenal's season seemed to depend on a growing injury list. The fans had already started to dream of the elusive Double, and so did the players.

There were so many memorable moments that season – not least the attraction of the club's biggest post-war attendance of more than 72,000 to see a 1–1 draw with defending champions Tottenham in late September. At Christmas Arsenal were in contention, tucked in behind the leaders Manchester United. The FA Cup also provided excitement for Gunners fans. The run began with a trip to Carrow Road to play Norwich of the Third Division (South), a match Arsenal won 5–0. Next up were Barnsley, who came to Highbury in the fourth round and were hit for four of which Reg Lewis scored a hat-trick. In the fifth Arsenal had to face Leyton Orient at Brisbane Road. The prolific Lewis scored again but was injured in the process. Arsenal held on despite being down to ten men and Doug Lishman added two late goals to flatter the North Londoners. Again, top-fight opposition was avoided in the quarter-finals as Arsenal were drawn against Luton at their compact Kenilworth Road ground. A tight game saw the Bedfordshire side ahead at half-time. But Whittaker took the opportunity to re-shuffle his team and two goals from Cox, who then set up the third for Milton, put Arsenal in the driving seat. A late penalty gave the score a respectable look but the semi-final place belonged to Arsenal. There was a familiar look to the semi-final, against Chelsea at White Hart Lane. But those who had witnessed the epic match-up two years before were disappointed this time. The first match ended 1–1 but the replay was a walkover with Arsenal winning 3–0 with two goals from Freddie Cox and another from Lishman. Next up at Wembley in the final were the holders Newcastle United.

The omens were not good for Arsenal as the demands of the season began to take their toll. The injuries were mounting as the climax to the campaign approached. There was no psychological damage inflicted on the respective teams when they met in a league game at Highbury after the semi-final but ahead of the final. The match finished 1–1. Then the cruel hand of fate began to take a grip on Arsenal's hopes in both competitions. Ray Daniel broke his arm in a goalless draw at Blackpool and the powerful Lionel Smith hurt his knee in a 2–1 defeat at Bolton. Such was the injury crisis that the rarely used Leslie Compton was drafted back into action. A brief revival kept alive flickering hopes of the league title but in the end the streak of realism inside Whittaker took over. He knew that if he kept pushing for the league and his team fell short not only would he have demoralized players on his hands going to the clash with Newcastle but also exhausted ones. Mercer, for one, was feeling the effects of a punishing schedule and Whittaker showed his hand when he left his captain out of the league game at West Bromwich Albion. Arsenal lost 3–1. As far as the title was concerned, that was the end of the road. In footballing terms, a miracle was needed in the last league game at Old Trafford against Manchester United. Not only had Arsenal got to win – they had to win by seven goals to better United's goal average. They were without Lishman, who was in hospital with suspected blood poisoning, and Reg Lewis was in the team for what was to be his last senior appearance. But it was all to no avail. Not only did United win – they romped to an emphatic 6–1 victory. It was a defeat that cost Arsenal more than the title. Arthur Shaw broke his wrist to rule himself out of contention for a place against Newcastle. Those two defeats meant Arsenal were destined to finish third behind United and Spurs. Two wins and they could have been champions.

So, it was Wembley or bust. In the run up to the game, Arsenal's treatment room was more like the casualty department in a hospital on Saturday night. The two main concerns were Daniel, who was under intensive treatment for his broken wrist, and Logie who, according to Whittaker had a hole in his thigh, ' big enough to take a small apple'. There was still concern over Lishman. But all three were desperate to play to rescue something from a season that had once promised so much but now threatened to finish with no silverware.

In the event, all three lined up for the start of the game – Daniel with a protective plaster that needed to be passed by the match officials, Logie clearly unfit for the demands of the draining Wembley turf (again it is important to stress that no substitutes were allowed) and Lishman desperate to make amends for his omission from the final team two years earlier. But the gamble appeared to be paying off, Arsenal settled quicker and Lishman went close. However, the curse of injuries was to blight Arsenal right until the end of their season. Ten minutes from half-time and with the game still goalless, the gifted Arsenal full back Walley Barnes badly twisted his knee and was a virtual passenger for the rest of the game. While there were question marks against the fitness of several Arsenal players, there was no doubting their character.

Adversity brought them closer and they performed heroically in the second half. Don Roper switched to right back to make up for the inability of Barnes to fulfill the role and Cox was a constant handful for Newcastle. Bravery looked certain to bring its reward when, with ten minutes left, Lishman headed goalwards and the ball went over the bar by inches. Daniel, already with a fractured wrist, contrived to break another bone in his arm while falling over Newcastle front man Jackie Milburn. The toll of the season was telling and both Holton and Roper were down injured as Newcastle attacked with five minutes left. With the ball still alive, referee Arthur Ellis, despite the pleas from Mercer, allowed the game to continue rather than stop the action to allow treatment. The inevitable happened. A cross came in and Newcastle's Chilean striker George Robledo headed in via a post. Alex Forbes somehow mustered the energy to produce a shot that rattled the Newcastle bar but it was not to be – Newcastle retained the FA Cup.

But the heroics of the battered and depleted Arsenal team were not lost on Newcastle manager Stan Seymour. After the game he made a point of going to Whittaker and saying, 'Ours is the FA Cup; yours is the honour and the glory.' Later that night, Mercer summed up the feelings of pride within the Club at the sterling performance from a team that had suffered so any handicaps before and during the game. At the post-match dinner he stood up and said, 'I thought football's greatest honour was to captain England. I was wrong. It was to captain Arsenal today at Wembley.'

Chapter Six

GLORY AND DEMISE

The championship of 1953 was
the last great triumph at Arsenal
for almost 20 years

No matter what any particular football supporters' loyalties were, there was justifiable cause for celebration in London when the 1952/53 season reached the halfway point around New Year. Gradually, the austerity of the aftermath of the Second World War was beginning to erode. In 1953, the policy of rationing came to an end. Christmas that year was a symbolic turning point in many ways – at last food became available in more plentiful supply. There was hope and a new optimism in society. And, for Arsenal fans, there was also the thrill of a hotly contested battle for the title with Preston that went down to the last day.

Arsenal started the campaign still feeling the effects of their Wembley combat with Newcastle. Walley Barnes was the most notable casualty because he was to miss the entire season with the knee injury that hampered Arsenal so badly against the Geordies. Thankfully, Whittaker was able to find the perfect replacement in Joe Wade. In goal a young Welshman called Jack Kelsey emerged as the new first choice, and in Don Oakes, they had a player who had waited seven long years for his chance to play up front and when it came he took it with both hands, scoring the winning goal in the win away at Aston Villa on the first day of the season. Four days later a second win, this time at Highbury over Manchester United, was blighted by a serious injury to Oakes, which resulted in him not being seen in an Arsenal shirt until the latter end of the following season.

Hard-earned triumph

But after that impressive start, Arsenal faded badly. They won only one of their next six games and the championship seemed light years away from reality. However, re-enforced by the return of Arthur Milton who came back from county cricket duties with Gloucestershire, Arsenal picked up dramatically as autumn set in. Portsmouth, Tottenham, Blackpool and Newcastle were all beaten, and Hibernian were hammered 7-1 in a floodlit friendly. It is generally reckoned that the immense performance from Jimmy Logie that night made his call-up by Scotland irresistible. He went on to win, at the age of 33, his one and only cap against Austria at Hampden. The honour had come too late in Logie's career for him to make any kind of impact at international level but it was just reward for the contribution the talented man had made to football in Britain. He was an artist and if he had played in the modern era, with its plethora of international fixtures, he would have been closing in on the half-century of caps rather than finishing 49 short of that mark.

He was certainly in inspired form again at the end of November as Arsenal produced one of their most impressive performances of that season with the 5-1 demolition of Liverpool on their own Anfield pitch. It was an astonishing and awesome performance. Ben Marden was drafted in from the reserves and scored twice while the powerhouse Cliff Holton scored a hat-trick. But Christmas Day witnessed an even more memorable encounter. In the 1950s Christmas Day was for the fans not the players. Modern players may moan about having to train on Christmas Day to prepare for the holiday programme, but in 1952, they were required to play on the day itself. Usually, the fixture list would pair teams with a local rival – in Arsenal's case Tottenham, Chelsea or West Ham. That at least cushioned the blow of having to play on what is traditionally a day for families. But that season Arsenal had to play Bolton at Burnden Park.

The ground was full – and the feast that those supporters had ready for them on their return was nothing compared to the banquet of attacking football that was served up to them during the game. Despite the final scoreline, goalkeeper Jack Kelsey finished as something of a hero. At half-time Arsenal were 2–1 ahead in what had been a high-tempo but not exceptional clash. Willie Moir had put Bolton ahead but Arsenal equalized through Arthur Milton and had then taken the lead through Holton. Two goals early in the second half, from Jimmy Logie and Don Roper, put the Londoners in a seemingly unbeatable position. But Moir struck again to pin them back. Arsenal's centre half Ray Daniel then converted a penalty to put his team 5–2 up. With ten minutes left Bolton threw men forward leaving spaces at the back, and sure enough, Holton scored again to put the result beyond doubt. Or so they thought. Bolton front man Nat Lofthouse – a muscular striker and no friend of goalkeepers – scored once and then again to make it 6–4. Bolton's hopes were lifted even higher when they were awarded a penalty with two minutes left. But just when they needed it, keeper Jack Kelsey came to the rescue and saved Langton's spot-kick. Although it had seemed unlikely, the points were finally secured.

That victory, which came at the end of a run of six unbeaten games, kept Arsenal in the leading pack. Preston and Wolves were their main rivals. A 4–1 home win over Bolton in the middle of April put Arsenal in pole position. But, on the last Saturday of the season, they were down to play Preston at Deepdale in the penultimate match. By then, Arsenal were two points ahead of their closest rivals but with a superior goal difference. They could afford to lose but not by a huge margin. They did lose, but it wasn't a disaster. The mercurial Tom Finney and Charlie Wayman got the goals in a 2–0 win for the

Lancashire club. Arsenal still held a narrow advantage and both teams had one game left.

Preston played first on the following Wednesday evening, beating Derby 1–0 courtesy of a Finney penalty. On the Friday night Arsenal played Burnley at Highbury. Only a win would clinch the title and 51,500 people were there to witness the event. The script was not going to plan early in the match as Burnley took the lead. Just three minutes had passed when Joe Mercer deflected a low centre from Burnley winger Roy Stephenson into his own net. Preston's spirits were lifted; Arsenal's were dampened. But not for long, as first Alex Forbes, then Doug Lishman and then Jimmy Logie all scored to give Arsenal a 3–1 lead before the half-time whistle sounded. Burnley – themselves a top six team and with talent aplenty in their line-up – refused to capitulate. If Arsenal were to be crowned champions that night, they were going to have to earn it. They pulled one goal back and from a policy of all-out attack, Arsenal reverted to one of dogged defence. The end of the match was nail-biting, with Mercer dominant and Swindin making some wonderful saves. But, it was enough... just. The 3–2 win secured the league title on goal average – 0.099 of a goal! Arsenal's players and supporters celebrated long and hard. It was the seventh league title, and probably the hardest earned.

The rot sets in

Just why Arsenal fell into such decline after this is not easy to explain. Maybe it was just their turn to suffer a dip in fortunes. It happens to all football clubs, even Manchester United had to endure a season in the old Second Division when they were relegated in the 1970s. It meant their fans had to look forward to such mouth-watering fixtures as away at York City. As their manager Tommy Docherty quipped at the time, 'I have not been there since I was demobbed.' Thankfully, Arsenal did not have to suffer that indignity. Thanks to Sir Henry Norris, Arsenal started life after the First World War in the First Division and it is a status they have held ever since. But a decline set in after the title win in 1953.

Even before a ball was kicked in the 1953/54 season, the Club suffered a huge emotional shock with the death of Alex James from cancer. Somehow it seemed symbolic. James was an iconic figure at the Club – something of a maverick as a player but blessed with supreme ability. James was indulged but he also repaid the Club for the faith that was shown in him. It was a sad time for all connected with Arsenal and it truly seemed an era was coming to an end. The team that had brought the league trophy back to Highbury was on the wane. There was even embarrassment away from competitive football when Arsenal were beaten 6-1 in a friendly against Rapid Vienna. Form was no better at domestic level. They went the first eight matches of the season without a win as they lost six and drew two. Arsenal could not even raise their game against London rivals Chelsea as they tamely surrendered in a 2-1 defeat. Then came humiliation at Sunderland – in a match that was to be the last for long-serving and loyal goalkeeper George Swindin. As is the case with many heavy defeats, there was no indication early in the game of the rout that was to follow. Indeed, Doug Lishman even gave Arsenal the lead at Roker Park. Then the floodgates opened... as Arsenal were beaten 7-1.

Manager Whittaker knew he had to act and looked for help from the most unlikely of sources. Tommy Lawton was one of the original superstars of the game but he was struggling in his job as player-manager of Brentford. And when Whittaker received a phone call from Brentford chairman Frank Davies indicating that Lawton was for sale, (Brentford had a cash flow problem and needed the money badly) Whittaker did not dismiss the idea out of hand. True, Lawton was now 34 years of age, but the more that Whittaker thought about it, the more he was convinced that Lawton could give the team and the supporters a lift. He was, after all, not much older than Ronnie Rooke had been when he signed for Arsenal and he went on to serve the club admirably. Whittaker acted quickly and signed his man in a hush-hush deal and on 19 September Lawton was paraded in front of the Highbury crowd ahead of the game against Manchester City. His arrival had the desired effect of lifting morale among the fans but it failed to have the impact that Whittaker wanted on the pitch. Lawton was to stay two and half seasons but he was never able to stake a regular place. 'I am a lucky young man,' said Lawton when he signed, but he was unable to live up to his billing. His best days were behind him, and it was several months before he was to score his first goal for Arsenal, in a clash with Aston Villa the following April. It could have all been so different for Lawton some 20 years earlier when he was a player with Burnley. He had been a target for Arsenal and manager George Allison made a bid for him. But so did Everton and Lawton decided to stay in the north west. 'The biggest mistake of my life,' said Lawton of his decision back in 1936. When Whittaker signed him, the Arsenal manager was desperate and at one stage Arsenal were bottom of the table. But in an 18-game run, Arsenal won ten, drew six and lost only twice. They eventually finished 12th behind champions Wolverhampton Wanderers. After the nightmare start, it was an acceptable finish.

If Arsenal were looking for glory in the FA Cup as compensation, they were to be disappointed as they were victims of yet another upset. The campaign had started in impressive enough fashion with an emphatic 5–1 against Aston Villa. Norwich at home in the fourth round had the look of a formality. It was to be anything but – and Arsenal also had to suffer the indignity of a sending-off for Alex Forbes after he had clashed with Norwich's Bobby Brennan. Then there was the indignity of defeat. Keeper Jack Kelsey could do nothing about two headers put past him by Norwich striker Tommy Johnston and though Arsenal launched all-out assault, it brought only one goal from Jimmy Logie.

Another indication that the Arsenal cycle of success was beginning to turn full circle came in April 1954. Whittaker, understandably, was becoming selective with the games for which he would select Joe Mercer. Mercer had been a fantastic servant to Arsenal, the Club where he had fulfilled his dream of winning the FA Cup. Liverpool were due at Highbury towards the end of the season and Mercer nagged away at Whittaker to be included. Whittaker relented. For Mercer it was a fateful decision because he broke his leg and made his farewell to the Arsenal fans on a stretcher. Arsenal won the game 3–0 but that was little consolation. A new, uncomfortable era was about to start at Highbury in which the word mediocre would figure prominently.

'Lead us out' Joe

Joe Mercer junior was born on 9 August 1914 in Ellesmere Port, Cheshire. He was the son of Joe senior who had played for Nottingham Forest and Tranmere Rovers. Mercer clearly inherited his father's qualities. He first emerged as a player with his local team in Ellesmere Port, where he earned a reputation as a man who would never shirk a tackle and who was blessed with tremendous anticipation to snuff out danger. Such talent did not go unnoticed at Everton. He was snapped up by the Goodison Park club and, by the tender age of 18 – in a more ruthless and harder world than confronts the teenagers of the modern era – was a first-team regular. He won honours with Everton including a League Championship in 1938/39, and between 1938 and 1939 he won five England caps. But come the Second World War Mercer was called to arms. He spent his time in the army where he rose to the rank of sergeant major. He also captained England on many occasions during the 26 times he represented his country in wartime internationals.

But as well as his talent, Mercer had character, and never was that better illustrated than when he bore the brunt of criticism from his Everton manager Theo Kelly. Kelly accused Mercer of not trying in an international against Scotland. In reality, Mercer was suffering from a serious cartilage injury and had consulted an orthopaedic surgeon. However, even after examining the surgeon's report, Kelly still did not believe him and Mercer was forced to pay for an operation to correct the problem himself.

In late 1946, Mercer joined Arsenal where his career was to experience a dramatic and memorable renaissance. He cost Arsenal £9,000, which was to prove the definitive bargain. But Kelly was resentful of Mercer leaving – so much so that he brought Mercer's boots to the transfer talks to deprive the player of any reason to go back to Goodison and thereby prevented him saying his farewells to the other players. He made his debut for Arsenal against Bolton on 30 November 1946 and was appointed captain within months, taking over from the popular Leslie Compton and with whose blessing he got the job. He managed to produce performances of a consistently high standard despite commuting from Merseyside and training with Liverpool. He was the inspiration of the team that enjoyed much success in the late 1940s and early 1950s. From a team that flirted with the wrong half of the First Division table the season before he joined, under his leadership they won the league in 1947/48. He won an FA Cup winner's medal in 1950 to fulfill a career-long ambition and was voted Footballer of the Year that same season.

He was a real captain, a great leader and, after losing the FA Cup final to Newcastle in 1952, he was an integral part of the side that regained the league title in 1952/53. He was due to retire at the end of that season but stayed for one more year. A decision on his retirement was ultimately made in April 1954 during a home game against Liverpool. He suffered a double facture of his leg after a collision with team-mate Joe Wade. In all, he played 275 times for Arsenal.

When he stopped playing, Mercer decided to run a grocery shop but the call of the game was too strong and in 1955, he came back into football as manager of Sheffield United. He was not an immediate success in his new role and United were relegated at the end of the 1955/56 season. Unhappy with managing a Second Division side Mercer took over at top-flight Aston Villa in December 1958. However, Villa were bottom of the First Division at the time and he could not keep them up and they too were relegated. But this time he stayed and began to blood a conveyor belt of young talent who became known as the 'Mercer Minors'. He led Villa to victory in the first-ever League Cup in 1961 but three years later suffered a stroke and, when he recovered, was sacked by the Villa board.

A year later he was back once again showing his grit and determination. He took over at Manchester City in 1965 where he was to enjoy tremendous success with the flamboyant Malcolm Allison as his right-hand man. The club won promotion from the Second Division in 1966 to regain what they regarded as their rightful place among the elite. Two years later, in 1968, City won the First Division title and the honours just kept on coming. They won the FA Cup in 1969, the League Cup a year later and, in that same season, the European Cup-Winners' Cup. During his time at Maine Road a whole host of top players came through – Colin Bell, Neil Young, Mike Doyle,

Mike Summerbee and Francis Lee to name just a few. But while Mercer was receiving the accolades, Allison grew resentful. He felt that his training ground tactics were just as responsible for City's success as Mercer's leadership. What seemed a perfect match ended in divorce in 1972 when Allison took sole charge of the club. Mercer, feeling that his position had been undermined, left to take over as manager of Coventry City. He stayed there for three years and remained a hugely popular and respected individual in English football.

In 1974 Sir Alf Ramsey quit as England manager following his team's failure to reach the World Cup finals in West Germany that year, and Mercer was asked to take temporary charge of the national side. He was in charge for seven games and had some success. The Home International championship was still going and England shared the title with Scotland. His record was – played seven, won three, drawn three and lost one. He quit as Coventry manager in 1975 but remained as a director of the club until his retirement from football in 1981. He had been given the OBE in 1976 as a mark of his contribution and services to football. He died in 1990 after suffering a stroke on his 76th birthday. He is regarded as one of the best loved and fondly remembered of all Arsenal captains.

The doldrums

For almost 20 years, Arsenal were unable to leave a mark on the English game. It wasn't a shortage of players because in that period they were to have their share of talented individuals. But the hard reality is that between 1954 and 1969 they only once finished higher than fifth – and life was not made easier by the emergence of other outstanding teams like the Busby Babes at Manchester United and the double-winning team from Tottenham in 1961. It was almost as though life passed Arsenal by from the mid-1950s until the end of 1960s. And with time came other, tragic milestones. None hit Arsenal harder than the death of Tom Whittaker in October 1956. He had managed to take a distinctly average Arsenal team into ninth place in the table, although the FA Cup run came to an end early in the competition with a fourth-round defeat against Wolverhampton Wanderers. Whittaker was feeling the strain. He had rebuilt a club that was relegation fodder when he took over into one that won titles and FA Cups on a regular basis. He had spent big at times but also invested wisely and adhered to the principles laid down by the man who had such a great impact on his career – Herbert Chapman.

There is a school of thought that Whittaker, in many ways Chapman's protégée, put so much mental and physical effort into the running of the Club he loved that he paid the ultimate price with his life. A year before he passed away, Whittaker had undergone an operation during the Easter of 1955. He never completely recovered. Instead of taking it easier after the surgery, Whittaker, if anything, increased his workload. And words that Whittaker had uttered some years before would come back to haunt him. 'Someone has to drive himself too hard for Arsenal,' he said. 'Herbert Chapman worked himself to death for the Club, and if that is to be my fate, I am happy to accept it.' They were prophetic words indeed. Before his 60th birthday, Whittaker passed away on 24 October 1956 at University College Hospital. He was still actively working as manager at the time – just like Chapman.

The players, those who had played for him in the past and those of that current squad, were devastated. 'Meeting him was the greatest thing that ever happened to me,' said Joe Mercer. 'Arsenal was his kingdom. In every football-playing country in the world he was acknowledged as a prince of the game. There has never been a greater man in football. It is a game of hard knocks but Tom never hit anybody. He never shirked making a hard decision, like sacking or dropping a player – or any of the other things that can hurt deeply. But the way Tom did it, it never did. Tom made bad sportsmen into good sportsmen. He made good footballers into great footballers. I know he never did a bad thing. All problems had just one solution – the one done with kindness. I saw Tom a couple of months ago. He looked ill but he had already started a new phase in Arsenal history. He realized the days of big buying were over. His plans only included youngsters. And every youngster who ever went to Highbury quickly learned one thing – the only thing that mattered was the Club. When he made a decision, if it was for the good of the Club, it was right.'

Whittaker, as Mercer said, was known and respected all over the world. Never was that more apparent than when he took Arsenal on tour to Brazil in the close season of 1949. Arsenal arrived in Sao Paolo in their ambassadorial role and Whittaker took pains to find out about the local supporters. He discovered that many had Italian roots and therefore a proportion would have been affected by the tragic Superga air crash, which had claimed the lives of the entire – and hugely talented – Torino team in 1939. At his suggestion, before the match both teams stood with their head bowed to pay their respects. He even insisted that the music 'Ave Maria' be played. The gesture was warmly appreciated. Mercer's description of Whittaker as a hard but fair individual was never more apparent than after Arsenal had taken a 7–1 hammering at Sunderland. Centre back Bill Dodgin blamed himself for an awful individual performance that had contributed to the defeat and went in to see Whittaker. He asked to be dropped because of his performance. Dodgin recalled later, 'I actually left his office quicker than I went in. He said that if there was any dropping to be done, then he would do it.'

The stress of the job was having a palpable effect on Whittaker's health and this did not go unnoticed within the Club. To ease his workload, Arsenal brought in Alec Stock from Leyton Orient in February 1956 as his assistant. It was an ill-fated appointment. Within six weeks Stock – later to find fame as manager of Fulham, taking them to the 1975 FA Cup final against West Ham – had gone. There was some unease among the players at his arrival because it was a job that was already being done as far as they were concerned, by former player Jack Crayston. Stock did not endear himself to the squad. His first team talk – or 'natter' as Stock called it – both alarmed and upset the players. 'At the end of the season,' he said. 'Twenty of you will be leaving.' They were stunned. 'We were just not used to be being spoken to in that way,' said goalkeeper Jack Kelsey. Further alienation was to come. Stock had his own ideas about how to attain the necessary fitness and emphasis was put on group sessions of sprinting and turning. A smoking ban was also introduced. These were the days when smoking was socially acceptable and many players indulged in the habit in ignorance of its harmful effects. Results were not good under the Stock regime with the players unhappy and disaffected with his methods. He abruptly left with the Club in 17th place in the table. Such was the relief at his departure that the team went on to win seven of their last nine games and finished in fifth place.

But when the time came to replace Whittaker, the Arsenal board decided that the demands of the job were too much for one man. Jack Crayston – a member of the team that won two league titles and an FA Cup before the war – was put in charge of the football while Bob Wall was promoted to secretary. The days of the one-man-band at Arsenal were over. The Club accepted that the stress, pressures and responsibility were too much for one man. There is even evidence of a fan who had applied for an FA Cup final ticket receiving a return letter rejecting his request – and it was signed by Herbert Chapman himself. Crayston was a logical choice. He had become Whittaker's right-hand man and had more status than an assistant. He had training as an accountant, so helped with the bookkeeping, and on occasions was also a trusted scout. He was an Arsenal man through and through. He had come through the reserves and become not only a first-team player with Arsenal but also represented England on eight occasions. He had been brought up in the traditions of Arsenal and was aware of the heritage that he had inherited. But although he worked hard enough to bring more success to the Club, it was to be a frustrating time for him and the fans.

Chapter Seven

SOCIAL CHANGE AND A NEW AUDIENCE

The 1960s was a period of huge social change in England – Arsenal were unable to keep up

Jack Crayston's time as manager came in an era of massive social change in Britain. The austere years of the war were fast fading into memory and there was a new wealth in the country, enjoyed by a new, brash generation. They demanded freedoms that were denied their parents in the tough years of unemployment and hardship in the 1930s and the immediate post-war years. They wanted independence and there was the emergence of a sense of rebellion against the establishment. The two generations that had preceded them had done little but engulfed the country in two world wars and the suffering and misery that came with them. No more, they said. They began to run their own lives.

Cultural revolution

They had their own music, the rock 'n' roll that had been imported from the United States – first by Bill Haley and his film *Rock Around the Clock* and then the iconic Elvis Presley. The youth began to make statements through fashion, through their winklepicker shoes, drape coats and greasy, swept-up hair. They were the Teddy Boys and they became the statement of youth in the mid- to late-1950s. While their parents had accepted authority largely without question, suddenly that authority was being ignored. While their fathers had no option but to satisfy their need to belong to a peer group by joining the armed forces, the sons found it by joining street gangs. They had their own music, their own slang and their own fashion.

In the slipstream of Elvis Presley came the British counterparts – Cliff Richard, Adam Faith, Billy Fury, Tommy Steele and Joe Brown. There were no more curfews for this generation. They wanted their own lives and demanded their own culture. The singer-entertainer Max Bygraves summed up the changing trends in society with his song, 'Fings Ain't What They Used To Be'. It included the lyrics, 'They changed our local palais into a bowling alley,' and, 'Once our beer was frothy but now its frothy coffee.' The young men and women wanted their own identity. Clem Cattini, drummer with the Tornados who hit No.1 in the pop charts with the tune 'Telstar', summed it up when he said, 'We just wanted our own lives. All our parents had known was war and fighting and unemployment. We wanted something different.' Cattini, a committed Arsenal fan who now works at the Club on a part-time basis, explained, 'We didn't want any more war. There was money about and not so much unemployment. I used to go down a lot to the famous Two Is coffee bar in Soho. It was where the wannabe pop stars used to go to perform, to get their names and voices heard. And they would also work there for a few extra shillings. I was served by Harry Webb and Terry Nelmes –you might know them better as Cliff Richard and Adam Faith. We wanted to enjoy ourselves, simple as that.'

The media was also expanding. There was the birth of musical papers aimed directly at the young, publications like the *New Musical Express* and *Melody Maker*. It was no longer a world simply for adults and the youth of the 1950s were alienated from their parents like no other. This was their time, this was their statement. Cinema was booming, many houses had televisions while radio output was developing. There was even a station to break the monopoly of the BBC based on mainland Europe called Radio Luxembourg. It played only pop records and although the reception sometimes faded, it was hugely popular. Record players were available in the shops – called Dansette Juniors – and smaller discs, called 'singles' that played at 45rpm, were in production to replace the larger 78s.

There was the advent of commercial television (ITV) and all the consumers' wants were satisfied. In the modern world, smoking is both frowned upon and dissuaded. There is one contemporary public service advertisement that shows a girl being approached by a man who is attracted to her – only for him to recoil when he realizes she is a smoker. By contrast, back in the mid-1950s, the man with the cigarette was the one who got the girl. The backdrop, of course, was one of global uncertainty. The Cold War was a constant reminder of the ever-present threat of nuclear conflict, which if it started, would wipe whole countries off the face of the earth. There were other ongoing conflicts too, like those in Korea and the Middle East. But rather than worry, the youth of the 1950s and 1960s opted to make the most of the leisure facilities that were opening up to them on a regular basis. Many were able to afford cars and there were also motorcycle gangs with their leather jackets and aggressive approach to life that imitated their mentors, the Hell's Angels of the United States, where youth was in a similar state of rebellion.

A new wave of television programmes and films had a more realistic edge and reflected true life rather than offering escapism. It was an era of HP – hire purchase – where a deposit was put down on one of the many goods that were beyond the reach of the pre-war generation and those in the years after the conflict. The goods were then paid for over a number of years. There was even a film that summed up the ethos of the times – *Live Now, Pay Later*. The old order had gone forever as the young took full advantage of their new world. Competition for their money and their attention was fierce. While professional sport, and football in particular, was the main recreational outlet in the preceding years, suddenly there was strong competition for the time and money of the growing audience of the Baby Boomer years.

Lack of funds

Arsenal tried to compete but they found themselves hamstrung by a lack of funds. While the late, great Sir Matt Busby had the vision and foresight to invest heavily in the youth policy at Manchester United in the post-war years, Arsenal had relied heavily on an ageing squad that constantly had to be rejuvenated. There were excellent young players who emerged – like Welshman Derek Tapscott for example, who finished the 1956/57 season as top scorer. But there was nothing like the strength and depth of the squad at United, whose potential was never to be fulfilled because of the Munich air crash tragedy. Their names were legendary – Tommy Taylor, Duncan Edwards, Eddie Colman, David Pegg, Roger Byrne and others. Crayston just could not compete with the players that were to become known as the 'Busby Babes'.

But Crayston was an intelligent man. He was aware of what was happening at Highbury. When he was officially appointed manager, in December 1956, he sounded out the board on cash to replenish his squad, going through a number of players he wanted to approach. On almost every occasion the answer was a firm 'no'. One pertinent case had been that of Welsh winger Cliff Jones who was emerging as a huge talent at Swansea. The Welsh club knew they had a special asset on their hands and would not sell at less than his true value. Eventually, he went, of all places, to Tottenham. Arsenal finished that season in fifth place, but Crayston could see the need for new blood and for new faces, and the Club's league performances the following season proved he was right. He was helped immensely by the appointment of Ron Greenwood in the winter of 1957, but even with the input from the man generally recognized as one of the brightest, most innovative and gifted coaches this country has ever produced, Crayston struggled. A mediocre league campaign saw the team get 39 points from 42 matches. The league season is chiefly remembered for the encounter with Manchester United at Highbury. A hugely entertaining game saw United win 5–4. It turned out to be the last time that the Busby Babes played in England. A few days after the game they flew to Belgrade for a European Cup clash with Red Star. It was on the way back from that match that the plane crashed, on the runway at Munich airport, killing nine players and 14 others.

The league campaign was bad enough, they eventually finished in 12th place, but what really hurt was the exit to the minnows of Northampton Town in the third round of the FA Cup. At the end of the season, Crayston decided to call it a day. No success, no funds, no success, he could see no way out of the cycle of despair. It was a huge decision for him. After all he had been attached to Arsenal for the best part of a quarter of a century. But he had had enough. He wouldn't be able to carry on under those conditions.

A new regime

The favourite to replace him was the ever-popular Joe Mercer who had been afforded legendary status by the Arsenal fans. And it was known that he would have relished the job of turning the club he had served with such distinction into a successful one once again. But the board chose former goalkeeper George Swindin and retained Greenwood as his assistant. They made a good pair. Swindin was all about tradition while Greenwood was all for new ideas. Swindin had cut his managerial teeth at Peterborough where, under his leadership, the club had earned a reputation as FA Cup giant-killers. For years to come, no one relished a game against the Posh, as they were nicknamed. And in his first season, Arsenal appeared to respond to his management and Greenwood's guidance on the training pitch. They finished third in the league behind Wolverhampton Wanderers and were unlucky to go out of the FA Cup at the fifth round stage to Sheffield United in a replay during which goalkeeper Jack Kelsey broke an arm.

Despite four years in the hot seat Swindin was unable to bring back the glory days to Highbury. It made matters considerably worse for the

Arsenal faithful to witness the Glory Glory days that were happening a few miles across North London at the time. In 1959/60 Arsenal finished 13th, Tottenham came third. The following season Arsenal finished 11th and Tottenham won the Double. The Double-winning Spurs side featured the likes of Danny Blanchflower, Dave Mackay and, ironically, Cliff Jones, the player that Jack Crayston had tried to sign. They were all-conquering and played football with style – and that was hard for Arsenal supporters to take.

Arsenal simply didn't have the wherewithal to compete with their successful neighbours and it was increasingly difficult for the Club to raise funds to buy players. No success, no players, smaller crowds. It was the same problem that had confronted Jack Crayston. There were exceptions, of course, like the powerful winger Danny Clapton – who incidentally remains the all-time favourite player of chief shareholder Danny Fiszman. Such was the dearth of talent at Highbury that Clapton became the first Arsenal player for five years to be capped by England when he was selected in 1959. This from a club that once provided the backbone of the England team. Another player in the news was George Eastham. Although technically a Newcastle player, the slight but talented midfielder was in dispute with his club and wanted to join Arsenal. The dispute was serious and had far-reaching implications. He was the Jean-Marc Bosman of the time.

The George Eastham saga

Eastham was the most unlikely of martyrs. He had football in his blood (his father played for Bolton, Blackpool and England, and his uncle for Liverpool). He was frail looking but behind that frame was a fighter and he was determined to fight for what he thought was right. He had started his career with Ards in Northern Ireland and joined Newcastle in 1956. In all he played 125 times for Newcastle and scored 34 goals. But in 1959 he fell out with the club over several issues. He was not happy with the house that had been provided for him or with the part-time job they had arranged for him to supplement his income of £20 per week – the maximum wage that players were allowed to earn. Eastham was also unhappy with the way that Newcastle tried to block his appearances for the England under-23 team. At that time, a system was in place known as 'retain-and-transfer'. The terms of the system meant that clubs had the right to say when a player moved. Eastham, with the backing of the club that wanted to sign him, announced that he thought this was unfair.

His contract was due to run out that year, he refused to sign a new one and demanded a transfer. Newcastle not only turned down his request but also stopped paying him. It was a ludicrous situation and Eastham later said, 'Our contract could bind us to a club for life. Most people called it a "slavery contract". We had virtually no rights at all. It was often the case that the guy on the terrace not only earned more than us – though there is nothing wrong with that – but he also had more freedom of movement than us. People in business or in other professions like teaching were able to hand in their notice and we weren't. That was wrong.' So Eastham started a process that was to end in a landmark ruling. During the 1959/60 season he went on strike and moved south to Guildford where he worked for an old friend of the family – Ernie Clay, later to become chairman of Fulham. He refused to return to Newcastle and was treated like an outcast by the Club.

But, come October 1960, Newcastle had to admit that matters had reached an impasse. True Eastham wasn't playing, but the Club recognized that a valuable asset was going to waste and decided to accept the £47,500 being offered by Arsenal. However, Eastham was not finished. He had the backing of the players' union (PFA), who financed him to the tune of £15,000, and eventually the High Court in his favour in 1963. Eastham, who had not let the litigation distract him from impressive form for Arsenal, argued that the situation of the footballer was an illegal restraint of trade and that Newcastle owed him not only £400 in unpaid wages but also £650 in unpaid bonuses. The judge, Justice Wilberforce, came down partly on his side. He agreed that the retain-and-transfer system was restraint of trade and unreasonable but he also said that because Eastham had refused to play for Newcastle during the period of his strike, any payment was to be at the club's discretion. Naturally they refused. But Eastham had won his case in so much as the whole transfer system had to be reformed. 'Retain' was all but eliminated from the procedure and certainly revised. Players could now look for more lucrative terms before re-signing for their clubs at the end of a contract and a transfer tribunal was set up to mediate on any disputes.

However, the stance he took made him a good few thousand enemies on Tyneside. When he returned to St James' Park with Arsenal in the 1959/60 season, he scored in a 3–3 draw, but he was faced with a barrage of constant jeering, called Judas and pelted with fruit. Eastham had six seasons with Arsenal and, by and large, he was a regular in the side. However, his stay at Highbury was also eventful off the pitch. The most unlikely-looking rebel became embroiled in another dispute in 1961, this time with the Arsenal board, following the abolition of the outdated maximum wage system. Eastham asked for a pay rise. At first his request was refused although the board later acceded to his demands. Then he fell out with manager Billy Wright at the start of the 1962/63 season when he was dropped from the team and replaced by striker Joe Baker. In a fit of pique he asked to be put back in the team or he'd leave the club. Again, he got his way. He was put back in the side, playing just behind Baker, and came off the transfer list. Despite the upheavals, however, Eastham reached a level of consistency that was lacking among his team-mates. He was called up by England and given a place in Sir Alf Ramsey's squad for the World Cup in 1966. Although he didn't get to play any games during the tournament and only those who played in the final were actually given medals at the time, FIFA recently backdated the awards and handed out medals to squad members as well. Thus Eastham became the first Arsenal player to possess a World Cup winner's medal.

Eastham played his last game for Arsenal at the end of the 1965/66 season and was sold to Stoke City for £35,000 in August 1966. His career, though, was far from over and he made history once again in 1972 when he scored the winning goal for Stoke against hot favourites Chelsea in the League Cup final. At the age of 35 years and 161 days, he became the oldest player to pick up a winner's medal at Wembley. He tried his hand at management at Stoke but left in January 1978 after just ten months in charge. He then moved to South Africa.

Clearly his time at Arsenal left a huge impression on him as he is now chairman of the South African Arsenal Supporters Club.

A revolutionary step

The man who signed Eastham, George Swindin, became a managerial casualty in March 1962. His time at Arsenal was up and could take the Club no further. The board decided to take a revolutionary step. Since the appointment of Chapman back in the 1920s, every successive manager had been found from inside the Club ranks, men who the board knew as individuals and who were aware of the traditions and values of the Club. When Swindin went, Arsenal decided to go outside for his replacement, and they opted for Billy Wright. Wright was a man with nationwide fame. At the time he held the world record for international caps at 105. He had captained a hugely successful Wolverhampton Wanderers side to glory – three league titles and one FA Cup. He was married to Joy, one of the Beverley Sisters, one of the most popular showbiz acts of the time. He was the Golden Boy of English football and seemed to have all the credentials needed to make it as a manager. He had cut his managerial teeth as the coach of the England under-23 side, but the step up to club management was a new challenge for him.

The appointment wasn't particularly successful. In hindsight, Wright seemed like a man out of time. His problems seemed to stem from the fact that he was too gentle to be a manager in a sport that was becoming increasingly competitive. His fame came at a time when the old order was still in operation, people knew their place, and respected others. At the beginning of the 1960s, society was in the process of radical change. For many a mild revolution was happening, out with the establishment in with the rights of man. This was the decade that would see evolution in technology and culture that had never been witnessed before in peacetime. On the music scene, four young men from Liverpool were starting to make an impact and putting Great Britain on the world map – The Beatles. 'I knew them,' said Clem Cattini.

'Paul McCartney became a personal friend over the years. But when I first saw them, they were just four ordinary blokes. They would have an ordinary roast dinner on Sundays when we were appearing at the same theatre in Blackpool.' Their emergence heralded the arrival of the first football superstar in George Best of Manchester United, a pop star in his own right, even though he was actually a footballer. And, perhaps most extraordinarily, towards the middle and end of the 1960s, there was the appearance for the first time of football hooliganism. This coincided with the gang culture that was first manifested in the Mods and Rockers battles of 1963 and 1964 in Clacton and Brighton. That was about fashion and contrasting tastes in music, this was about football allegiances. But it was pretty much the same thing.

Some argued that the root of the problem lay in the abolition of National Service in 1957. Without the two years' military service, the argument went, there was no release for the energies that would have been sapped and shaped on the parade ground. Instead, the tribal mentality took over and youngsters were drawn early in the decade to the Beatnik culture, that was pro-peace and anti just about everything else, or into the Mods or Rockers. You couldn't do both. Along with the music came rebellion through the likes of the Beatles and, more especially, the Rolling Stones who appeared to champion the use of recreational drugs. West End clubs, like the Marquee and Tiles, were a haven for the Mods and the less formal venues attracted the Rockers. The common ground was the seaside resorts they invaded en masse and where scores were settled. But, just like any other fad, the Mods and Rockers faded gradually out. They grew up, had families of their own or found steady work.

The gang mentality needed a new home and it found a permanent one in following football clubs. Towns became territory to be either invaded or defended. And certain areas of the ground became the ultimate scalp. The police were totally unprepared for this kind of violence. In the 1940s and 1950s less than 20 police could look after crowds of 60,000. There were no confrontations, and no need for segregation. Opposing fans could stand side-by-side, cheer for their team and still walk out of the ground together at the end of the game. Suddenly with the emergence of a win-at-all-costs society in which the biggest crime of all was to lose or be associated with the losing side, it became the vogue to be part of a gang that would terrorize the opposition. The atmosphere at matches began to change. Fights were frequent and trains – the so-called football specials – and buses were wrecked every Saturday.

Wright man, wrong results

Wright did not thrive in this atmosphere. He knew a good player when he saw one, however, and a list of those who came through while he was in charge makes impressive reading. He signed Frank McLintock from Leicester and he was to prove an inspired arrival. He also gave Geoff Strong his chance and Strong went on to be a huge success at Liverpool – as did David Herd at Manchester United. In the youth team were Pat Rice, Sammy Nelson, Peter Storey, Jon Sammels, John Radford and Peter Simpson. It was also in Wright's managerial reign that goalkeeper Bob Wilson was signed. Joe Baker proved to be an excellent buy and Ian Ure gave great service before he, too, left for Old Trafford. And on apprentice forms was Charlie George who was later, with his rebellious streak and long hair, to become the darling of the North Bank. But there was no mean streak in Wright to combine all these talents into a mean winning machine. It was happening at Leeds where Don Revie was moulding a team that not only had ability but was also made up of fierce competitors like Billy Bremner, Bobby Collins and Norman Hunter. Wright's record was certainly not the best. Not one major honour came Arsenal's way during his tenure.

In his first full season, 1962/63, the team could finish no higher than seventh behind league champions Liverpool. In the FA Cup they beat Oxford and Sheffield Wednesday comfortably at home but another home draw, against Liverpool in the fifth round, ended in a 2–1 defeat. The following season, they again went out in the fifth round at home to Liverpool and finished one place lower in the First Division. There was also the first competitive foray into Europe in the Inter-Cities' Fairs Cup (now the UEFA Cup). Stavenet of Norway were no match in the first round as Arsenal hammered them 7–1 in the first leg at Highbury. This made the second leg a formality, though Arsenal suffered an embarrassing 3–2 defeat. But in the second round, the clever and technical Belgians from Liege ended Arsenal's interest. After a 1–1 draw at Highbury, Arsenal were beaten 3–1 away.

It got worse in the 1964/65 season. In the league, Arsenal plummeted to 13th while the FA Cup was to provide Wright with his most embarrassing moment as Arsenal manager. Darlington had provided sturdy but limited opposition in the third round and were beaten 2–0 on their own ground in the north east. But in the fourth round came the banana skin of Peterborough at London Road – and Arsenal lost 2–1, to become the victims of the biggest FA Cup shock that season. It was a match that summed up Wright's benign approach. As the dispirited players slumped into the seats in the crowded and silent dressing room, they expected a hammering from the manager – and rightly so, they thought after losing to such inferior opposition. 'This was when Billy should have brought down the iron fist,' said Frank McLintock. 'But that wasn't in his nature. He was too nice, too kind.'

Stay away supporters

Worse was to come in 1965/66 for Wright as the new breed of fans, who would stay away after a poor result, rather than the one who would turn up wind, rain or shine, made their statement. Arsenal's league form had been poor. They went into the second last game of the season knowing that a mid-table place was the best that could be anticipated after another mediocre campaign in which the Club seemed to heading nowhere. They were in fact to finish 14th – their lowest placing since 1929/30. The FA Cup provided no solace either as they were convincingly beaten 3–0 by Blackburn Rovers at Ewood Park in the third round. Liverpool's star, meanwhile, was in the ascendancy and they were a team that was to haunt Wright. Not only had they beaten Arsenal twice in the FA Cup during his four years, in 1966 they reached the final of the now defunct European Cup-Winners' Cup where they met Borussia Dortmund of Germany. It was a match that was screened live on television on 5 May – the same night that Arsenal were to play a talented Leeds team who were at that time second in the league. The attendance was to cause immense concern among the Highbury hierarchy. A mere 4,544 turned up to watch the match. It was the lowest attendance at a top-flight match in England since the end of the Second World War. Arsenal also lost 3–0 and that was to prove the death knell for Wright's time in charge at Arsenal.

Wright then made what is regarded as one of two fatal mistakes in football when times are bad. One rule is never to let the chairman play golf with well-heeled fans. The other is not to go on holiday. Wright committed the latter sin. He went away to refresh himself ready for his commitment to the BBC as part of the pundit team for the World Cup which was staged in England that summer. While he was absent, there was a board meeting. The directors were alarmed at the Club's failure to progress under Wright's management and decided there should be a change. On Wright's return, chairman Denis Hill-Wood broke the news. Wright put on a brave face. For public consumption he took the decision in good grace, but inside it cut him deep and he admitted his natural relaxed manner had played its part. 'It was heartbreaking for me,' he was to say later. 'Maybe I was too nice but that is the way I am. I wanted so much to make Arsenal great again and I felt that with the young players we were moving along the right lines.' But Arsenal's decision proved to be the correct one. They reverted to their old style when it came to appointing managers and opted for an insider, a name many people outside the Club were unfamiliar with.

Chapter Eight

RETURN OF THE GOOD TIMES

From physiotherapist to manager – Bertie Mee restores pride to Highbury

Speculation was rife about who would take over from Billy Wright. Many high-profile names were linked with the job but in the background Denis Hill-Wood had already identified the man he wanted to be the new manager. And it was a name to shock football – to many outsiders the question was, 'Bertie Who?' In Bertie Mee, the Arsenal physiotherapist since 1960, Hill-Wood saw a man of integrity. Mee knew the players and they respected him. He had also had experience of working with other managers having run a number of courses on the treatment of injuries at FA headquarters in Lilleshall. He also had the ability to spot a player. 'I was playing for the universities team while I was studying at Loughborough,' said Bob Wilson who was registered as an amateur with Wolverhampton Wanderers. 'Bertie had seen me play and suggested I go to Arsenal.

He was a good judge of players – and a disciplinarian. As soon as he was appointed we all said as one, "Oh no!" The days when it was a bit free and easy were over. Billy Wright was a lovely man, one of the nicest I had ever met. But Bertie was different. We knew straight away that discipline would be tight, that it was going to be a suit and tie job on match days. We all got them as well... beautiful blue ones from Austin Reed. He was very strong on discipline on and off the field. He was very regimental.'

Mee initially expressed surprise at the opportunity to be a manager. 'It was a surprise but a very pleasant one. I had not planned to become a football club manager. I was enjoying my career and I was getting job satisfaction from it. But I was used to positions of responsibility. I had run organizations of various kinds. So my response was that, if that was what the board would like, then I would give it a go.'

Mr Organization

If there is one word that sums up Bertie Mee it is 'organization'. Both on and off the pitch, he always made sure his players were prepared. So stunning was his appointment that there were two schools of thought. Some said it was a stopgap, temporary affair until the man that Arsenal really wanted was available. Others thought he wouldn't last in the cauldron of the professional game. Players are past masters at testing out new managers and it was felt they would get the better of Mee. The cynics were wrong on both counts. Mee was to prove not only a survivor, but also a highly successful one.

After the somewhat lax ambience of the Billy Wright years, the players were suddenly faced with a dapper authoritarian figure. Mee's knowledge of tactics was not deep and he didn't pretend otherwise. He left the finer points of how the team actually played to a man who was destined to be one of the great coaches of his generation – Don Howe. Howe's enthusiasm was infectious and his ability to transmit to the players what he wanted was a true gift. He knew when to encourage and when to bawl people out. 'At half-time,' said Wilson, 'it would be Don who spoke first. If he was pleased he would let you know but spell out how we could give more. If he wasn't pleased, he would let you know in no uncertain terms. But invariably he was spot on with his assessment. Then Bertie would speak. It would more measured, less emotional than Don. That is why they worked so well together as a team.'

At the start of his reign, Mee appointed another coach, Dave Sexton, to work alongside Howe. This was a stroke of genius. As McLintock said a few years later, 'I haven't come across many people in the game who have his ability to get through to players without shouting the odds and screaming at them. I don't know what it is that Dave has, maybe it is a gift of leadership. All I know is that he could have persuaded us to do anything. He thinks deeply about football and pointed out things I wouldn't have dreamed of – and before he came I thought I knew most of it.' Few groups of players had the benefits enjoyed by those Arsenal players of working with two gifted coaches like Howe and Sexton. The players were soon impressed with Mee's serious approach. 'That was his skill,' said Bob Wilson. 'He was the disciplinarian, almost to a fault. At times, you could say he was way over the top. But what he did was surround himself with such excellent coaches.' Howe was quick to point out to Mee how to get under the skin of the players by reminding them, in subtle fashion, of past glories and how they now had their chance to make history. It had been 17 long years since Arsenal had won a major honour and when Mee took players into the staff room at Highbury for a private chat, he would encourage them to look at the photographs on the walls showing the triumphs achieved by Tom Parker, Joe Mercer and Denis and Leslie Compton. 'The players would say that they wanted those bloody pictures down,' recalled Howe. 'But Bertie refused. He said that when we won something, then we could take them down.'

Highbury as a stadium was mightily impressive to the players. 'It was like a cathedral, not a football stadium when I first went down the tunnel on to the pitch,' said Wilson. 'The whole place just looked solid and dependable,' said Frank McLintock. 'Marble halls, marble staircases. The marble even extended into the dressing rooms.' The trappings were there. All Mee had to do now was mould the squad into one that would end that drought of trophies. The players knew him primarily as a physiotherapist. They had experienced his no-nonsense yet highly professional approach to the treatment of injuries. They knew that as manager he would stand for nothing less than 100 per cent commitment and professionalism from them. Mee certainly wasn't overawed. He was also shrewd enough to insure himself in case his venture into management did not pay off. 'I asked the chairman if I could initially take the job for 12 months and that if it didn't work out I could revert to my previous position. He agreed. So I began by approaching the task in terms of management, from a purely management point of view. There was nothing radically wrong at the club – we just had to be more professional from all angles. We needed a general tightening-up. The players were a good bunch but they needed to be more dedicated. The danger was that mediocrity was being perpetuated.'

First fruits

Mee immediately started laying the foundations of his new team. He started by selling George Eastham to Stoke. His replacement was Jon Sammels, a youngster who did not possess the guile and craft of Eastham, but who had what they term in football parlance 'a great engine'. George Graham was signed from Chelsea. Initially a wide player, Graham was converted into a deeper role by Mee and Howe. And from Huddersfield came the cultured left back Bob McNab. The impact of this new ethos at the Club was not immediately apparent. In his first full season, 1966/67, Arsenal finished seventh in the league and were beaten in the fifth round of the FA Cup by Birmingham City. His second season was almost a rerun of the first in terms of the league and the FA Cup. But the seeds had been planted and in the League Cup that year the first fruits of return were there to be seen. Coventry, Reading, Blackburn, Burnley and Huddersfield were all beaten as Arsenal reached their first final in a major competition for 16 years. The opposition at Wembley were Leeds United who, for all their promise and all their talent that had been nurtured by Don Revie, had so far failed to win the first trophy in the history of the club.

The match will not go down as one of the most memorable in the history of the old stadium. It was a match of the times in many ways – hard, tense and competitive. Footballers were becoming better, more durable athletes and a certain cynicism was creeping into the game. There was a greater sense of professionalism and urgency and it is not unfair to say that Leeds were the masters of this new mindset. They were uncompromising and brought a whole new definition to the word gamesmanship. Terry Cooper, the England full back, scored the only goal in a 1–0 win. It was a bitter pill for everyone at Arsenal to swallow, but in particular for McLintock. He had already lost twice at Wembley as a Leicester player, beaten by Tottenham in 1961 and Manchester United in 1963, and now he had to suffer the walk up the Wembley steps as a loser yet again.

But Mee was not without hope. He had seen a togetherness and a tenacity about his team that had been absent before. Others too were taking notice of the new players and international recognition came from England for striker John Radford and left back McNab. Bob Wilson was emerging as a goalkeeper of some standing and he was to be ever-present in the 1968/69 league campaign. Mee was also pleased with Peter Storey – a man not known to take prisoners. Equally effective at right back or in midfield, his abrasive style encapsulated the style of the new ball-winning midfield player. Those qualities were also recognized by England manager Sir Alf Ramsey. In the first leg of a European Championships qualifier in 1972 England had been beaten 3–1 by Germany at Wembley. The man who had done most damage was the brilliant Günter Netzer. While never admitting that it was a lost cause before the second leg in Berlin, Sir Alf wanted to ensure there was no repeat performance. He picked Storey and his instructions were simple – stop Netzer. He did. The game ended 0–0, which meant England were eliminated, but the only kicks Netzer got were from hard-man Storey. Indeed, the German spoke after the game to say, 'Peter Storey is not such a bad guy. He gave me his autograph. It is all down my legs!' Every successful team in that period needed such an individual and Mee acknowledged that.

Also coming through were the understated central defender Peter Simpson and the re-born George Graham who was revelling in his new midfield role where he could make full use of his sharp football brain. And waiting in the wings was a youngster destined to become the idol of the North Bank. Charlie George, born in Islington, was an Arsenal fan through and through. Never the best at school, all he wanted to do was play for the Club. And boy could he play. Long-haired, scruffy and no respecter of authority or of reputations – the younger fans were able to see something of themselves in him. 'He captured the imagination of the supporters,' said McLintock. George had phenomenal talent. He wasn't scared of anyone. He could dish it out and take it at a time when self-protection was the order of the day for attack-minded players. Verbally and physically, George was equipped to handle himself. He was good in the air and his control was magnificent. He was tall and never shirked his responsibilities on the field. He was to be the wild card, the maverick that was to complete the jigsaw being assembled by Mee.

Another failure

There were signs of further progress in the 1968/69 season. The campaign started with a 2–1 win at Tottenham and a six-game winning run between November and January saw the Club high up the table. In the end they finished in fourth place. The FA Cup was disappointing with Arsenal dumped out by holders West Bromwich Albion in the fifth round. But there was success once again in the League Cup. Victories against Sunderland, Scunthorpe, Liverpool and Blackpool set up a two-legged semi-final against Tottenham. Rivalry between the two clubs was now becoming more bitter and intense. A resurgent Arsenal were giving their own fans cause to believe that they could get the better of a team who had lorded it over them for more than a decade. The first leg at Highbury was typical derby fare – full-blooded and close. The fear of losing seemed to eclipse the ambition to win. It was goalless until the last minute when John Radford gave Arsenal a precious lead to take to White Hart Lane. The second leg was a nasty affair, both sides making it plain that they did not want to lose. Tottenham took the early advantage with a goal from Jimmy Greaves.

But up popped that man Radford again to equalize and take Arsenal to Wembley for the second year running.

The day of the final dawned with optimism. The opponents that day were Third Division Swindon Town. Surely silverware was on its way to Highbury again. But, as we have already seen, Arsenal's cup history is littered with disappointment, and 15 March 1969 must go down as one of the most humiliating in the Club's history. The match was played on a pitch that had hosted the Horse of the Year show a few days before. It was a bog, with a heavy, cloying surface that made slick football impossible. But even that cannot excuse a horrible performance from Arsenal. Scottish central defender Ian Ure and keeper Bob Wilson were responsible for the first goal as a mix-up between the two allowed Roger Smart to nip between them and give Swindon the lead. That lasted until the 86th minute when Peter Downsborough in the Swindon goal attempted to hack the ball clear but instead hammered it against Arsenal striker Bobby Gould. The ball rebounded goalwards and a gleeful Gould was able to head it into an unguarded net. Gould was so emotional that he cried and a huge wave of relief spread among the Arsenal fans as the match went into extra-time. This was surely to be the moment.

But Gould's tears were almost prescient. Don Rogers, Swindon's talented winger, put Swindon ahead as the first half of the added period came to an end and then produced a thrusting run that took him from his own half into the Arsenal area before he scored the goal that won the cup. McLintock, in particular, was devastated. He had now been in four Wembley finals and lost the lot. He had been sent a good luck telegram from Don Revie ahead of the game telling him, 'to be first up the steps this time'. What Revie had overlooked was that Wembley tradition dictated that losers go up first for their medals.

The tide turns

Mee remained convinced that he had a team of winners on his hands even if the record books were yet to reflect that. There is an old adage in football that more is learned about an individual in defeat than in victory and Bob McNab was of that school of thought. 'I truly believe that the rise of the team that won the Double stemmed from that afternoon at Wembley,' he said later. 'We came home to headlines going on about the "Shame of Arsenal". That made a lot of us determined that would never happen again. It made us crave success even more.'

McNab and his determined colleagues did not have long to wait. Their fourth-place finish in the league meant Arsenal qualified for the 1969/70 Inter-Cities' Fairs Cup. The team started the league in poor form but Charlie George made his debut and there were other promising youngsters waiting for their chances including Scottish midfield player Eddie Kelly and striker Ray Kennedy. Mee loved Kelly. 'My midfield tank,' he called him, while Kennedy was coming through as the perfect supplement to Radford. The season ended with five wins in eight games but 12th place was disappointing. The domestic cups brought little joy too. Blackpool beat Arsenal in a replay in the third round of the FA Cup while Everton did the same thing to ensure there was no third consecutive League Cup final for Arsenal.

But in Europe, things went well from the start. Arsenal's form was little short of magnificent in a campaign with few scares. Indeed, there were several superb performances. Northern Ireland's Glentoran were brushed aside with ease in the first round as Arsenal won 3–0 at Highbury. True, they lost the second leg 1–0 but the outcome of the tie was never in doubt. From then on Arsenal proved themselves to be a genuine European force as there followed convincing wins over Sporting Lisbon, Rouen and Dynamo Bacau of Romania – which included a 7–1 hammering at Highbury. But it was in the semi-finals that Arsenal's real pedigree was to come through. They were paired with Ajax of Amsterdam and this was the embryo of the team that were to make them the Dutch masters of Europe in the years to come. The first leg witnessed Arsenal at their irrepressible best, winning 3–0. Still to complete his first full season for the first team, George was not a great one for reputations. The object of his attentions that night was Johan Cruyff. Already a rising star in world football, George gave the Dutchman the benefit of his best 'verbals' throughout the game. Cruyff was not totally impressed. 'That man – is he the chairman?

He has so much to say for himself,' said Cruyff afterwards. But George had also done his 'talking' on the pitch, scoring twice. Ajax won the second leg 1–0 and Arsenal duly went through.

The final, against Belgian giants Anderlecht, was massive. It was a two-leg tie, the first leg to be played in Brussels. For the Belgians, the visit of a world famous club like Arsenal was an honour. In order to make their guests welcome Arsenal were asked to play in their famous home strip so that Belgian fans could get to see it in the flesh so to speak. And Arsenal's travelling supporters were given a warm welcome too and told to make themselves at home. But when the match started Arsenal did not play as though they felt at home. At one stage Anderlecht were 3–0 up, with two goals from Jan Mulder, and cruising. Three goals would have been a near-impossible hurdle to overcome but with just a few minutes left on the clock, Ray Kennedy scored with a powerful header. Where there was despair, there was now hope. Bob Wilson said, 'We were still down in the dumps, despite that late goal. Frank McLintock was cursing all over the place. He could see another loser's medal coming his way. Then he went for a bath and came out a different man. He must have sat there thinking about it and decided that Ray's goal had given us hope that we could still win. He was a different man when he came back to get dressed. He was shouting at us all and telling us that the cup was still ours if we wanted it bad enough. That was a big, big moment. It changed the mood of everyone and we came home confident that we could win.'

A comeback of some stature was needed in the second leg at Highbury though. McLintock can clearly recall those two matches against Anderlecht to this day. 'They were a good team, no question and in Jan Mulder and Paul van Himst they had two special players. But I didn't fancy them at all at the back. They looked uncertain when we went at them and their centre backs looked poor in the air. I honestly believed we could do it and I wanted to ensure that the rest of the team believed it as well.'

The second leg was a memorable occasion. It was on Tuesday 28 April 1970, a day when Frank McLintock emerged as a true leader and an inspiration in his new role in central defence. So well had he played that season that Scotland recalled him to international football after three years in the wilderness. But it was one of the new breed who struck first. Arsenal needed an early lift to boost their confidence and they got it from Eddie Kelly, who rifled a shot into the Anderlecht net. Now Arsenal had genuine hope and that was reflected in their high-tempo game. 'Are you on drugs?' one Anderlecht player asked McLintock. The only drug they needed was adrenalin. And that was generated by ambition – ambition to have their photographs up on the wall in Bertie Mee's staff room alongside a major trophy, ambition to stop the talk of past glories at the club being rammed down their throats at every opportunity. McLintock had been spot on about the vulnerability in the air in the centre of Anderlecht's defence and Radford exploited it to the full to head Arsenal further ahead. Driven by the unwelcome souvenirs of two successive League Cup final defeats at Wembley, Arsenal went for the kill. True, because of the strike by Kennedy in Brussels, Arsenal were level on aggregate and ahead on the away goals rule. But Anderlecht still had class and there was a wake-up call when the ever-dangerous Mulder hit the post. But it was a homegrown who finally secured victory. As Anderlecht became more adventurous, so space appeared and Jon Sammels capitalized on the gaps to score the third. Finally, 17 years after the trophy cabinet was last opened, it had to be opened again to take in the Inter-Cities' Fairs Cup. The long wait for silverware was over for Arsenal and for Frank McLintock.

Delirium – but it has be stressed, good-hearted delirium provoked by euphoria – broke out at the end of the match as thousands of joyous fans invaded the pitch and mobbed the players. To this day, Charlie George can't pinpoint what happened to his shirt as it was ripped from his back. The Fairs Cup had stayed in England as Arsenal continued the trend set by Leeds and Newcastle before them. The trophy was presented to McLintock by FIFA President Sir Stanley Rous and he was carried round the pitch once it had been cleared. George Graham, later to manage the Club, reckons the match was a watershed clash in Arsenal's history. 'After that we grew in confidence and we grew in belief,' he said. 'We looked down and out but we came back to win. That was one hell of a comeback and one hell of an achievement.'

The Double dream begins

But if those scenes were memorable, they were nothing compared to those that greeted the end of the following season. No question, Arsenal wanted the league. Yes, cup success was welcome – indeed after such a long wait, any success was welcome. But the league title is the blue riband for any club. Arsène Wenger will say now that, as much as he would love to win the Champions League, the main test for any team is to win the league. 'The Champions League is great and produces great drama. But does it always produce the best team in Europe? I don't know that you can say that. But the league never lies. It has to be won by consistency and invariably the best team in the country wins it. That is why it is the priority for me every season. That will not change.'

There was a similar school of thought back in 1970. The word 'champions' has a ring about it that cannot be equalled and Mee was determined to build on the Fairs Cup success. That was to be the start, not the finish. Yet they did not start the 1970/71 season as favourites despite their moment of European glory – and understandably so. They had finished way down the league table that season and little was expected of the squad that Mee had assembled. But outsiders had reckoned without the lift in confidence, morale and self-belief that the Fairs Cup win had given the players. The likes of Chelsea, Leeds, Everton and Liverpool were among the teams hotly tipped to take the championship. Arsenal hardly got a mention and that worked massively in Mee's favour. He and Howe were of the same mind. With players like Charlie George, John Radford and Ray Kennedy Arsenal were always capable of scoring goals. With the speed of tenacious little winger George Armstrong and the midfield input of George Graham and Eddie Kelly there would always be plenty of ammunition for the front men. What they needed was a rock-like defence, one that would not concede goals readily or easily. And with Pat Rice, Frank McLintock, Peter Simpson and Bob McNab in front of the ever-reliable Bob Wilson, Arsenal had the formula that Mee wanted.

Not that his plans included a knee injury to the dependable Simpson ahead of the first league game at Everton on 15 August. But a reliable deputy was found in John Roberts, a sturdy Welsh defender, who slipped in alongside McLintock in an almost seamless transition. Everton were the champions and played like them. At the time they boasted what is reckoned to be the most gifted midfield in the club's history – Howard Kendall, Alan Ball and Colin Harvey. Storey, now in midfield after the promotion of Rice, was given the job of looking after Ball who was pinpointed as the man who made Everton tick. He did a more than adequate job but could not stop Ball scoring. Joe Royle added another but Arsenal replied with two of their own from Charlie George and George Graham to take a share of the points. Arsenal's resolve was plain to see and McLintock, in his sixth year at the Club, reckoned it was the best Arsenal line-up he'd played in. Further evidence of that assertion was to come in early September when mighty Leeds came to Highbury with an unblemished record in the league – and it seemed that would be preserved when Kelly, in a show of impetuosity, was sent off after just half an hour for a kick at the provocative Billy Bremner. But Arsenal rose to the challenge and Rice was showing the qualities that would one day make him one of the greatest captains the Club have ever had. Leeds met resistance all over the park and the match ended goalless. Mee, while in no way absolving Kelly for his petulance, said, 'This was the best performance I have seen from an Arsenal team against a side of the calibre of Leeds. I am proud of them and if they can survive this, they can survive anything.'

This was a great sentiment, but it was not quite true. On 23 September Arsenal travelled to Stoke. Stoke City were never regarded as one of the major players in the league and a trip to the old Victoria Road ground held few fears. But on this occasion it did. Arsenal, with a defence earning a reputation as one of the toughest and most uncompromising in the country, were totally dismantled and beaten 5-0. It was an inexplicable defeat, totally out of context with what happened before that match or indeed afterwards. Bob Wilson, honest as ever, went public with an explanation of the goals that had been conceded and that prompted an immediate and irate reaction from Mee who felt such analysis belonged behind closed dressing room doors. But once again the character of the Arsenal squad came through. They could have let the defeat infect the squad with self-doubt. Instead, they

Arriving at Highbury in tin hats for ARP training are, left to right, Cliff Bastin, Arsenal and England manager Tom Whittaker, George Male and goalkeeper George Marks, 13 October 1939.

◀ **33 May 1950:** Arsenal's Joe Mercer (1914–90) holding the FA cup after his team's win against Liverpool in the Final at Wembley. The final score was 2-0.

5 August 1936, Arsenal footballers back in training for the imminent start to the new season are taken for long walks around the streets of London's Tufnell Park (left to right) Wilf Copping, Jack Crayston, trainer Tom Whittaker, Alex James and Frank Moss.

1 Feb 1958 League Division One – Arsenal v Manchester United. United's Mark Jones (c) and Duncan Edwards (r) playing against Arsenal at Highbury in their last match before the Munich Disaster, in which they were tragically killed.

10 December 1960 League
Division One – Arsenal v
Bolton Wanderers –
Highbury. (Left to right)
Bolton Wanderers' Graham
Stanley challenges Arsenal's
George Eastham as the latter
lashes the ball into the
crowd. Eastham scored twice
in a 5-1 win for the Gunners.

◀ **7 July 1965** Billy Wright,
Arsenal manager,
with the Arsenal squad
in the background.

12 August 1966 new manager Bertie Mee meets some of his new players at Highbury (left to right) Mee, Terry Neill, John Radford, Tommy Baldwin, Frank McLintock, Bob Wilson and Don Howe.

1 August 1969 Arsenal Photocall at Highbury. Frank McLintock (right) looks on as team-mate Charlie George poses for the camera.

8 May 1971 Charlie George scores for Arsenal v Liverpool to win the FA Cup and seal the double.

9 May 1971 Arsenal fans, standing in Upper Street, Islington, celebrating winning the FA Cup with Arsenal captain Frank McLintock.

Frank Stapleton scores Arsenal's second goal against Manchester United during the 1979 FA Cup Final.

7 December 1959 Football League Division One – Arsenal Training. Jack Kelsey (left) and David Herd (right) ruffle the hair of new signing, 17-year-old Terry Neill.

◄ **David O'Leary,** 17 July 1978.

Liam Brady, 1978/79 season.
▼

▲ **20 October 1990,** League Division One – Manchester United v Arsenal. Arsenal Manager George Graham shouts from the dugout.

▲ **11 August 1998** (left to right) Lee Dixon, Tony Adams, Steve Bould and Nigel Winterburn with some of the spoils for their magnificent careers: the FA Cup, the Premiership trophy and the Charity Shield.

treated is as a wake-up call and it merely made them tighter as a unit. They proceeded to go on a 14-match unbeaten run in which only three of those games were drawn.

In November, Arsenal were dumped out of the League Cup, beaten 2–0 by Crystal Palace in a fourth-round replay. But there were no tears, league form was pretty good and anyway there were bigger fish to fry. As holders, Arsenal were entitled to defend the Fairs Cup. In the first round they were given an exacting task against Lazio. In those days, Lazio did not play at the Stadio Olimpico. Theirs was a compact, atmospheric ground and the ambience was anything but friendly. However, Arsenal drew 2–2 – but that was not the end of the hostilities. At the post-match dinner Ray Kennedy was set on by a number of Lazio players. Soon, everyone was involved and Mee, while not condoning such behaviour, encouraged the players to stick up for one another. McLintock, a fiery Scot who could handle himself, was in the thick of the action and would back down to no one. There was an immediate inquiry launched by UEFA into the events and they duly found the Italians were to blame and the club was fined.

The second leg was something of a formality as Arsenal cruised through 2–0. But Mee was wary of over-commitment. He quietly fancied Arsenal's chances of the league title and thought that Europe could become a distraction. In later rounds, Arsenal beat Sturm Graz of Austria and Beveren of Belgium, but they eventually surrendered their grip on the trophy losing on away goals to FC Cologne of West Germany. Arsenal won 2–1 at Highbury but lost 1–0 away.

Making sacrifices

That defeat came on 23 March, just when the league was getting tight and the pressure was becoming more intense. Mee chose his words carefully after the match. He did not want to be seen to be happy in defeat. That just did not fit in with the winning culture he was trying to introduce at the Club. But at the same time, he knew that their elimination would mean they had fewer games in the last two months of the season. 'It could be a blessing in disguise,' was as far as he would go. The Club had been performing consistently in the league and they were well placed just behind front-runners Leeds. Their form in the FA Cup too was good. With Yeovil and Portsmouth beaten, the draw for the fifth round took Arsenal to Maine Road for a tie with a talented Manchester City side. The match was called off on the Saturday because rain had made the pitch unplayable and in the re-arranged clash the following Wednesday, Charlie George stole the show and the headlines with a two-goal performance that took Arsenal into the quarter-finals. Indeed, one commentator was moved to describe George as having the same gifts and talents as Charlie Buchan. Praise indeed. Mee could see the potential that lay in the season and Bob Wilson recalls a speech that the manager gave the players as the season approached its climax with Arsenal in the sixth round of the FA Cup and just three points behind Leeds in the league. 'He called us altogether for a talk and I swear he was shaking as he spoke to us. He told us, quite simply, that for the next two months we would be playing two games a week and that, if we were successful in those matches, we could make history. He said he thought it was possible with the players we had to win both the league and the FA Cup but in order to do that we had to make sacrifices. For just this once, the families and social lives must come second. He said we may never get an opportunity like this again in our lifetimes and that we had to take advantage of it. The message got home.'

Arsenal responded by winning game after game in their pursuit of Leeds. It may not always have been pretty, but the players called on reserves of determination and willpower to stay in a challenging position in both the league and the FA Cup. Between early February and the last week of April, they lost only once, a 2–0 defeat at Derby. In the FA Cup, Arsenal again refused to do things the easy way. They were drawn against McLintock's old club Leicester in the quarter-final and they were expected to enjoy an easy passage through to the semi-finals. The 55,000-plus fans at Highbury were expectant but were soon hushed and then relieved as a Leicester strike was ruled out. And with only seconds left until the interval, Charlie George rose majestically to head home a George Armstrong corner. Leicester responded with a committed second-half performance but it was not enough and Arsenal were in the last four. Along with them were Liverpool, Stoke and Everton.

The draw paired the two Merseyside clubs and Arsenal were to play Stoke – the team that had given them such a shock earlier in the season. Stoke were massive underdogs but they did not play like that in the match at Hillsborough. At half-time, Stoke led 2-0 courtesy of goals from Denis Smith and John Ritchie – the second thanks to a howler from Charlie George whose weak back pass was intercepted and prodded past Wilson. And it could have been worse because Jimmy Greenhoff blasted wide when clean through on goal. But with Gordon Banks in inspired form in the Stoke goal, the lead looked comfortable enough. However, Arsenal used the half-time break to re-group and refocus. The message from McLintock was clear and concise – Arsenal had not come all this way in the FA Cup to get beaten now. The new attitude paid dividends when Arsenal reduced the arrears early in the second half. If Greenhoff had kept his nerve it could have been 3-0 but with half an hour to go it was suddenly 2-1 with a goal from the unlikeliest of sources. Ray Kennedy caused a moment of havoc in the previously stolid Stoke defence and the ball broke to Peter Storey at the edge of the area. He unleashed an unstoppable shot from 20 yards that not even Banks could save.

Game on, as they say. But Stoke were stubborn and their refusal to bend seemed to be paying off. Not only were Arsenal losing the game but they also lost Charlie George who was replaced by Jon Sammels for the last 15 minutes. However, no cause was a lost cause to this Arsenal team and in time added on, Arsenal forced a corner. George Armstrong floated the ball in, it eluded Banks and there was McLintock with a header that was goalbound until John Mahoney handled it. There could be no greater pressure on the penalty taker but Storey had nerves of ice as he calmly slotted home the equalizer. 'The rest of the lads were hugging each other as though we had scored but I still had to take the kick,' said Storey. 'And I had to put it past Gordon Banks.'

Double talk

It was almost as if Stoke knew their chance had gone when the replay started at Villa Park. George Graham put Arsenal ahead from a cross by Armstrong in the 13th minute. The match was effectively over in the 47th minute as the Radford-Kennedy partnership proved fruitful once again – Kennedy sliding home a cross from Radford. McLintock was in no doubt after the game of the significance of the result. 'We are going for the Double,' he said. 'There is real character in this side, enough to achieve that. I have lost four times at Wembley in finals. This must be my chance now to be a winner.'

But that prospect had to be put on the backburner by Mee and his men. There were ten league games left and that was Arsenal's priority. Leeds were showing signs of strain. They had lost at home to Liverpool and away at Chelsea, and Arsenal's cup run had given them games in hand. If Arsenal won all their games, they would catch the Yorkshiremen. And the Londoners still had to visit Elland Road.

Sure enough, the winning streak continued. There was no hangover from the FA Cup celebrations and a matter of days after the replay against Stoke, Arsenal beat a strong Chelsea side 2-0 at Highbury. They now had the scent of the Double in their nostrils. Maximum points came against Coventry, Southampton and Nottingham Forest to set up a teasing afternoon on Saturday 17 April. Both Leeds and Arsenal were at home – West Bromwich Albion went to Elland Road while Newcastle were at Highbury. It was assumed that they'd both be home wins. But, of course, that's not how it worked out.

By now any thoughts of entertainment were out the door. This was the business end of the season when titles and cups are won and lost. All that mattered was the result and Arsenal looked to have gained that winning mentality. At Highbury Newcastle were stubborn and Arsenal looked lethargic. But after 70 minutes, Charlie George hit the winning goal, a stunning drive after working himself room in a crowded penalty area. 'I don't suppose anyone will remember the game,' observed winger George Armstrong afterwards. 'But they will all remember the result.'

For Arsenal fans there was even more good news. Word drifted into a disbelieving Arsenal camp of a serious setback for their nearest rivals –

and the finger of blame was pointed quite firmly by Leeds manager Don Revie at referee Ray Tinkler. With the match against West Brom goalless and 20 minutes left on the clock, Tony Brown ran clear into the Leeds half. In front of him, totally isolated and palpably offside, was Colin Suggett. Brown hesitated on seeing his team-mate, but Tinkler, ignoring the linesman's raised flag, waved for play to continue. Brown crossed for Jeff Astle to stroke the ball into the net. The whole of the stadium – save for a pocket of Albion fans and the Albion bench – were enraged. Furious fans invaded the pitch, but the goal stood and Leeds lost the game.

With five games left, the title was Arsenal's to lose. A 1-0 win over Burnley came thanks to a Charlie George penalty. But then came the inevitable hiccup. Arsenal could only manage a 2–2 draw with West Brom at the Hawthorns while Leeds were trouncing Southampton 3–0 at the Dell. That evening Arsenal sat on top of the table with 61 points from 39 games, Leeds were a point behind but had played one game more. The next fixture paired the two title chasers at Elland Road.

McLintock started the mind games ahead of the clash. 'It will be hard but the odds are still in our favour. I am sure Leeds would be happy to swap positions with us.' Indeed, a win for Leeds was essential while Arsenal were happy to settle for a draw. The clash was potentially explosive, and an experienced and respected referee, Norman Burtenshaw was put in charge. He was superb and kept a tight lid on the game, which did look like ending in stalemate. But as the minutes ticked down Arsenal, perhaps, were guilty of dropping back too deep and they paid the price. The architect of the goal was the much-underrated Paul Madeley. A forging run took him deep into the Arsenal half and his pass allowed the dynamic Billy Bremner to set up Jack Charlton with a shooting chance in the Arsenal area. Charlton prodded the ball past Bob Wilson but against the post. As it came out it hit a defender and rebounded over the line. Arsenal were furious. They were convinced that Charlton had been offside and protested first to referee Burtenshaw and then to the linesman. But the goal stood. In frustration, Charlie George kicked the ball into the stand and was cautioned. George Graham went close after the game resumed but the final whistle served only to prompt more protests from the Arsenal players.

After the game Mee paid tribute to the performance of his men when he said, 'Never was a defeat less deserved.' Arsenal's complaints were later seen to have little justification, however. Television replays suggested that Arsenal had been slow to push out and that Charlton had indeed been onside and that Burtenshaw was right.

Now there were two games left for Arsenal and one for Leeds. Leeds duly won their last match with ease. Billy Bremner and Peter Lorimer scored the goals that beat Nottingham Forest. Arsenal did not have it so easy in their home game with Stoke, a team that had given them problems all season. There seemed to be more on the horizon as the team from the Potteries held Arsenal to a goalless first half. It seemed the occasion had got to Arsenal. But this was the moment for Eddie Kelly to make an impact as he came on in the second 45 minutes for injury victim Peter Storey. With his youth came an absence of fear and he started and finished the move that gave Arsenal the lead combining with John Radford and George Graham before blasting the ball past Gordon Banks. It proved to be the winner and now Arsenal had the title within their grasp. Only the small matter of a match against Tottenham at White Hart Lane stood between them and the championship.

Bedlam on Tottenham High Road

The scenario was complicated. A 0–0 draw would see Arsenal awarded the title on goal average, but any other kind of draw would have handed it to Leeds. Mee and Howe knew the folly and the pitfalls involved in setting out for a 0–0 – especially as Tottenham had motivation above the need to deny their great rivals. They needed three points from their last two games to secure a place in Europe the following season. Mee knew that nothing less than a win would do.

The build up was fierce and partisan. George Armstrong was confident because of Arsenal's impressive away form, which had often seen them soak up pressure and then break forward with menace. He was even heartened by Tottenham's attacking philosophy. 'It is in our favour that Tottenham are not a defensive side,' said the winger. The Tottenham mood was summed up by their captain Alan Mullery. 'Arsenal have as much chance of being handed the title as I have of being given the Crown Jewels. They are the last people we want to win the title. And if we win, we will have won the League Cup and finished third. Not too bad.' Tottenham were well prepared for the clash by manager Bill Nicholson. He hated Arsenal with a vengeance and even frowned if any of his players turned up in a red car. He also had the incentive to protect the prestigious achievement of winning the Double a decade earlier. 'I suppose some club will do it again in the future but we will be determined to make sure it isn't Arsenal.' Mee, of course, had other ideas. He was not deterred by the sights that he witnessed from the Arsenal team coach as it crawled towards White Hart Lane. 'It just added to the sense of occasion,' he said. 'I didn't think for one minute that we were going to be beaten.' Even referee Kevin Howley – officiating in his last game – did not escape the fall-out from the seething masses trying to get to and into the stadium. Frustrated and fearing that he would miss the kick-off, he abandoned his car a mile from the ground and walked the rest of the way. This was a time when partisan support of teams had reached its zenith and Tottenham High Road was chaos that night. 'It was crazy, unbelievable,' said McLintock later. 'Nothing was moving. Nothing. It was just a sea of fans and a sea of noise.'

The match was a typical high-tempo derby clash, watched by over 50,000 breathless spectators. Tottenham were laced with potential match-winners like Martin Chivers and Alan Gilzean, while Arsenal had the menace of Charlie George and the sheer endeavour of Ray Kennedy and John Radford. Despite this, with only three minutes left the match was goalless. Such games are often decided by a horrendous mistake or a flash of genius – sometimes a combination of both and that was the case that night. Charlie George caught Joe Kinnear in possession and his cross was pinpoint perfect on to the head of Radford only for Pat Jennings to pull off a wonder save. While most of the players anticipated the ball going for a corner, Armstrong, never one to give up, chased it and was able to produce another cross. This time the header from Ray Kennedy was too good even for Jennings.

Arsenal were there... almost. McLintock was aware that in the time left, Tottenham were going to mount a barrage of attacks. And he knew better than anybody that a 1-1 draw would mean the title went to Leeds. He desperately mustered his troops. 'That was the longest three minutes I have ever known,' said Kennedy. 'As Tottenham came back at us, I remember thinking it might have been better if my header had not gone in. A 0-0 would have been enough for us but now Tottenham would not want to be beaten at their own ground.' Amid a crescendo of noise, the two teams played out the last few moments of the game.

But, with the resilience that had been their hallmark that season, Arsenal held on to spark scenes of bedlam at the final whistle. Players' shirts, shorts and even boots were taken by fans after they invaded the pitch. Bertie Mee lost his tie as he made his way from the directors' box and Don Howe became fearful of the players' welfare. 'I was genuinely concerned for them,' recalled Howe. 'I mean the fans were not only taking the shirts off their backs but they were trying to get their boots as well. There were thousands of fans on the pitch, literally thousands. Yes, they [the players] were celebrating but without any boots on, there could easily have been an injury – and these players had an FA Cup final to play on Saturday. Yes, I was worried.'

Maybe not as worried as referee Howley. He was the nearest person to Bob Wilson when he blew the whistle for the last time that night and was on the receiving end of a massive hug from the Arsenal goalkeeper. But when the players eventually found their way back into the dressing room, there was a crate of champagne waiting for them, courtesy of Tottenham. 'It was a great gesture,' said Mee. 'They could not have done more to help us celebrate our great night.' And night became morning as the Arsenal players found their way home. No one was more joyous about the feat than Charlie George, the local boy made good. There is nothing that football supporters like better than to watch what they would call 'one of their own' make the grade. He can feel what they feel, he can suffer what they suffer and celebrate like they celebrate. There is a bond – and George had that bond with the fans.

The party moves to Wembley

Mee allowed the festivities to go until Tuesday and gave the players an extra day off. They could unwind, recharge their batteries and then turn their thoughts to Liverpool. Wednesday was down as the traditional media day when all the interviews were done for newspapers and television. After that day, no more. All distractions were erased. Their focus was to be on the FA Cup final. As a physiotherapist, Mee was more aware than most about the need for the right physical preparations. He had an interesting theory about cramp, which had been the curse of the lush Wembley turf over the years and had afflicted many players. He was basically of the opinion that it is all in the mind. 'It is an emotional problem rather than a physical one,' he said. 'It can be brought on by stress and pressure. I wanted that stress to be eliminated so after Wednesday, no press, radio or television'.

On the training ground, Don Howe left nothing to chance as he prepared his team for Wembley. Arsenal had lost two cup finals in their recent history and during both matches question marks were raised over Arsenal's readiness for the energy-sapping Wembley conditions. So a pitch with the exact measurements of those at the national stadium was marked out and the grass was allowed to go uncut to simulate the surface that could be expected. A major lift for Mee was that Peter Storey was declared fit. He had missed the match at Tottenham but came through a fitness test to assure his manager that his considerable presence in midfield would be available. Mee was delighted. As for Liverpool, they had the irrepressible Bill Shankly in charge. He never missed a trick and he wasn't going to start now. As the Arsenal players took a stroll round the pitch on the eve of the final, they were amazed to see Shankly standing there and the legendary Scot could not resist the opportunity to plant a seed of doubt in Arsenal minds. It had been a showery week and as Bob Wilson walked by him he said, 'Bob, it's going to be a nightmare out there tomorrow for goalkeepers.' Wilson, however, was not the impressionable kind.

Come the day of the final the sun was blazing and heat was very much in evidence. Liverpool arrived at the stadium in a state of high anxiety, for Arsenal it just seemed like another matchday in an extraordinary season of matches. The demanding league programme, with its dramatic finale at White Hart Lane just five days before, meant that Arsenal had distractions to keep their mind off the FA Cup final. Liverpool had no such luxury. They were out of the title race long before the season reached its climax and had more than a month of questions and more questions about one issue only – the final. Arsenal could not allow themselves to even think about Wembley until late on the Monday night at Tottenham. Five days of focus compared with five weeks of it. 'I think that worked in our favour,' said McLintock. 'We were all thinking about the league and the league and then again the league. After we had beaten Stoke, it was pushed largely to the back of our minds. Of course you think about it every now again. But we were caught up in the league title contest and that took up the vast majority of our time.'

As kick-off time approached, Mee managed a rarity – he got one over on Shankly. FA Cup final protocol demanded that the teams assemble at the top of the tunnel at 2.45 pm, ready to march on to the pitch together. Liverpool obliged immediately when asked to come out, Mee asked for more time to finish his last-minute instructions. Not once but three times. Liverpool were left standing and Shankly was not happy. The game started amidst high tension. Chances were few and far between, although George Graham had a header cleared off the line, but there were few genuine alarms. It was 0–0 after 90 minutes.

Eddie Kelly came on for Peter Storey as the match went into extra-time. Suddenly, the deadlock was broken. Two minutes into the extra-half hour, Liverpool struck through Steve Heighway who beat Bob Wilson at his near post. Arsenal responded by pushing George Graham into a more forward role and playing an exhausted Charlie George deeper. Four minutes from the break it paid off when John Radford hooked the ball hopefully into the Liverpool area and Eddie Kelly prodded the ball forward at a snail's pace. Suddenly Graham appeared on the scene and his presence unsettled Ray Clemence in the Liverpool goal and the ball trickled into the net for the equalizer. Graham claimed it but dozens of television replays from a series of angles proved that he did not, in fact, touch the ball. The goal was Kelly's.

Don Howe, for one, would have taken a draw and a replay at that moment. There were no penalty shoot-outs to decide the showpiece occasion back then. 'I just didn't think it was our day,' said Howe. For the second half of extra time, George Graham reverted to midfield and Charlie George was pushed back up front, more as nuisance value than anything else because he really did look like a spent force. But appearances can be deceptive as George showed with less than ten minutes left on the watch. From somewhere he found the energy to surge upfield and, after swapping passes with Radford and he fired an unstoppable shot past Clemence from 20 yards. The attempted tackle by Liverpool central defender Larry Lloyd may well have given the ball enough off a deflection to wrong-foot Clemence but the goal was George's. He lay, prostrate, on the turf waiting for his team-mates to pick him up. Liverpool just could not find another response and the FA Cup and the Double were Arsenal's.

Skipper McLintock was in so much of a hurry to collect the trophy that he had to be hauled back by Wilson who was aware of the tradition that the losers went up first. 'I also shouted at him that he should take it all in, really savour the moment because it might not happen again,' said Wilson. Just to round off a memorable Treble, Arsenal also won the FA Youth Cup that season and the three trophies were on show during an open top bus parade the following day through Islington. Mee was aware what victory meant for McLintock who had suffered heartbreak in four major finals. 'I wanted the team to win the FA Cup for Frank,' said Mee during the celebrations. 'The League Championship, that was for my chairman. As for me, I wouldn't mind the European Cup next season.'

Departures and arrivals

There was a disappointment for Mee before the next season was underway with the departure of Don Howe from Highbury. There is no doubt it was a huge blow. But Howe, arguably one of the most gifted coaches this country has produced, had a burning ambition to go into management to stretch his talents further, and when West Bromwich Albion offered him the chance to take over at the Hawthorns, he jumped at it. 'I rate him very highly as a coach and I am very sorry to see him leave,' said Mee. What Howe had wanted, it emerged in the years to come, was the chance to manage Arsenal once Mee had stepped down. He had also been prepared to wait, 'five or ten years if it was necessary,' he said. 'But nobody said anything about it.' To compound Arsenal's loss, Howe took club physiotherapist George Wright and youth coach Brian Whitehouse with him. And chairman Denis Hill-Wood left no doubt about his anger as the loss of three key personnel when he said, 'Loyalty is a dirty word these days. But there is nothing I can do about what West Bromwich Albion have done except ignore them.'

To fill the vacancy, Mee promoted Steve Burtenshaw from the reserves, but there was a general sense that the Arsenal squad had reached its peak and fulfilled its potential. It was a disconcerting time for Mee. This was not the pre-season that he had envisaged after such a glorious finale to the previous campaign. Despite this off-the-field confusion, Mee took time out to strengthen his squad. He knew that a team was always at its most vulnerable when it had been successful. Complacency can creep in and over the years the great managers have always refreshed their respective squads after they had enjoyed success. Shankly was a master at it and Bob Paisley, who followed him, showed the same talent. It is also an art that has been mastered more recently by Sir Alex Ferguson at Manchester United and Arsène Wenger at Arsenal.

Mee's primary target was England World Cup winner Alan Ball. Ball was a fiery competitor and also a born winner. He arguably had the best game of his life when he destroyed West Germany's world class left back Karl-Heinz Schnellinger in the 1966 World Cup final. Everton had acted on that performance and taken Ball from Blackpool to Goodison Park. Now Mee wanted to inject Ball's enthusiasm into his squad to keep his Double-winning team on their toes. Mee reasoned that the rest of the country now knew all about Arsenal, that there was no surprise element – no 'X' factor if you like. Ball was signed to provide that. Mee also had Peter Marinello up his sleeve. The 19-year-old had been signed from Hibernian in January 1970 as an investment for the future. Arsenal had paid £100,000 for him – the first time that Arsenal had paid a six-figure sum for a player. Mee was convinced that the youngster could be developed into a star for the future. With his pop-star looks and swagger he appeared to be another George Best.

Unfortunately, it turned out that Arsenal, and London in particular, was the wrong environment for the youngster. Marinello could play, but, like Best, he found it hard to deal with life outside football. Arsenal's strength had been to excel without the need for an individual. The team ethic was everything. Marinello couldn't fit into that structure and he represents probably the only major misjudgement in Mee's dealings in the transfer market. In three years, Marinello made only 38 appearances and scored only three goals. He was homesick for Scotland and tried to overcome that with a somewhat colourful lifestyle. He also suffered a knee injury, which meant he missed the Fairs Cup run in 1970. He played in only four matches during the Double-winning campaign. In the next two seasons he played only 21 league games and he left Arsenal in July 1973 to join Portsmouth.

His chequered career also took him to Motherwell, Fulham, Phoenix Inferno in the United States, Hearts and Partick Thistle. He was made bankrupt after a business failure in 1994. During his time at Highbury Mee tried to defend him by saying, 'Give him time, be patient.' However, he never did come through. 'I had an agent and received so many offers,' Marinello was to reveal later. 'I was asked to open nightclubs, appear on *Top of the Pops*, to model and even make a record.' London needed its own George Best and Marinello was supposed to be the answer. 'Bertie Mee said I was being bought for the future so it was usually me that was left out for the big games. I did play against Ajax in that European Cup quarter-final at Highbury and Johan Cruyff said to me afterwards that I had a good game,' added Marinello in a revealing interview in the *Observer Sport Monthly* in 2007. 'But I missed a good chance to score and I am still reminded of that by Arsenal fans. At the end of three and a half years at the Club I made the mistake of chasing the money and joined Portsmouth. I would never be the same player again.'

Another trip down Wembley Way

Despite the talent at Mee's disposal, the 1971/72 season was to end in anti-climax. Mee's great dream had been to win the European Cup but that ambition was to evaporate at the quarter-final stage. All was going well in the first two rounds with Stroemsgodset of Norway beaten 3-1 away and 4-0 at home. Zurich Grasshoppers were supposed to provide a sterner test but it was one that Arsenal passed easily. Mee's men won 2-0 in Switzerland and 3-0 at Highbury. But the competition really began in the last eight, and Arsenal were found wanting against Ajax. This was a different team to the one that Arsenal faced in the Fairs Cup of 1970. The Amsterdamers were developing the nucleus of the team that would represent Holland in successive World Cup finals in 1974 and 1978. And they were world class and it was Arsenal's misfortune to meet them just as they were beginning to blossom. Gerrit Muhren scored twice in the first leg in Amsterdam but Arsenal were given hope with another of Ray Kennedy's speciality away goals. A 1-2 deficit meant that a 1-0 home win in the second leg would be enough to reach the last four. In the event George Graham scored a memorable goal. The problem was it was past Bob Wilson into his own net, and Arsenal went out.

The league season wasn't much better. They started well with wins against Chelsea and Huddersfield, but that was followed by three defeats on the bounce, against Manchester United, Sheffield United and Stoke. Those defeats meant that Arsenal were always playing catch up and they eventually finished fifth behind new champions Derby County. Sheffield United also brought the League Cup quest to a halt after Barnsley and Newcastle had been beaten. If there was to be glory, then the FA Cup appeared to provide the most likely route.

The third round handed Arsenal the type of tie that all high-profile clubs dread – away to opponents from a lower division – January weather, a less than perfect pitch and the whole country waiting for a giant-killing. And it was against the team who had embarrassed Arsenal in the League Cup final just a few years earlier – Swindon. But Alan Ball hadn't been part of that team that day at Wembley and he showed no fear as he set about the minnows. First he made the opening goal of the game for George Armstrong to settle Arsenal nerves and, if the Wiltshire club had any dreams of fighting their way back, they were ended when Ball scored the second. There was a similar formula in the draw for the fourth round, which took Arsenal to Fourth Division Reading. They played at Elm Park in those days, and the ground was packed with 25,000 enthusiastic supporters. It was a tight game, but with an own-goal and then a rare strike from Pat Rice, Arsenal reached the last 16. They were drawn away again – this time against champions-elect Derby County. The match ended 2-2 with Alan Hinton and Alan Durban scoring for Derby and Charlie George replying with two goals for the Gunners. The replay at Highbury was tense and finished goalless, even after extra-time. The second replay, at Filbert Street, Leicester, was decided by a Ray Kennedy goal.

It was back onto the banana skin for the sixth round with the draw pairing Arsenal with Leyton Orient at Brisbane Road. Third Division Orient had already provided one of the great upsets of that season's FA Cup when they had beaten mighty Chelsea in the fifth round. Arsenal held no fears for them. But Orient held no fears for Ball either. The red headed dynamo revelled on that stage and scored the winning goal early in the second half. Arsenal were on their way into the semi-finals and kept alive their hopes of retaining the FA Cup. The omens were good because Arsenal were once again drawn against Stoke City in a tie to be staged at Villa Park. Again there was drama. George Armstrong had put Arsenal in front but then goalkeeper Bob Wilson had suffered a serious knee injury. It was decided to keep him on but the ploy backfired when Peter Simpson headed into his own net when trying to clear a cross that a fit goalkeeper would have gathered with some comfort. Enter hero John Radford. He took over in goal and managed to frustrate Stoke's attempts to get past him. The match ended 1-1. The replay was at Goodison Park – a homecoming for reserve goalkeeper Geoff Barnett and Ball, both signed from Everton. Jimmy Greenhoff and Charlie George both converted penalties. Then George set up the winner for John Radford and Arsenal were back at Wembley.

Their opponents at the national stadium were Leeds United, who had cruised past Birmingham City in the semi-final, and were on-course to emulate Arsenal's Double triumph of the previous season.

Arsenal went into the match without keeper Bob Wilson who needed surgery on the knee injury he suffered in the semi-final. The best thing about the match was the winning goal – unfortunately for Arsenal fans it was scored by Allan Clarke, who headed home a superb cross from Mick Jones. The rest of the game, which started with an Arsenal defender begin booked for a scything challenge on Peter Lorimer, was poor and littered with niggly fouls. Leeds captain Billy Bremner held up the trophy with pride – it was the only time the Yorkshire club has won the FA Cup in its history.

Cold comfort

It was cold comfort that Leeds lost their final match of the season, 2–1 at Wolves, and so failed to emulate Arsenal's Double. The Arsenal team seemed to be lacking the special qualities that had been in evidence the previous season. Not that they were the only English Club in the doldrums. There was little success for English teams on the European stage during these years, and the national team fared even worse. They failed to qualify for the European Championships in 1972 and 1976 and for the World Cup in 1974. The players were there – Ball, George and Kennedy at Arsenal, Keegan at Liverpool, Coppell at Manchester United, Martin Peters and Chivers at Spurs, Bell at Manchester City, Hunter and Clarke at Leeds to name but a few. But either through bad luck or bad judgement, successive England managers – Sir Alf Ramsey, briefly Joe Mercer and then Don Revie – could not find the right formula. Add to that the growing menace of hooliganism and the game was not in the healthiest of states. Thugs were now organized and terrorized towns and cities up and down the country every Saturday. And by the end of the 1970s, they began to export their criminal behaviour to unsuspecting locations on mainland Europe.

For Arsenal there were hints of a revival in the 1972/73 season. It started with a seven-match unbeaten run. But there was still something missing. Two games in particular stood out in exposing the limitations of the squad. The first was a 5–0 thrashing by Derby County and the second was a 6–1 drubbing at Leeds. Both matches exposed a lack of defensive discipline, which was a huge concern for Mee. Arsenal went on to finish second in the league behind the winners Liverpool. But the season as a whole was disappointing. The quest for the League Cup was ended by Norwich, who won 3–0 at Highbury. And though there was a good FA Cup run to warm the hearts and hands of supporters during the winter months, that too ended in disappointment. Arsenal met Second Division Sunderland in the semi-final at Hillsborough and were on the wrong end of a 2–1 scoreline. Again there was cold comfort as Sunderland famously went on to beat Leeds in the final.

At the end of the campaign Mee knew that he had to ring the changes. George Graham was signed by Manchester United manager Tommy Docherty. United had endured a barren patch and Docherty was brought in to reverse the trend and wanted Graham's experience to help him. Jeff Blockley had been brought in the previous summer as a long-term replacement for the ageing Frank McLintock. Though physically strong, he had been a bit of a disappointment. Despite this McLintock was put up for sale and he was snapped up by former trainer Dave Sexton then manager of Queens Park Rangers. It was a decision that did not go down well among the fans who had seen his replacement Blockley struggle to make any kind of impression. 'A grievous error,' is how Bob Wilson described the decision to let McLintock leave. In retrospect it seems that Mee doubted the wisdom of his own move. 'It was my biggest mistake,' he admitted later. It also brought the curtain down on the career of a famous Arsenal captain.

Frank McLintock

On the night of 16 September 1970, the Arsenal players and those of Lazio of Rome were dining in the same restaurant after a 2–2 draw in the Inter-Cities Fairs' Cup. An argument broke out and several of the Italians started on young striker Ray Kennedy. As captain, Frank McLintock was having none of that. To call it a mass brawl would be inaccurate. It was as one-sided a fight as you could ever see because the Italians who provoked the situation were given a good hiding. And leading the charge was McLintock. His players were his family. Attack one and you attack them all. Clearly he is one of the most inspiring leaders the Arsenal team have ever had. But to associate McLintock merely with violence away from the pitch would be wrong. He was enthusiastic, determined and both proud and honoured to be captain of Arsenal.

His upbringing had been tough. He was born in the winter of 1939 in the Gorbals district of Glasgow. He had to learn very quickly to stand on his own two feet. He survived that most fearsome of environments to flourish in schoolboy football. At 17 years of age, he was invited down to Leicester City and he made his debut in 1959 as a midfield player. With the Midlands club he appeared in two FA Cup finals and lost them both. In October 1964, he was signed by Arsenal manager Billy Wright and was immediately installed in the first team. In 1967, Bertie Mee, who had succeeded Wright the previous year, made him captain. 'One of the proudest moment of my life,' he said. Mee converted him into a central defender; a role where the manager felt McLintock could exert more influence and authority as well as make use of his ability to read the game. McLintock duly led the club to two League Cup finals at Wembley in 1968 and 1969. In that close season, McLintock almost let the frustration of losing both finals cloud his judgement when he asked for a transfer. Mee was determined to hang on to the man he felt could lead Arsenal to the success that he believed was close. After a long heart-to-heart talk, McLintock opted to stay and found for himself a place in Arsenal history.

Inside two years, he picked up three major trophies. In 1970, it was his inspirational team talk that helped win the Fairs Cup. The match was played over two legs and Arsenal had lost the first leg in Brussels 3–1. But McLintock blocked out his immediate disappointment to stress to his men that victory was still theirs if they wanted it badly enough. Arsenal duly won the second leg 3–0. The following season, McLintock led the team to the league championship and the FA Cup inside five dramatic days. That year he was also voted Footballer of the Year. In 1972, he captained the team back at Wembley in the FA Cup final but they lost 1–0 to Leeds. He was made an MBE that year. In 1972/73 Arsenal finished as runners-up in the league. Then, in June, he was sold to Queens Park Rangers. In total he had played 403 matches for Arsenal and scored 32 goals. He stayed four years at Loftus Road and was an important part of the team that finished runners-up in 1976 to Liverpool and qualified for the UEFA Cup. When he retired from playing he went into management at Leicester and then Brentford. His return to Leicester was not a memorable one and they were relegated from the First Division during his only season in charge. He was at Brentford between 1984 and 1987 and then moved to Millwall, where he was assistant manager to John Docherty as the team reached the top-flight for the first time in their history.

The Double team breaks up

Clearly he had left too soon. Cracks were appearing in the Arsenal team, which had once seemed so bonded but was now slowly being dismantled – on and off the pitch. Mee turned to QPR for a new first-team coach when he replaced Steve Burtenshaw with Bobby Campbell. The Liverpudlian was earning a reputation as one of the brightest coaches in the game and his arrival was seen as something of a coup.

But Campbell could only be as good as the material with which he was working and the 1973/74 season will go down as distinctly average. The opening day saw a false dawn. Manchester United, with new signing George Graham, were the visitors at Highbury and left on the wrong end of a 3–0 result. But early optimism gradually gave way as the season wore on. Sheffield United gave out a 5–0 hammering to Mee's men and early in February 1974 a mere 20,789 turned up at Highbury to see a 1–1 draw with Burnley. These were not good signs and it could be argued that Mee's judgement was now being called into question. Arsenal finished tenth in the league as Leeds United again asserted their authority by winning the title. There were also early exits from the domestic cup competitions. They lost at home to Tranmere Rovers in the League Cup and went out of the FA Cup at Villa Park in the fourth round.

Perhaps the most heartening moment of the season was the debut of 17-year-old Irish midfield player Liam Brady in a 2–0 away defeat at Tottenham. Part of a footballing family, he had been spotted in Dublin as a 13-year-old. He came to the Club and excelled in a trial game and proceeded to spend his school holidays at Arsenal where he was earmarked as a talent for the future. He moved over permanently at the age of 16 and while he admitted to often feeling homesick for his native Ireland, he was determined to make the grade. He played 13 league games that season and through the gloom that shrouded the Club at that time, Brady's deft touch and immense talent shone through. Despite the lack of success, Brady had no reason to change his first impression of Arsenal. 'You knew you were coming into a top club, a place with style and swagger.'

It is hard to explain the decline of a team that had won Double glory three years before. Somehow, Liverpool and Leeds managed to maintain their challenge for honours over a decade but Arsenal's seemed to be extinguished almost as quickly as it started. It might well have been that they missed the influence of Don Howe. It was evident that the Club failed to enjoy anything like the success they had when he was coach. And, gradually, the players that had brought so much glory continued leaving the Club.

At the end of the season, Ray Kennedy left to join Liverpool for a meagre £150,000. He was Bill Shankly's last major signing and was to go on to have tremendous success at Anfield and as part of the England team. To take Kennedy's place, Mee bought Brian Kidd from Manchester United. As an 18-year-old, Kidd had been a revelation in United's European Cup win of 1968 against Benfica. Now Docherty regarded him as surplus to requirements. And that close season, Bob Wilson decided to retire and was replaced by Jimmy Rimmer who had been bought a year earlier from Manchester United to be groomed as his replacement. Eddie Kelly joined McLintock at Loftus Road in 1976 but while McLintock flourished in the new environment and looked just as effective as he had done at Arsenal, Kelly was unable to reproduce the form he had shown while at Highbury. He seemed to have everything that was needed for a central midfield man except pace. But he made up for that with a steely determination and an eye for a goal as well as including a neat passing game in his repertoire. But something was missing, whether it was his attitude or a case of a young player unable to handle sudden fame is not clear. But Eddie Kelly was one of the most gifted young players of his generation and should have illuminated the midfield more often than he did.

Last knockings for Mee

By any standard the 1974/75 season was a poor one. Two wins in the first 13 matches, out of the League Cup by 18 September, things went from bad to worse. They managed to stop the rot during the early part of winter but once again it was the FA Cup that seemed to offer the only hope of silverware. Arsenal reached the last eight the hard way. The minnows of York City held Arsenal to a draw at Highbury in the third round but the replay was won 3–1. In the fourth round, a draw at Coventry was followed by a comfortable 3–0 win in the replay. Three attempts were needed to dispose of Leicester as Arsenal exacted revenge for their defeat in the League Cup. Then came a sixth-round home game with West Ham and Arsenal were strongly fancied to reach the last four. But West Ham had their FA Cup talisman that season in diminutive striker Alan Taylor and he scored twice as the Hammers went through. Another season of failure saw the Club finish in 16th place and Mee was not free from criticism.

He shocked the Highbury faithful in the summer of 1975 by selling Charlie George. To many of the fans that was close to sacrilege. Yes, he could be a handful and he had already had a number of run-ins with the manager. He was something of a loose cannon and his obscene two-fingered salute to barracking Derby fans after scoring did not go down well. But his value to Arsenal was summed up by Bob Wilson who said, 'Without Charlie, I don't think we would have won the Double. In a tight, disciplined team, he was our free spirit.' But Mee clearly felt that George had given his best days to Arsenal and he was sold to Derby for £90,000 to be suddenly adored by the fans he had once taunted.

Mee had tried to refresh his squad for the 1975/76 season by signing tenacious winger Alex Cropley from Hibernian. 'A tough, hard little bugger,' as John Radford once described him. And there was a glimpse of a compatriot of Brady's who was to represent Arsenal with immense distinction for the next 17 years – David O'Leary. Born in Stamford Hill while his father was working in London, O'Leary moved back to Ireland while still a baby. His talent was evident before he entered his teens and he became a target for Arsenal. 'This boy is some player, trust me,' said Mee ahead of O'Leary's debut, a 3–1 defeat at Manchester United that was to be the first of a record 558 league appearances he would make for the Club. These, however, were not good times. Arsenal went out of the League Cup and the FA Cup with something of a whimper – losing to Everton and Wolves respectively. In the league they finished a poor 17th.

At that point Bertie Mee had endured enough. He wanted out. Management had taken its toll and he opted for retirement. Arsenal's choice to succeed him was something of a shock and proof that it is possible to bridge the great divide between the North London clubs as they went for Terry Neill. Neill had been an Arsenal captain and a Northern Ireland international of some standing. He had cut his managerial teeth at Hull and then Tottenham. It has to be said that he was not an outstanding success at White Hart Lane where they had flirted with relegation. True, Bill Nicholson, who had stepped down in 1974, had been a hard act to follow and Neill had worked hard to bring the 'Glory Glory' days of the early 1960s back to Tottenham. Now he was to try his luck at the other end of the Seven Sisters Road.

Chapter Nine

FINALS AND FRUSTRATION

Arsenal exhibit flair in cup competitions, but league success proves elusive

No one could doubt that Terry Neill showed anything but the utmost professionalism when he was at White Hart Lane. True, honours were non-existent, but Spurs fans who question his commitment should remember that when Neill arrived at the club in 1974 Steve Perryman was on his way out. Bill Nicholson had put Perryman on the transfer list and Coventry were extremely keen to sign him, but Neill immediately blocked the move, telling the man who would, over the next decade, go on to lead Tottenham to success at home and in Europe, 'You are going nowhere.'

It was also Neill who gave a Tottenham first-team debut to a precocious youngster called Glenn Hoddle, but when Neill came back to Arsenal there was always the feeling that he had returned to his spiritual home, and he acted quickly and decisively to make changes on and off the field. First, aware of the contribution that Don Howe had made both prior to and during the highly successful Double year, he brought Howe back from Leeds and into the fold.

On the field, Neill was quick to bring in new blood and discard players he felt had either outlived their usefulness or were not the type of player he wanted. Brian Kidd left and, to fill in alongside young Stapleton, Neill paid £333,333 to Newcastle for Malcolm 'Supermac' Macdonald. It was stunning coup. Macdonald was massively popular on Tyneside, arriving at St James' Park in a Rolls Royce and showing the kind of cockiness and self-assurance that the Geordie public adored, plus he scored goals for fun. That was the quality that Neill wanted at Arsenal as he sought to rebuild his team. The Newcastle fans never forgave their manager Gordon Lee for selling Macdonald and he was soon out of a job because of the decision.

Neill now had the strike force he wanted – the bravery and youthful zest of Stapleton, and the pace and power of Macdonald. The emergence of Stapleton allowed Neill to release one of the Double heroes, John Radford, to West Ham, and he then turned his attention to midfield. Neill and the opinionated Alan Ball were never going to see eye-to-eye and, as he tried to establish himself as manager, Neill saw Ball as too big a character and a negative influence, so Ball went to Southampton, where Lawrie McMenemy once again managed to extract top-class performances from a player that many felt had his best years behind him (it was a trick McMenemy performed time and time again with the likes of Mick Channon, Mick Mills, Kevin Keegan and Dave Watson). Alan Hudson was next in Neill's sights. Hudson had been a star at Chelsea, no question about it. Indeed, he looked to be the best midfield player of his generation, but he'd been snared by the Kings Road syndrome, which also trapped the likes of Peter Osgood and Charlie Cooke, and, having fallen out with Stamford Bridge manager Dave Sexton had been transferred to Stoke. Hudson was always more Primrose Hill than Potteries, though, and needed little persuasion to come back to the capital.

It was all falling into place for Neill, although he clearly needed time for his new players to gel. That made 1976/77 a season of transition, but not the most difficult fans have had to endure over the years. In the league

Arsenal finished eighth – a vast improvement, it has to be said, on the two previous campaigns. In the FA Cup Notts County and Coventry were disposed of without too much fuss, but in the fifth round Middlesbrough handed out a 4–1 beating, which served as a reminder that there was still work to be done. In the League Cup Arsenal battled past Carlisle, needed three games to beat Blackpool and then produced an impressive performance to conquer Chelsea, but Queens Park Rangers, enjoying a highly successful season, won 2–1 at Loftus Road.

A staggering signing

Neill felt Arsenal were progressing, but decided to strengthen the team further in the close season with a signing that took everyone by surprise. Pat Jennings, the new Tottenham manager Keith Burkinshaw had decided, could leave White Hart Lane. Burkinshaw made several inspired decisions in his time at Tottenham, where he had been brought by Neill to be first-team coach. He signed Ossie Ardiles and Ricky Villa, while Garth Crooks and Steve Archibald were a front pair that would terrorize defences. However, to let the legend that is Jennings leave the club was beyond belief. The Northern Ireland international was nowhere near past his best and at £40,000 he was the bargain of this and many other seasons. The Tottenham fans despaired at his departure, the Arsenal fans welcomed him with open arms, but such is the character and popularity of the man that, to this day, he is loved and revered by both sets of supporters – and not many have achieved that particular 'double'.

Neill also had the acumen to understand that football was entering the era of specialized coaches and he wanted one of this new breed to take the goalkeepers. He immediately turned to Bob Wilson, who was delighted at the prospect of working for the Club where he had made his name. Neill explained, 'I had begun to realize the need for a specialist goalkeeping coach, but Bob asked me, "What on earth am I going to do with someone like Pat Jennings?" I just said, "Keep him happy." And he did!'

Now the pieces of the jigsaw were beginning to fit together and in the 1977/78 season Arsenal began to make a real impact in both the league and the FA Cup. There was another talented youngster coming through in Graham Rix, who was to go on to win England honours at under-21 and full level. Indeed, he played a significant role for the national side in the 1982 World Cup finals in Spain. Arsenal had also been strengthened by the October 1977 arrival of striker Alan Sunderland from Wolves. He cost £500,000 and was a mobile, neat striker who would add another dimension to the team and increase the attacking options for Neill.

In the league Arsenal showed further improvement as they finished in fifth place. In the cups the potential of the team was also evident. Arsenal reached the semi-finals of the League Cup, but, frustratingly, failed to overcome a 2–1 deficit from the first leg at Anfield and drew 0–0 at Highbury. However, there was still the FA Cup to play for.

The Club's 1978 FA Cup run started at Bramall Lane where Sheffield United were comprehensively beaten 5–0. Wolves, Walsall and Wrexham were also overcome at the first time of asking, and Arsenal's luck in the draw held out in the semi-final, when they were paired with that season's shock team of the competition, Leyton Orient. Under the shrewd management of former Arsenal player Jimmy Bloomfield, Orient had the free-scoring Peter Kitchen up front and among their victims that year had been the durable Middlesbrough side that had been put together by Jack Charlton. The final scoreline of 3–0 belied Orient's brave and committed efforts at Stamford Bridge, and it has to be said that any luck that was around went Arsenal's way. Indeed, one of Arsenal's goals was credited to Macdonald, but it took at least two deflections before ending up in the net.

Through to the FA Cup final

Ipswich Town, managed by future England manager Bobby Robson, were the opposition at Wembley and the fact that they were the clear underdogs helped the East Anglian team no end. There is pressure enough in an FA Cup final and to be burdened with the tag of being favourites is not one that many teams relish. Arsenal also had problems off the field, with star front man Macdonald struggling with an ankle injury and Liam Brady battling to be a hundred per cent fit. Neill also had a huge midfield selection dilemma.

Graham Rix had emerged as a real talent for the future. He was slightly built, but brave as a lion. 'I remember Tommy Smith, that tough Liverpool defender, once saying to me that if I tried to make him look silly he could chop me in half! Of course he didn't, but there was a menace in his voice and he not only looked hard, he was hard,' said Rix. 'But you have to deal with that. It is part and parcel of the game. If you're frightened by it then don't bother going into football.' Rix certainly wasn't one to be intimidated. He could handle the verbals, no problem, and his wiry frame belied a durable streak. Arguably, he had also been Arsenal's best player in the semi-final win over Orient, but Neill opted to leave the youngster on the bench and gambled on the fitness of Macdonald. It was not a move that was to pay off.

Ipswich were relaxed and confident. Their own central defensive pairing of Allan Hunter and Kevin Beattie was intact, after Northern Ireland international Hunter passed a fitness test at the team hotel on the morning of the final, and they were highly-motivated – none more so than goalkeeper Paul Cooper. 'I had a good game,' said Cooper later, 'and that was largely thanks to Jack Charlton. He was on the television the night before the game and he slaughtered me. He said I was too small and that I was the weakness that Arsenal would expose. That really geed me up.' It must have had the same effect on the rest of the team as well, as Ipswich played with a freedom and a fluency that belied their underdog status.

In contrast, Arsenal just couldn't get going. Brady was forced to come off and Rix was given his opportunity, but by then the force was with Ipswich. In Paul Mariner the East Anglians had a striker of height, power and excellent touch. He worried Arsenal throughout the game and in the first half he thundered one drive against the bar. Somehow it was goalless at the break, but Ipswich served notice that they were going to be as focused during the second half as they had been in the first 45 minutes, and it was only a stunning save from Pat Jennings that kept out a goal-bound effort from George Burley. The reprieve was only temporary, though, as Ipswich finally got the goal their play deserved. David Geddis beat Arsenal's Northern Irish full back Sammy Nelson and crossed into the area. Willie Young, who had moved across North London with Neill from Tottenham, managed to make some contact, but only succeeded in diverting the ball into the path of Ipswich midfielder Roger Osborne, who scored from close range. A Suffolk boy playing for his local team, Osborne was overcome with emotion and had to be taken off with nervous exhaustion. Ipswich held on without any problems and the upset was complete.

There was an inquest some days later in which Neill and Howe asked the players for their versions of why it had gone wrong. 'For me,' said Hudson who was never slow to voice an opinion, 'the wrong team went out there. We should have had Graham Rix in the line-up.' Neill and Hudson continued to clash, and in the end the single-minded midfield player left Arsenal in October 1978 for a new career in the United States with Seattle Sounders. It was a decision that Hudson always regretted. 'Leaving Arsenal was the worst day's work I ever did,' he was to say. 'I just couldn't get on with the manager Terry Neill and I was fed up with the way things had gone for me, on and off the pitch. In fact, my last game was the 1978 FA Cup final against Ipswich. I remember Don Howe saw me at the airport as I was leaving and couldn't believe it, but I had made up my mind and I was off.' Macdonald was on the McLintock trail. This had been his third final and, after two unsuccessful appearances with Newcastle, his third defeat, but unlike for the Scot, there was to be no happy ending for Macdonald. The week after the final he went into hospital for the first of a series of knee operations that were to blight his career and end it prematurely.

The following season, 1978/79, was never going to bring glory in the league and Arsenal eventually finished seventh, although it did include one incredible derby game against Tottenham at White Hart Lane just before Christmas. Rarely are these encounters one-sided affairs and whoever is having the most difficult spell at the time invariably raises their game. Not on this occasion, however. This was the Liam Brady show. He was in quite magnificent form and to this day many Arsenal fans regard it as his best performance in the Club shirt.

Arsenal won 5-0 at White Hart Lane and Brady just could not be contained. He ripped Tottenham apart and that gave Arsenal hope for the FA Cup campaign.

In the League Cup Arsenal had suffered the humiliation of a defeat at lowly Rotherham, and the players and Neill were so upset that they refused to give any post-match interviews. Howe was particularly furious. Arsenal enjoyed a better run in the UEFA Cup, where their travels took them into Eastern Europe at a time when the Iron Curtain was still very much in place. The East Germans of Lokomotiv Leipzig were easily beaten, 3-0 at home and 4-1 away. Then came Hajduk Split of the former Yugoslavia, who were a much tougher proposition. Arsenal were grateful for an away goal from Brady in a 2-1 defeat and the winner at Highbury came from an unlikely source, when central defender Willie Young scored to put Arsenal through on the away-goals rule. It was back to Yugoslavia again for the next round and this time the campaign came to an end. Arsenal were beaten 1-0 by an excellent Red Star team in Belgrade and were held to a 1-1 draw at home, with Frank Stapleton scoring the goal.

Another shot at the FA Cup

However, the FA Cup, and a possible second successive final, were still to come, although Arsenal needed an extraordinary total of five third-round games, plus some heroics from Brady, to dispose of Jack Charlton's well-organized Sheffield Wednesday. A 1-1 draw at Hillsborough brought a replay at Highbury. Brady hit the net for Arsenal, but it finished with the same scoreline as the first game. In a third replay at Leicester Brady was on the mark again, along with Alan Sunderland, as Arsenal were held 2-2. A fourth replay – unimaginable these days with penalty-shoot-outs coming after the first replay if the match is undecided – ended in a thrilling 3-3 draw, before Arsenal finally saw off Wednesday's challenge with a 2-0 win, and goals from Stapleton and Steve Gatting, the brother of former England cricket captain Mike Gatting.

The start of 1979 saw another new arrival in Brian Talbot, who had made a huge impression on Neill and Howe the previous May when he'd played for Ipswich at Wembley. They liked his dynamic, foraging style and eye for a goal. They inquired about him and, with Ipswich manager Bobby Robson looking to Holland, where he had identified Frans Thijssen and Arnold Muhren as future targets, and with the impressive youngster John Wark establishing himself in the ranks, an offer of £400,000 was accepted.

Talbot and Young scored the goals that saw off Notts County in the fourth round of the FA Cup, but an almighty clash was predicted for the fifth round, when Arsenal were paired with Nottingham Forest at the City Ground. This was to be Stapleton's day. From the raw youngster who was so close to a release from Arsenal, Stapleton had developed into a striker with the ability to hold the ball up and the awareness to bring others into the game, but it was his goalscoring that was to be of value that day. Forest, managed by the late Brian Clough, were a formidable team. They took the game to Arsenal and were on the front foot for most of the encounter. However, as Clough memorably remarked, 'It only takes a second to score a goal,' and when Stapleton's positional play left Forest central defender Larry Lloyd struggling, the Irishman rose to head home a memorable winner. The quarter-final opponents were Southampton and after a 1–1 draw at the intimidating arena of the Dell, Arsenal won the replay 2–0. As much as a semi-final win can be comfortable, Arsenal eased past Wolves to set up a final with Manchester United.

The first half was Arsenal's and they led 2–0, courtesy of strikes from Brian Talbot and Frank Stapleton. United, now managed by former Arsenal coach Dave Sexton, just couldn't get to grips with the game and if it had been a boxing match the opinion of many was that it would have been stopped to prevent the infliction of any further punishment. The second half, in searing heat, appeared to be drifting towards an inevitable conclusion until it suddenly took a different turn with a period of drama and contrasting emotions that it seems only football can produce. With only around five minutes left, Neill decided to inject some fresh legs into the team to help run down the clock. On came Steve Walford. 'To be honest, it was a great feeling,' said Walford in the aftermath of the final. 'I had come on just to add some presence, but it seemed that before I had touched the ball United were level. It was weird.' United's comeback started when central defender Gordon McQueen swept the ball home, but worse was to come as, within two minutes, Sammy McIlroy set off on a mazy run that took him inside the area and he prodded the ball past his Northern Ireland team-mate Pat Jennings.

An anonymous final had suddenly been ignited and it wasn't over yet, much to the relief of Arsenal, and Walford in particular. 'I came on expecting to see out time and then pick up a winners' medal,' he said. 'Then suddenly it's 2–2!' Not for long, though, as Brady, keeping his head amid the bedlam, secured possession in midfield and spotted Graham Rix running down the left wing. With a superb measured pass, Rix was able to run clear and cross deep to the far post, beyond United goalkeeper Gary Bailey, where Alan Sunderland was waiting to rifle home the winner and set off on the victory run that is shown time and time again on television replays. Arsenal had won the 1979 FA Cup 3–2.

Within touching distance of trophies

After the heartbreak of the previous year there was now promise for 1979/80, but it was to be a season in which Arsenal came tantalizingly close to a great deal, but in fact won nothing, becoming victims of a crowded fixture list that eventually took its toll. The league campaign started superbly with a 4–0 win at newly promoted Brighton, but it was to be mid-September before Arsenal won again. A spell like that so early in the programme can leave a team with too much ground to make up in the months ahead and Arsenal were eventually to finish fourth – close, but no cigar.

The cup competitions, however, were becoming Arsenal's forte. A League Cup run which was to end in defeat at Swindon in a fifth round replay included a 7–0 thrashing of Leeds, but in the European Cup-Winners' Cup (now merged with the UEFA Cup to make one competition in which domestic league placings and cup success are rewarded), Arsenal went as far as the final. This was thoroughly deserved, with tough matches all the way to the clash against Valencia in Brussels. Fenerbahce of Turkey, Magdeburg of East Germany and Gothenburg of Sweden were all beaten and the reward was a semi-final clash with Juventus. The first leg was at Highbury and an own-goal enabled Arsenal to take a 1–1 draw to Turin. Surely this was not to be enough – not only did the team have no win to defend, but they had also conceded an away goal? Arsenal, though, were confident. 'The pressure is on them now,' said the canny Howe. 'Let's see how they handle that.'

Juventus had had Marco Tardelli sent off in that first game and David O'Leary had been the victim of a horrendous tackle from Roberto Bettega, but he was thankfully fit for the return, in which Arsenal were to have an unlikely hero. Most Italian teams would back themselves to play out a goalless draw on their own turf and, said Neill, 'We knew that would be their mindset. All we needed then was one chance, one break and we would be through.' On the day, the strategy worked to perfection. Juventus were content to go forward when the occasion arose, but refused to over-commit for fear of being caught on the counter. The Juve players were confident, the home crowd were confident, but so were Neill and Howe. With the clock running down in the second half they sent on young striker Paul Vaessen and he scored. Juventus were stunned, Arsenal were delighted. That was one final achieved and they could turn their attentions to another competition – the FA Cup.

Cardiff, Brighton, Bolton and Watford had all been beaten and now it was a semi-final against Liverpool, which was to turn into a record-breaking, four-game marathon. In truth it was the last thing Arsenal needed. With cup replays allied to excursions into Europe, the league programme was becoming a drain on resources and towards the end of the season Arsenal were playing three games a week. That was to be crucial in the final reckoning. The first clash with Liverpool finished goalless and the second ended 1–1, with Alan Sunderland scoring for Arsenal. Sunderland was on the mark again as the third clash ended 1–1, but Talbot eventually concluded the saga at the fourth time of asking. Two finals now beckoned inside four days.

Through to two finals

At Wembley, Arsenal faced a West Ham team managed by the late John Lyall, who succeeded in pulling off a tactical masterstroke. West Ham were even more unfancied than Ipswich had been two years earlier. They were part of the old Second Division and had not even clinched promotion that year, but in Lyall they had the perfect man for the job. If anyone had the know-how, then it was Lyall. His plan was simple – use a lone front man to occupy the Arsenal defence, swamp the midfield, then catch the opposition on the break. He also included in his team a 17-year-old called Paul Allen, who was to be denied a moment that would have lived with him forever by a crude challenge from Willie Young.

The plan worked a treat. On a scorching hot day, with Stuart Pearson alone up front, Arsenal found themselves overrun in the department in which they felt so strong. They completely failed to impose themselves on a team superbly led by Billy Bonds and must have known it wasn't going to be their day when they went behind to that rarity in football, a header from Trevor Brooking, as Pearson drove the ball into a crowded area following a run and cross from the elusive Alan Devonshire. Arsenal had territory, but no penetration and it was a desperate movement from Young that denied Allen his moment. While Arsenal were clearly paying the price for their punishing schedule, Allen was full of youthful energy and it was a surge forward late in the game that appeared to leave him one on one with Pat Jennings – until Young unceremoniously hauled him down. These days, Young wouldn't have bothered to wait to see the red card. In 1980, a yellow sufficed.

Drained and demoralized, Arsenal now had to try to lift themselves for a better-prepared Valencia team in the 1980 Cup-Winners' Cup final. To their credit, Arsenal matched the Spanish team, took the game into extra-time and then forced a penalty shoot-out. Liam Brady was, for once, let down by one of the most cultured left feet in the game and that was followed by a similar strike from Rix. Arsenal lost 5–4 and it was Rix who had to carry the can. 'Most people seem to forget that "Chippy" missed as well!' said Rix. 'It seems it was all down to me!

But to be honest, we were all out on our feet. The season caught up with us.' Brady's last game for Arsenal was at Middlesbrough in the league five days later and Arsenal lost 5–0. A campaign that had started with such promise ended with nothing. After 70 games (no English team has played so many in a season) all the players had to show for their efforts was two runners-up medals.

Without Brady, Arsenal lacked their iconic figure, although there were positives to emerge from this testing time, notably the way in which Paul Davis fitted into midfield. A graduate of the youth policy, Davis described his elevation to the Arsenal first team as 'a dream come true,' adding recently, 'I was playing for the Club I had supported as a kid. I seem to have spent most of my life at Highbury.' In the midst of one of the strangest transfer sagas in the Club's history, there was also the arrival of Kenny Sansom from Crystal Palace. In summer 1980 Arsenal had signed Queens Park Rangers striker Clive Allen for £1 million. The son of former Tottenham player Les Allen, he looked to be one of the brightest prospects in the game and his arrival was regarded as something of a coup. He went on a pre-season tour with the Club, but was not at Highbury long enough to play a competitive game as, out of the blue, he was swapped with Crystal Palace defender Sansom before the season had started. Neill also signed John Hollins from Queens Park Rangers and Peter Nicholas from Palace, and another young striker, Brian McDermott, was emerging from the academy. However, although there was another solid league campaign in which Arsenal finished third to Aston Villa, there was no joy in the knock-out competitions as Neill's men lost their 'cup kings' label.

Departure of a proud player and captain

Another loyal and long-serving player who left the Club in 1980 was Pat Rice. Although he was born in Belfast in 1949, Rice moved to North London when he was five and, like most kids in the area, he played football morning, noon and night, in the streets and in nearby Finsbury Park. He was just eight when he went to see his local team

Arsenal play the great Manchester United side of the Busby Babes era. He didn't pay to get in – 'It was easy to bunk in in those days, the crowds were huge,' he recalls – and United won 5–4. 'You couldn't help but love the football United played,' he says, 'but I came away a real Arsenal fan. Maybe it was this thing of loving the underdog, because that's what everyone was when they played that Manchester United side. From then on, though, it was Arsenal for me.' However, the date was February 1958 and the significance of that first professional game Rice attended emerged five days later, as it turned out to be the last match United played in England before the Munich air crash tragedy.

By his own admission Rice was not the most gifted player to wear an Arsenal shirt, but no one has worn it and shown the same commitment or as much pride. There was a dogged determination about him, a refusal to quit, and that's what impressed the Arsenal scouts who saw him play as a teenager. On leaving school Rice went to work in a greengrocer's in Gillespie Road, only giving it up when he was offered an apprenticeship by Arsenal in 1964. He became a full-time professional in 1966 and made his first-team debut in the League Cup against Burnley on 5 December 1967. Arsenal won 2–1, and it was to be the start of a connection with the Club that lasts until this day and was only interrupted by the four years at Watford between 1980 and 1984. 'I loved my time there,' said Rice, 'but the reality is that there is only one Club in my life and that has been Arsenal.' In his time as a player at Highbury, Rice also played 49 times for Northern Ireland.

For his first three years at the Club Rice was essentially a squad player, but his breakthrough came in 1969/70, when Arsenal won the Fairs Cup, and he was a regular in the team that won the League and FA Cup Double in 1971. In 1977 Terry Neill named him captain. 'In football, that was my proudest moment,' he says. 'You have to remember I grew up near the Club, I worked near the Club before I was signed on and it was a real dream come true to play for the Club – to be captain was incredible. I was captain for three successive FA Cup finals in 1978, 1979 and 1980. Yes, we lost two of them. I have to admit in the first one, against Ipswich, I didn't have one of my best games – Clive Woods, the Ipswich winger, gave me a terrible time – but the following year we beat Manchester United and I can assure you there was no one prouder than me in the whole world when I went to lift up the FA Cup for Arsenal – no one.'

When Graham Taylor was looking for an experienced head to help his young Watford team adjust to life in the top flight he turned to Rice, but after finishing his playing career at Vicarage Road Rice returned to Arsenal as youth team coach. He held that job for 12 years before he was made assistant manager by Arsène Wenger in October 1996.

A downward trend

In general, this was not a good time for English football. The hooligan problem was getting worse and England performed woefully in the 1980 European Championships finals in Italy. Indeed, it was during this tournament that football witnessed the first export of hooliganism. After Belgium had equalized in a game in Turin, England fans rioted and tear gas was used to quell the disturbance. The game was suspended, because England goalkeeper Ray Clemence was temporarily blinded by the gas. England went home in disgrace and, since then, the national team's fans have been regarded with suspicion and subjected to high security whenever they travel abroad.

Back at Arsenal, there were to be no cups on display at the famous old stadium at the end of the 1980/81 season. Interest in the FA Cup ended in January at the third round stage as they lost 2–0 at Everton. The League Cup saw Swansea and Stockport knocked out before a defeat at White Hart Lane against Tottenham, and there was no repeat of the 1980 heroics in the UEFA Cup. Two wins against Panathinaikos were followed by a tie with Winterslag from Belgium and Arsenal were eliminated on the away-goals rule. While Arsenal were consistently achieving top six finishes in the league, they seemed to have lost their knack of winning trophies – and that, in the end, is the currency in which all managers are judged.

In the summer of 1981, Stapleton left Arsenal to join Manchester United and with him went much of the goal potency. In 1981/82 Arsenal scored only a meagre 48 goals without him and, although they finished fifth, they did not seem to be a team that was progressing. The FA Cup draw was again unkind as the third round took Arsenal to Tottenham, who won 1-0, and Liverpool ended the League Cup charge in December with a resounding 3-0 replay win at Anfield.

In the close season of 1982, in a bid to solve the goalscoring problem, Neill signed striker Lee Chapman from Stoke and Tony Woodcock from FC Koln. One transfer worked, the other didn't. Woodcock proved himself to be an asset to the Club. Neill had clinched the deal after four or five months of hard work behind the scenes, but his patience paid off. 'He is a marvellous player,' said Neill. Chapman was not so much of a success, but maybe it was a move that was destined not to work out. His first game was against the Club he had left, Stoke. Arsenal lost 2-1 and Chapman was subjected to incessant derision from the crowd. His home debut was a 1-1 draw with Norwich and how different Chapman's Arsenal career might have been if a goal that looked perfectly legitimate had not been disallowed for offside, as it would have gone a long way towards helping him win over the Highbury fans, who were somewhat sceptical about him. Chapman was big, brave and fearless, but lacked real guile and would never be accused of being elegant. The longer the goalless spell went on, the harder he tried and the worse it got. He managed a paltry three goals all season and never totally convinced the Arsenal audience.

In the 1983 League and FA Cups Arsenal reached the semi-final stages – only to be beaten by Manchester United in both competitions. The UEFA Cup run didn't get past the first hurdle. The first leg against Spartak Moscow appeared to be going Arsenal's way when Chapman and Stewart Robson put Arsenal two valuable away goals up. The Russians responded with a remarkable comeback to win 3-2, but Neill and Howe were still confident Arsenal would progress. Little did they know, though, what was in store as Spartak put on one of the most impressive performances seen at Highbury by any team in European competition. Arsenal were just blown away and lost 5-2. Their opponents were applauded off and a shell-shocked Neill had to admit that Arsenal has been well and truly taught a lesson in swift, counter-attacking football. 'They murdered us,' he said. 'It was a bit of a shock to the system, but the Arsenal fans recognized a good performance.'

The fans may have been impressed with the Russians. They were not impressed with their own team, who finished halfway up the league and not a cup in sight. The trends were not good and Neill decided that Arsenal needed a new hero, so he went north of the border to Scotland, the nation that had been so productive for Arsenal in the past, and in June 1983 Neill bought Charlie Nicholas from Celtic for £625,000. Champagne Charlie was ready to burst on to the London scene and he lapped up all the attention he immediately attracted. He had the looks and the talent, and the fans loved him, especially as, in the years to come, he proved to be such a thorn in the side of Tottenham. Neill reckoned that Nicholas would bring the star quality the team lacked and which the fans so wanted to see. And Nicholas wasn't shy, either.

Graham Rix tells one story about the Scot, who spent his first few months with Arsenal living at a country club in Hertfordshire, where he was somewhat isolated from the fans. He never saw them except on match days, so Graham Rix decided that he should take Nicholas out to a pub in Hackney that was frequented by hard-core Arsenal supporters. 'Dress as you would normally dress,' Rix told Nicholas. 'Just be yourself,' but much to Rix's astonishment Nicholas turned up in a cream leather suit. 'Well you said be yourself and that's what I'm doing,' said Nicholas – and off to the pub he went. He was eventually approached by a large individual who didn't look like the kind to be messed with. 'You're Charlie Nicholas aren't you?' he said. Rix feared the worst, but Nicholas remained his normal assured self. 'I am,' he replied. 'Well, I can head a ball better than you, I have a better right foot and left foot than you, and I can run faster than you,' said the fan. 'I believe you can do all those things,' said Nicholas, 'but can you do this?' And he promptly took a £20 note out of his pocket and tore it up in front of his inquisitor. Rix waited – and the fan proceeded to give Nicholas a huge hug. 'You'll do for me, Charlie boy,' he said. The fans loved Nicholas' flamboyance and flash image. He could also play, but not even the talents of Charlie Nicholas could save Neill.

There had been a spectacular 6–2 win at Aston Villa in the league, but highlights like that were few and far between. The nadir was reached in November with a 2–1 home defeat by Walsall in the League Cup.

Arsenal had been rejoicing just a few weeks earlier when they'd won 2–1 at White Hart Lane in the same competition, but that night the fans turned on the team and the management. 'They don't seem to know what it is to hunger for goals and glory,' said Neill, after the shock that was to mark the end of his reign. 'On some days I think they just want to pick up their money and go home, but I'll tell you now, we'll finish in the top six again this season. Whether or not I'll be around to see it is another matter.' He was right. Arsenal did finish in the top six, but by Christmas 1983 he had gone. Chairman Hill-Wood said, 'Some of the decisions that Terry was making were somewhat strange and when he started talking about bringing Alan Hudson back to the Club, well, that was it for me.'

Howe finally gets the top job

In all, Don Howe had spent 15 years as a coach at Arsenal. He yearned for the chance to manage the Club and it was the lack of assurance that he would get that opportunity that prompted him to walk out on the Double-winning side in 1971. Now he was installed by the board to succeed Neill and one of his first matches in charge was the league game at Tottenham on Boxing Day. Rafael Meade scored twice, as did Nicholas. Afterwards, Howe dedicated the win to Neill and there was genuine hope that the trend had been reversed. Once again the FA Cup draw was not the kindest, though. Middlesbrough on their own Ayresome Park patch were never an easy proposition and a 3–2 third-round defeat ended the Wembley dream for another year.

Howe, however, had been encouraged by the young talent coming through the ranks and was convinced that within two or three years Arsenal would have the players to push for the ultimate prize, the league championship. He had seen the likes of Niall Quinn and Martin Keown coming through and breaking into the first team, but he felt the dressing room needed a bouncy character and for that he turned to Paul Mariner. As Arsenal coach at Wembley, back in 1978, Howe had seen what the heavy-metal fan could do on the pitch, and with his work for England in the qualifying games for the 1982 World Cup and the finals in Spain he had seen that Mariner was a positive dressing room influence. 'I needed someone noisy in there, someone to liven everyone up,' said Howe soon after he signed Mariner from Ipswich in February 1984. 'Paul did that well and he was an excellent player as well.' Howe had also planned for the inevitable retirement of goalkeeper Pat Jennings. For the long term he had bought England youth goalkeeper John Lukic from Leeds and blooded him in April 1984 against Stoke. Arsenal won 3–0 and Howe kept him in for a four-game spell.

In the 1984 close season came two faces – Steve Williams from Southampton and Viv Anderson from Nottingham Forest. Romford-born Williams was a self-assured and confident individual who knew his own mind and was not afraid to express his opinion. That often caused friction with Howe and his new coach John Cartwright. Williams was unable to accept that he wasn't automatically in the team and wasn't afraid to say so. 'It's like buying a Rembrandt and keeping it in the cellar,' he said. He also disagreed with Cartwright's coaching methods. Anderson was less of a handful for the Arsenal backroom team. He was an England defender who had contributed much to the Nottingham Forest success story, but he was not to enjoy the same glory with Arsenal. In the 1984/85 season they finished in seventh place in the league – decent enough for many clubs, but not for Arsenal fans who'd been reared on success. And there were two massive embarrassments in the domestic cup competitions.

In the League Cup an uncharacteristic error by Jennings led to a 3–2 defeat at Oxford United on Halloween night. In the FA Cup, after comprehensively beating Hereford 7–2 in a third-round replay Arsenal were drawn at York City for the game on 26 January. The cold snap had forced York to cover the pitch at Bootham Crescent with bales of straw, and it was still frozen when the protective covering was removed, but it was decided that the game would go ahead. The conditions made football a lottery, but Arsenal appeared to have survived to force a replay. Then, late in the second half, Williams was adjudged to have given away a penalty by pulling back one of the York players. Keith Houchen gave Lukic no chance from the penalty spot and Arsenal were out. It would be of little consolation to Arsenal fans that the same player, Houchen, would score a memorable goal for Coventry against Tottenham in the FA Cup final two years later.

The 1985/86 season would prove to be Howe's last. Yet again, Arsenal failed to impose themselves in the league and they finished seventh behind Liverpool. The League Cup seemed to offer more hope, but after beating Manchester City and Southampton, Arsenal went out to Aston Villa in a replay. In the FA Cup, after a 2–2 draw at Luton in the fifth round Arsenal failed to make home advantage count at Highbury and the match finished goalless. In the second replay Arsenal were comprehensively beaten 3–0.

In the wider footballing world, May 1985 had seen the horrors of the Heysel Stadium, when 39 Juventus supporters were crushed to death after a battle with Liverpool fans before the European Cup final in Brussels. English teams were banned from European competition and the reputation of English fans, at club and country level, was tarnished forever. It was a sad, hollow time, interest in the sport was dwindling and Arsenal, like many other clubs, was experiencing a decline in attendances. Gates dropped to below 20,000 for the first time in some 60 years and the board needed to act. The rumour was that Howe would be replaced at the end of the season and Howe knew it. He said, 'The chairman Peter Hill-Wood said to me, in a nice way, "I think we are going to have a change." I said, "Fine."' On 22 March 1986, after a 3–0 win over Coventry, Howe resigned.

There had been talk of Terry Venables taking the job. He had excelled at Barcelona, but the Catalan club made it known that they would block any move, so Arsenal went to one of the heroes of 1971, who had been making a name for himself at Millwall, where he had turned a struggling team into one which would win promotion to the top flight a few years later. In May 1986, George Graham returned to Highbury.

Chapter Ten

THE GEORGE GRAHAM ERA

Graham revived Arsenal and brought the Club honours on an almost annual basis

As the manager of Millwall, George Graham had earned a reputation for discipline and organization. As a player with Arsenal he had won three major trophies between 1970 and 1971, and knew about the traditions and expectations at the Club. To Peter Hill-Wood the combination of those factors made him the man to re-establish order at Arsenal. Graham recalled, 'We met at the chairman's house in Chelsea, and I was thrilled and honoured to be given the chance to take over at the Club I loved. What a great challenge. It was made clear to me that finances were a bit tight and that there wouldn't be millions to spend or anything like that, but I could work with that. I knew the kind of players they had at the Club and I believed they could be successful. I couldn't wait.'

What Graham found when he took over was a squad of what he called 'three factions'. He didn't elaborate on exactly what he meant, but clearly there were the superstars, the journeymen and the youngsters on the periphery. His first job was to unite them and he did just that. Everybody knew where they stood. 'There were no favourites,' said Graham. 'I told the players that we all started with a clean sheet and that everyone would get their chance to show what they could do.'

What Graham did bring to Arsenal was a deep knowledge of players outside the top flight. 'I had to do that at Millwall,' he explained. 'It was no good me looking at the players in the top clubs, was it? The only time I saw the likes of Tottenham, Chelsea and Arsenal was when I went to see their reserves. I had to make the most of very little money at Millwall. I knew the lower reaches. I knew the players that I felt could make it at the highest level. That was one of my strengths.'

On his scouting trips for Millwall, Graham had noted a lively, speedy Colchester winger by the name of Perry Groves. At £60,000 he wasn't the most expensive signing in Arsenal's history, but he was to become a terrace hero. 'I liked what I saw when I was watching him and he gave me a pacy option,' said Graham. In his first season as manager Groves was Graham's only signing as, true to his word, he gave the existing players an opportunity to prove their abilities.

The new manager takes charge

There may have been one or two who thought they would test out the new boss, but Graham, who was in the old-school mould of Bill Shankly, Bill Nicholson and, in the modern era, Sir Alex Ferguson, was always going to come out on top. For instance, he would only ever have one bed in the treatment room, reasoning that if there was more than one there would be more than one player injured. As Gary Lewin, the former Arsenal player who was to serve as Club physiotherapist for 20 years before joining the England medical staff full-time, recalls, 'My job was simple under George – basically patch them up and send them out – although it wasn't just George, as that was the school of thought at the time.' The treatment room at the old training centre in London Colney, Hertfordshire, was small and dark. Injured players were kept away from their team-mates and Lewin would attend to them there in the mornings. 'Then George would send them to Highbury for more treatment in the afternoons,' says Lewin. 'His thinking was simple. The ones who wanted to get fit would then get fit quickly. Those who didn't care when they got fit, well, they would be heavily inconvenienced by having to go from London Colney to Highbury every day.'

Many felt that Charlie Nicholas would be the first to suffer under the new hard-line regime, but, said Graham, 'I never had a problem with Charlie. He trained well.' It was also Nicholas who gave the Graham managerial reign a good start with a 1–0 win over Manchester United at Highbury. There were setbacks against Coventry and Liverpool, but a victory against Sheffield Wednesday put Arsenal back on the winning track and, on the date of the Club's centenary in December, they were top of the league – a fitting tribute. Arsenal celebrated their landmark by beating Southampton 1–0 at Highbury on 27 December and many great names of the past were there to witness the occasion, including Joe Mercer, Ted Drake and George Male.

The League Cup campaign was also just beginning to gather momentum. Huddersfield, Manchester City, Charlton and Nottingham Forest had been beaten and there was now the prospect of a titanic, two-legged semi-final with Tottenham. This was to show Arsenal and Graham at their best. Tottenham had a 1–0 lead from the first leg, courtesy of Clive Allen, the man who had been on Arsenal's books so briefly in 1980. Tottenham needed only a draw at White Hart Lane to reach Wembley, but Arsenal won the second leg 2–1 and then the replay with goals from the late David Rocastle and Ian Allinson, signed on a free transfer from Colchester by Terry Neill in the summer of 1983. 'We never panicked,' said Graham. 'We always had faith in ourselves. In effect we were 2–0 down when Tottenham went ahead in the second leg, but we kept our shape and we kept our discipline. That saw us through.'

Arsenal were back at Wembley to face the formidable challenge of Liverpool. Under the management of Kenny Dalglish, Liverpool had battled hard to restore their reputation as a football club and to maintain their tradition of competing for the major prizes. Arsenal's league position had now slipped, so Graham rested several key players ahead of the First Division game against Liverpool on 10 March. Rush scored the winner in this match and many took it as an omen for the final, but Graham knew better.

His management had brought out the best in Nicholas, Michael Thomas was looking the part in central midfield and David Rocastle was blossoming as a gifted wide midfield player. In goal, John Lukic was proving to be a popular successor to Pat Jennings and, with the experience of Viv Anderson, David O'Leary and Kenny Sansom at the back to help support fledgling star Tony Adams, there was a genuine belief that this Arsenal team could do something special. Frank McLintock observed, 'Like us in the 1970s, they have got players who hate to be beaten. I don't remember us losing when we were a goal up. That team has the same mentality.'

Granted, there had been an upset to cope with in the shape of a 3–1 home defeat by Watford in the FA Cup. It was a game Arsenal were expected to win, but when John Barnes scored what Arsenal thought was a clearly offside goal, the match was settled. Watford manager Graham Taylor had been accused of putting pre-match pressure on the officials by pleading for a fair deal for his club and the abrasive Williams – never one to hold back with an opinion – confronted Taylor at the final whistle. Accusations flew, but Taylor shrugged his shoulders and kept his cool.

Graham challenges for his first trophy

Attention now turned to the League Cup and Wembley, but before the final Graham showed his renowned ruthless streak. Giant striker Niall Quinn was stalling on a new contract. The Bosman ruling, whereby players can move on a free transfer at the end of their deals, was not yet in force for domestic football, but there was nothing to stop a player changing clubs when his contract was up and if a fee could not be agreed between the clubs then it went to a tribunal. Graham had already agreed to buy Alan Smith from Leicester for £600,000, but what he wanted to do was hold on to the highly effective Quinn to keep his attacking options open in what was increasingly becoming a squad game. So he gave Quinn an ultimatum – sign a new deal and show your commitment to the Club or you could miss the final. Quinn signed and started at Wembley.

Forget that league game the month before. With Viv Anderson, David Rocastle and Steve Williams back in the team Dalglish knew this would be a more formidable outfit, and so it proved. That day at Wembley also dispelled one of the great myths. The records show that when Ian Rush scored, sometimes Liverpool did lose. After 23 minutes, he scored in his last game at Wembley ahead of his move to Juventus that summer, converting the kind of chance he rarely missed from a neat Craig Johnston through-ball. But Arsenal remained unruffled, Adams stayed in command at the back and Arsenal were level by half-time. It was not a classic strike by Charlie Nicholas, but it was a vital one as he prodded the ball home after a skirmish in the Liverpool penalty area. Arsenal's confidence went up a notch, Liverpool's looked dented. In the second half Perry Groves came on for Quinn, to stretch the tiring Liverpool defence with his pace, and it was a tactic that paid off seven minutes from time. Groves cut through several attempts to dispossess him and set up Nicholas in the penalty area. The shot from the Scot was hardly venomous, but it took a deflection and crawled over the line, with Bruce Grobbelaar in the Liverpool goal helpless. The League Cup was Arsenal's – a perfect present for the Club's hundredth birthday.

To Graham, however, this was just the start. He had fierce drive, burning ambition and he wanted to build on the League Cup success, again using his extensive knowledge of football's lesser lights to strengthen his squad. In came spiky and industrious left back Nigel Winterburn from Wimbledon for a bargain £400,000, drafted in because Kenny Sansom's best years were now behind him, while Graham paid Watford a mere £200,000 for versatile midfielder Kevin Richardson.

Allied with the arrival of Alan Smith, and despite the loss of Viv Anderson to Manchester United, Arsenal had strength in depth to compete with the Merseyside clubs and United.

However, the 1987/88 season did not start well, with an expectant crowd at Highbury witnessing a 2–1 defeat to the beaten League Cup finalists Liverpool. In midweek came a goalless draw at Old Trafford against Manchester United and then a 2–0 defeat at Queens Park Rangers. The hangover was still evident. Changes had to be made and the first to suffer was Charlie Nicholas. The match-winner at Wembley was dropped and by January, as the Graham restructuring began to take effect, a disillusioned Nicholas was sold to Aberdeen. In the league there was consistency without there ever being a genuine threat to title-winners Liverpool. In the FA Cup, a 2–1 win over Manchester United was very much the highlight as Arsenal went out in the sixth round to Nottingham Forest. In the League Cup there was consolation in an easy-enough passage to the semi-final with wins over Doncaster, Bournemouth, Stoke and Sheffield Wednesday. A more exacting task awaited Arsenal in the semi-final, but again Graham proved to be the master of cup ties. Against the odds, Arsenal beat Everton 1–0 at Goodison Park, thanks to a Perry Groves goal, and in the second leg Arsenal completed the job with a 3–1 win, with Michael Thomas, David Rocastle and Alan Smith on the scoresheet.

Another League Cup final

When it came to the final, Luton, now managed by the late Ray Harford and still searching for the first trophy in their history (they had lost 2–1 in the FA Cup semi-final against Wimbledon and been hammered 4–1 by Reading in the final of the Simod Cup) appeared to hold few fears. Everything pointed to an Arsenal win, so there was surprise when Luton took the lead early on through Brian Stein. A blast of the hairdryer treatment from Graham (Sir Alex never had copyright on that tactic) saw Arsenal rejuvenated in the second half and they went level through Martin Hayes and then ahead through

Alan Smith. With only eight minutes left Winterburn was given the chance to finish Luton off when Rocastle earned a penalty, but Andy Dibble in the Luton goal pulled off a stunning save. Arsenal were to regret that miss, because three minutes later Luton were level after defender Gus Caesar lost possession in his own area and Danny Wilson scored. In the last minute Stein scored his second and Luton's winner. It ended 3–2 to Luton.

Graham knew he needed more players and that summer he did attempt to spend big on one player, offering £2 million for West Ham striker Tony Cottee. Explaining his buying policy, Graham said, 'I love hungry players, players who want to win something, players who have drive and want to get football's big prizes.' Cottee, however, opted to go to Everton, but that provided an opening for Paul Merson, who would capitalize on the opportunity the following season. Winterburn, coming to terms with his League Cup final miss, began to settle down, but described the pressures he felt fitting into his role. 'I was worried about being compared to Kenny Sansom,' he said. 'After all, he's won more caps than any other England left back. Then I realised that comparisons would be made anyway, so I just concentrated on my own game. Arsenal is a bit like Wimbledon really. When I was there we were always getting criticised, but we drew strength from that. The mood is the same in the Arsenal dressing room.'

Graham had also solved the right back problem that had been an issue since the departure of Anderson by paying Stoke £400,000 for Lee Dixon. 'This was again down to my knowledge of the lower divisions,' said Graham. 'I had seen Lee and thought he would have what it takes to succeed at the top level. Few clubs take chances like that in the modern game, but I didn't see it as a risk… I can assure you, without bragging in the least, that no one knew more than me about the good players in the lower divisions at the time when I went to Arsenal. I used that knowledge to get the likes of Kevin Richardson, Steve Bould, Perry Groves and Lee Dixon to the Club without spending a fortune. And they all had great careers there, especially Steve and Lee. I can't recall how many honours and medals they have won.' Richardson had already been a title-winner with Everton in 1985 before moving to Watford. 'I was buying experience, quality and, as much as that, I was buying a player in Kevin who already knew what it took to win a title,' said Graham. Steve Bould arrived at Arsenal that summer from Stoke, as did Brian Marwood from Sheffield Wednesday. Graham was now assembling a squad that he felt could at last challenge for the league.

A season of ups and downs

The 1988/89 season got off to a somewhat bumpy start with a 5–1 away victory at Wimbledon – never an easy place to win – followed by a 3–2 home defeat by Aston Villa and then a 3–2 away win at Tottenham. A strange mix indeed, but then that season was to have more than its fair share of strange results. Basically, Graham's team played with a 4–4–2 formation. 'Even the flowers in his garden are set out in that formation,' was the joke at the time, but it wasn't rigid. Often Graham would play with three central defenders and he loved his full backs to overlap. The team may not have been overloaded with fantasy players, but neither were they the negative outfit of popular belief. What they did, they did well. Alan Smith was emerging as the focal point of the attack and his hold-up play was highly impressive in a season when he also contributed his share of goals. 'They have massive midfield strength,' was the observation of future Arsenal manager Bruce Rioch.

While the new players gelled, Arsenal managed to stay near the top and in early November they were in second place behind surprise leaders Norwich. The East Anglian challenge was to fade as the season progressed, but Arsenal, limpet-like, held on. 'We had a great mentality,' said Graham. 'We just refused to accept defeat. It was that hunger coming out in the players.' The rest of the country began to take Arsenal seriously when they played Nottingham Forest at the City Ground on 6 November. Forest were taken apart with Steve Bould, Tony Adams, Alan Smith and Brian Marwood scoring the goals. Come January and Arsenal were five points clear after a 3–1 win against Everton at Goodison Park.

So much for the league. In the FA Cup it was a different story. A 2–2 draw at West Ham in the third round should have given Arsenal the home advantage to go through to the fourth, but they were beaten 1–0. In the Littlewoods Cup a win over Stoke earned a clash with Liverpool, who won a second replay 2–1 at the end of November. With no European football because of the UEFA ban, it was to be the league or nothing. Richardson sensed that Arsenal could do it. 'For me it's like history repeating itself,' he said after the mightily impressive display at Goodison Park. 'It's the same team shape, tactics and balance that we had at Everton when I won the title. That's why it is so easy for me to fit in. The manager wants us to close down opponents, deny them space and put good-quality balls into the box. Now we have the experience we need. Arsenal have led the table on occasions over the last two years, but now we have a five-point cushion to help us. If we don't win it now, it will be the fault of the players and nobody else.' The chairman Peter Hill-Wood was hugely impressed with the development of the team under Graham. 'My feeling is that whether we win the league or not, I see no reason why we shouldn't go on to have a great deal of success with this team. I have never been so hopeful of the future in my time at the Club.'

However, success meant Arsenal had become favourites for the title and they weren't quite so impressive with the weight of expectation on their shoulders. In short, they began to wobble, with quality performances contrasted by several indifferent displays. Hot on their tails were Liverpool, who, from the turn of the year, went on a remarkable 28-match unbeaten run and made up what was once a 19-point difference between themselves and Arsenal. In the 17 games between outclassing Everton and the eventful last match of the season at Anfield, Arsenal lost three and drew five. It looked as though that would be an expensive dip in form and a five-game spell that started in February was regarded by many as the one which would cost them the league title. They drew at Queens Park Rangers, and at home to Millwall and Charlton. They were beaten at Coventry 1–0 and were comprehensively defeated at Highbury by Nottingham Forest. The one victory in that sequence was a 2–0 home win against Luton. Liverpool, meanwhile, relentlessly closed the gap.

The team were becoming too predictable and vulnerable to attacks. The defence, which had looked so solid, was now leaking goals at vital times, so Graham decided that a change of formation was necessary, dropping 4–4–2 and introducing a sweeper system, with David O'Leary playing just behind Bould and Adams. He said, 'I like to think that I have always tried to learn from any situation and it was up to me to learn from the problems that we had faced. The team were willing to try it and it worked for us.' The system was first employed at Old Trafford on 2 April, a bitter-sweet day for captain Tony Adams. He and his co-defenders had adjusted well to the new demands on them and he himself had put the team ahead, but he also had the misfortune to score an own goal and the match finished 1–1. Arsenal had played well enough, though, and the response to that awful five-match spell earlier in the year had been to win four and draw one (at United).

However, amid all the excitement of a close and intriguing title race came a tragedy that would change the face of football forever. On 15 April Liverpool were due to play Nottingham Forest in an FA Cup semi-final at Hillsborough. By kick-off time thousands of Liverpool fans were still waiting to get in and, rather than delay the start, the authorities inexplicably and unforgivably allowed the match to begin punctually. The result was panic as hundreds of fans tried to cram into the end where the Liverpool fans had collected and those already inside the area were crushed against the fencing. Ninety-six supporters lost their lives that day and this horrendous event prompted the Taylor report, which was to recommend the end of terracing and standing areas, and the creation of all-seater stadia. The whole scenario created chaos and confusion as the Football League considered their response. Liverpool were duly granted permission to postpone fixtures arranged for the weeks after the disaster and one of them was a clash with Arsenal at Anfield. Arsenal were told to carry on as normal but, understandably, refused and didn't play again for more than a fortnight as the football community mourned the events in Sheffield.

The league title goes to the wire

Arsenal resumed playing on 1 May and were convincing 5–0 winners over a Norwich outfit that had found the going tougher and tougher as the season progressed. Leaders of the First Divison at Christmas, they had folded and were overwhelmed at Highbury. 'We were outclassed and outplayed,' said Norwich manager Dave Stringer afterwards. 'It was a hammering. We finished as also-rans and on that performance Arsenal will walk away with the title.' It was anything but a stroll, though. The away game against relegation-threatened Middlesbrough was always going to be hard and it took a strike from substitute Martin Hayes – his first goal of the season – to clinch the win.

If they won their next two matches at home, Arsenal would need only to draw the postponed game at Anfield, now the last of the season, to secure the title for the first time since 1971, but the pressure once again began to tell and Derby, inspired by Peter Shilton in goal, came away from Highbury 2–1 winners. 'We didn't take our chances,' said Graham. 'It was as simple as that. Maybe we were too enthusiastic, too keen. Instead of building from the back like we have been doing, we started to hit too many long balls. I want the players to be patient, but that isn't so easy when there is such a prize to play for. We have to bounce back and we have shown already this season that we can do that. I wouldn't write us off yet.'

There were two games left, one at home to Wimbledon and the last one at Anfield, but Graham didn't anticipate an easy game against the team Arsenal had thrashed 5–1 on the opening day of the season. 'I liked Wimbledon, because of their spirit,' he said. 'I knew they would be difficult opposition. The culture of the club was that they liked nothing better than giving one of the big clubs a bloody nose. They had nothing to play for, but that didn't mean anything where Wimbledon were concerned.' True enough, Wimbledon gave Arsenal a real battle at Highbury and came away with a result that could easily have cost Graham's men the title. Winterburn scored against his old club and Alan Smith, who'd got a hat-trick on the opening day of the season, found the back of the net, too, but with a typical display of grit and determination Wimbledon achieved a 2–2 draw.

Liverpool completed one half of the Double by beating Everton in the Merseyside FA Cup final and now seemed destined to add the championship to their already impressive trophy cabinet. All they had to do was avoid defeat by two goals. They could lose 0–1 or even 1–2 and still be champions. Arsenal hadn't won at Anfield for 15 years and if ever there was a test of Arsenal's resolve, and Graham's ability to prepare his men for a one-off match, this was it. 'There was nothing special in the build-up, nothing at all,' he recalled. 'I was always confident that we had the system that would bring us the win and the players to play in that system. We trained as normal that week and went up to Liverpool the day before the game. I was stressing to the players the whole time that we could do it. The threat from Liverpool came from Ian Rush and John Barnes with little Ray Houghton providing the ammunition. We keep those three quiet and I was confident we would create chances of our own. We had shown all season that we were capable of creating chances and taking them. It would be hard at Anfield and I acknowledged that, but all the pressure was on them, not us. They were wary of playing their normal attacking game, because they knew we only needed two shots on target and we would take the title from them. We were very relaxed.'

At half-time Graham still felt as though Arsenal would get the win they needed. 'We knew we still needed the two goals, but we still had the chance to get them... I was still confident.' And the manager's confidence was justified as, after 52 minutes, Arsenal took the lead. Steve Nicol gave away a free-kick and Winterburn took his time to size up how to make the best use of Alan Smith's potency in the air. 'This was one of those opportunities I knew would come our way at some stage,' said Graham, 'and we took it.' The ball was flighted into the area and Smith gave it the most subtle of deflections to put it past Bruce Grobbelaar into the net and send the Arsenal fans massed behind the goal into raptures. Arsenal now had hope.

Liverpool were already without Rush who had gone off in the first half after testing John Lukic with a ferocious shot – 'He gave it a right belting, I can assure you,' said Lukic – and now they looked to be in panic mode and unsure what to do. If they dropped too deep they would be inviting trouble by surrendering territory to an Arsenal team in search of the second goal that would bring the championship to North London. If they went forward in waves in search of the equalizer that would make the title safe, there could be gaps for Arsenal to exploit. Liverpool, with Peter Beardsley on for the injured Rush, looked to have ridden the storm when, 15 minutes from time, Richardson threaded the ball through to Michael Thomas around 12 yards from goal, but the midfield player failed to make a powerful connection and Grobbelaar saved with ease. Surely that was it, but as McLintock had observed earlier in the season, this was an Arsenal team that would not accept failure, a team that would fight until the end.

And with a minute to go came Liverpool midfield player Steve McMahon's famous televised gesture as he urged a final effort from his team-mates. With his index finger in the air, he turned round to the remainder of the Liverpool players and could be seen mouthing, 'One minute! One minute! One minute!' That was all the time that Liverpool had to survive, but it was to prove time enough for Arsenal to win the league. A long ball from Lee Dixon found Alan Smith and inside him Michael Thomas made his run towards the Liverpool goal. Smith found him and as Thomas ran goalwards Steve Nichol came over in an attempt to intercept. The ball bounced off the Liverpool defender and put Thomas clear – and he gently prodded the ball past Grobbelaar. The midfield player produced a series of forward rolls in celebration. Liverpool's attempt to score the goal that would have rescued their league title hopes proved to be in vain. Fittingly, their last attack was ended by Thomas, who passed the ball back, in ice-cold fashion, to John Lukic. The whistle went and there were scenes of delirium from the Arsenal bench, the Arsenal players and the Arsenal fans.

Graham took the moment to declare that this was the start of a glorious era, not the end of one. 'We have laid a foundation of belief at Highbury. If you lose hope or belief you might as well get out of football. There is no doubt we had a mountain to climb. A lot of people thought we would get carried away by the moment and the result we needed, and play gung-ho football, but in fact we were very controlled.' The manager was fulsome in his praise of his players and Tony Adams, in particular. This had been the season when Adams had been subjected to donkey jibes and 'hee-haw' taunts from the terraces, but

Graham was quick to defend him. 'He has suffered a lot of stick, which has been very undignified and done little for football, but he has proved his strength and character – and all the team did that at Anfield. It is the players who have to go out and do it on the pitch, and they did that. It was great for Michael Thomas to score that all-important goal, which has earned him a place in Arsenal history. In the first half of that season he was the best midfield player in the country. His form dropped off for a spell, but he battled through that like all good players do. He got his reward.'

Down to earth with a bump

Arsenal were not the first team to find out that after a season of such drama there is frequently a season of anti-climax and that was their fate in the 1989/90 season. The European ban was still in place so there were no journeys to mainland Europe as a reward for their efforts. The league campaign could not have got off the a worse start with a 4–1 defeat at Manchester United and, although Arsenal were to finish fourth, there was nothing like the buzz of the season before. 'I suppose that was inevitable, because of the drama,' said Graham, 'but for me it was not a good season. We should have done better and built on what we did.'

The domestic cups were to provide no routes to glory either. By the end of November Arsenal were out if the League Cup after a 3–1 defeat at Oldham. In the FA Cup they saw off Stoke in the third round, but were then held at home in the fourth round by a Queens Park Rangers team organized by, of all people, Don Howe. Rangers won the replay 2–0. That was effectively the end of Arsenal's season as Liverpool ensured there were no last-day dramas again by winning the league before the final day.

Graham knew he had to inject new blood into his squad and his first signing in the close season was goalkeeper David Seaman from Queens Park Rangers. Graham had tried to sign him the previous season, but it had fallen through. Graham was determined to get his man, though, and succeeded that summer. 'I always rated David very, very highly, but it was never going to be easy for him,' said Graham. 'The fans loved John Lukic, because of the part he played in winning the title, but I thought David was world-class, although he had to win over the fans. Can you believe they actually gave him stick early on at Arsenal!' To freshen up his strike force Graham signed Swedish winger Anders Limpar from Cremonese and as security for the defence Andy Linighan arrived from Norwich.

A losing streak

The start of the 1990/91 season was everything that Graham could have wanted, with the livewire Limpar, his darting runs and impressive finishing, proving to be a huge success. He was not the stereotypical predictable, robotic Swede, perhaps because his background was Hungarian, and he had a streak of individuality that pleased the fans and a work ethic that delighted Graham. After a relatively easy start, Arsenal's true potential was seen in a conclusive 4–1 win over Chelsea, in which Limpar scored one goal and made a major contribution to the other three. Arsenal were not to lose a league game until February, when Chelsea won 1–0 at Stamford Bridge, but in between came two headline-grabbing clashes with Manchester United.

On 20 October, Arsenal and Manchester United players were involved in a mass brawl at Old Trafford. Arsenal won 1–0 thanks to a Limpar goal, but the match was memorable for the touchline clash that started with a difference of opinion between Nigel Winterburn and United's Brian McClair, and escalated to involve most of the players in an unseemly scuffle. It did not make great viewing and the respective managers – Ferguson and Graham – made their views known to one another. The Football Association launched an inquiry and a five-man commission sat for three and a half hours at Old Trafford on 13 November to decide what action would be taken against the clubs. Both were fined £50,000, but it was the points deduction that hit Arsenal hardest. They had two points taken away, while United lost one point. With a league title as the priority, Graham was fearful that the punishment would inflict irreparable harm on their championship campaign. The decision left Arsenal eight points behind Liverpool, but if ever there was a manager who excelled at developing the siege mentality among his players and encouraging them to use it to their advantage, then it was Graham.

Arsenal's response to the FA decision was to hammer four goals past Southampton at Highbury. 'We wanted to show that as a unit we were strong,' said Graham, but there were shocks in store for Arsenal on and off the field in the build-up to Christmas. In the League Cup, Arsenal were left reeling by a 6–2 home defeat to Manchester United as Sir Alex Ferguson's team gave a master class in lethal counter-attacking football. Graham rallied his shell-shocked troops and his inspirational team bonding was never more necessary – because the next match was against Liverpool at Highbury. 'If we had gone into that game feeling sorry for ourselves, then Liverpool were just the team to take advantage,' said Graham and his re-grouping exercise paid off handsomely as Arsenal were convincing 3–0 winners.

However, in the week before Christmas there was another crisis as skipper Tony Adams was convicted in Southend County Court of reckless and drunk driving, and given a four-month jail sentence. 'It was a difficult time for everyone,' said Graham. Arsenal were deprived of a highly influential player, but again Graham used adversity to inspire his team. Adams' imprisonment had come as a shock, but there was a determination among the players to continue their impressive form that season despite his absence.

Come the New Year and cup football was back on the agenda. Sunderland were beaten 2–1 at home, but then came a mighty saga of matches against Leeds in the fourth round. Two draws at Highbury and one at Elland Road meant that a fourth replay was necessary at Elland Road, with Lee Dixon and the inspired Anders Limpar finally getting the goals that secured a fifth round clash with Shrewsbury. In between those gruelling clashes, which included two sets of extra-time, came that league defeat at Chelsea where Arsenal lost 2–1. 'It was a day that it just didn't happen for us,' said Alan Smith, 'but there was no ranting or raving from George afterwards. He just said, "No problem.

We have been on one fantastic run and now we'll have to start another one." Simple as that.' Lee Dixon felt the setback badly. 'That defeat hurt,' he said. 'A couple of years earlier, Liverpool had threatened to go unbeaten all season until they came unstuck in a local derby against Everton. I suppose it was inevitable that we would lose our record in a local derby as well. We were really beginning to believe that we could go through the whole season unbeaten in the league, even though, deep down, we knew it was unrealistic.'

By the end of February Adams was out of prison and Graham decided to bring him back for the FA Cup tie at Shrewsbury. The reasoning made sense. It would enable Adams to return to the competitive fold away from the glare of a huge stage like Highbury or another top-flight ground, and the opposition was never going to be the strongest, despite the potential for a cup giant-killing. Adams coped superbly and Michael Thomas scored the goal to ensure his return would be a victorious one. The quarter-final, though, was not the walkover that many had anticipated. Indeed, for long periods the sixth round clash with lowly Cambridge United looked to be a candidate for the 'Arsenal cup disasters' category in the Club's annals. Cambridge manager John Beck was not a great one for reputations and, reflecting their irreverent approach, Cambridge were described as 'Wimbledon with attitude'. Arsenal had duly taken the lead through Kevin Campbell, a huge physical and athletic presence who had a significant impact during that season, but Cambridge were far from done and managed to equalize through Dion Dublin. For a while the highly unlikely seemed a distinct possibility. To the rescue came Adams with a header and the scare was over. Now there was the little matter of the semi-final against Tottenham.

Controversially, the FA decided on Wembley as the venue. The official reasoning was that it was the only stadium which could satisfy the demand for tickets, and obviously no one wanted the possibility of a repeat of the horrific and tragic scenes at Hillsborough just a few years before, but the winners of this semi-final would already have played in the stadium where the final would be held, which would give them an advantage over the winners of the Nottingham Forest versus West Ham semi-final, which was at Villa Park. Graham's view was that,

'Staging the match at Wembley was the only sensible solution.' He said, 'I don't think it devalues the glamour or the pomp of the FA Cup final just because we are staging a semi-final there as well.'

Arsenal were clear favourites. In the build-up to the semi-final they had been on an impressive league run that included wins over Leeds and, impressively, a 5–0 triumph over Aston Villa. Tottenham, under Graham's close friend Terry Venables, were in a state of financial flux. It was said that winning the FA Cup would be the key to their survival, but a combination of the uncertainty that is part of FA Cup history and the unpredictability that goes with local derbies produced a major upset. Paul Gascoigne was in inspired form for Tottenham and Gary Lineker was at his predatory best. Arsenal weren't out-played, they were simply out-gunned. Gascoigne hit the first from a free-kick and Lineker then scored a second from Gascoigne's audacious back-heeled pass. Alan Smith prompted an Arsenal revival by reducing the arrears to 2–1, but Lineker made the match safe with his second strike and the Double dream was over. 'The damage was done in the first 20 minutes,' said Graham. 'You can't give a highly motivated team a two-goal start in a match like the FA Cup semi-final. They will then fight tooth and nail to protect it. It was a bitterly disappointing experience for my players, but the true test of their character now is whether they can bounce back from these things.'

Cause for celebration

With four games to go, Arsenal were in a strong position. True, they had a tricky home game with Queens Park Rangers while Liverpool were at home to Crystal Palace, but Liverpool, under Graeme Souness, were looking creaky and suspect in defence. Arsenal went into the QPR game three points clear and the status quo prevailed afterwards. Arsenal won 2–0 and Liverpool, for all their frailties, won 3–0. Then came the May Bank Holiday and it was to be a definitive time in the title race. Chelsea beat Liverpool 4–2 and Arsenal drew 0–0 at Sunderland. The difference was four points with two games left, but television dictated the kick-off times on the Monday: first Liverpool at Nottingham Forest, then Arsenal at home to Manchester United. Liverpool had to win. A draw was of little use, because it would need two defeats by catastrophic scorelines for Arsenal to lose the title. The Arsenal players were at Highbury at lunchtime, even though their match was an evening kick-off. Graham saw no harm in their early arrival. Together they would find out what they had to do against United, which turned out to be nothing, as Liverpool lost with Ian Woan scoring the winning goal.

An electric atmosphere had been anticipated, but it was a party that ensued. Pubs near the ground were heaving with celebrating fans. The turnstiles were opened early, and Manchester United and their fans were the reluctant gate-crashers at what had become a North London carnival. David Seaman, Lee Dixon and Michael Thomas wore comic hats. Seaman then took pot-shots at goal. Anders Limpar treated the crowd to a ball-juggling act. Dixon then conducted the singing. George Graham had never overseen a pre-match warm-up like it before or since. Despite Graham's steely professionalism he could see that it was a time to be joyous, but he was equally determined that the season would not end in the anti-climax of a defeat. 'I wanted to win the game and I let that be known to the players,' said Graham. 'I didn't want to lose, it was as simple as that.'

In their relaxed frame of mind, the players did not let him down and there was none of the ill-temper or rancour that had marred the corresponding league clash at Old Trafford earlier in the season. Alan Smith put Arsenal ahead from a Dixon cross and added a second before half-time. Smith completed his hat-trick from the penalty spot and Steve Bruce scored a consolation for United near the end. Adams, who had endured such a traumatic season, led the players on a lap of honour in front of their adoring public. Graham, though, didn't join in. 'Why should I?' he said. 'I didn't think it was important for me to join in. The players are the ones who did it. They deserved all the credit and the limelight. The fans pay their money to watch them play football, not look at me sitting in the dug-out.'

Manchester United had their consolation by winning the European Cup-Winners' Cup a few weeks later. The European ban that had been imposed by UEFA after the Heysel tragedy had been lifted and United were the first beneficiaries, but Arsenal now had the chance to compete for the most prestigious tournament of all, the European Cup. 'That is the big one,' said Graham and, after a final league game in which Arsenal destroyed Coventry in some style, 6–1, Graham could begin planning for it.

Graham signs Ian Wright

Graham reviewed his squad and decided that it did not need re-enforcement, but the start to the 1991/92 league programme was disappointing – a home draw with Queens Park Rangers followed by defeats at Aston Villa and Everton. This was not in the script and, come mid-September, Graham decided to freshen up his strike force by signing Ian Wright from Crystal Palace for £2.5 million. 'He has this fantastic desire to win, to be part of something successful. He has character and he has belief in his ability to get goals,' said Graham.

Wright had instincts honed on the mean streets of South London. He lived five minutes walk from Millwall's ground – 'or ten minutes by bus!' – and always wanted to be a professional footballer, but the breaks didn't come his way until after he signed for non-league Greenwich. He was scoring goals for fun and was snapped up by Crystal Palace, where he formed a lethal partnership with Mark Bright. The chance to play the game at professional level was the realization of a dream for Wright. 'You know what I love?' he said. 'I love to hear the ball hitting the back of the net. That sound – I spent so many years playing football where the goals didn't even have nets – it was fantastic.' When he moved to Arsenal, with all its history and tradition, he said, 'I couldn't believe the quality that was around me when I joined.'

Wright was, however, signed too late to be registered for the first rounds of the European Cup, but initially that didn't seem to be too much of a problem. Austria Vienna at home was the first match and the performance and result seemed to augur well for the rest of the European campaign. The Austrians were beaten out of sight and overnight Arsenal became one of the most feared teams in Europe. Alan Smith, looking just as much the complete front man as he had the previous season, scored four times, with Andy Linighan and Anders Limpar completing the comprehensive rout. The second leg was a formality. Arsenal lost it 1–0, but their place in the next round was assured.

Waiting for them were Benfica of Portugal. Because of the ban on English clubs, many of Arsenal's players had not experienced European football. True, some had played against continental opposition when they had represented their countries, but as a unit they were raw, almost rookies. However, this was not the Benfica of old, the team that had established themselves as one of the most feared in Europe, the team that gave the world the legendary Eusebio. The side that Arsenal faced had neither charisma nor class, and Graham, thorough as ever, had watched them and believed Arsenal had every chance of progressing.

For the first encounter at the Stadium of Light. Paul Davis was given a specific duty. Scouting reports on Benfica suggested everything went through Brazilian-born midfielder player Isaias and Davis was nominated to quell his threat. It worked – and not only did Arsenal draw but they also managed an away goal from Kevin Campbell. All that was needed at Highbury two weeks later was a goalless draw. Arsenal were not content with that, however. Graham reasoned that by playing their normal game they wouldn't fall into the trap of playing too deep and the start was a dream one. Colin Pates, signed some 18 months earlier and making only his tenth start, scored and Campbell hit the post. Benfica were breathless, but only a goal down. While that scenario remained, they still had hope. They also had Isaias. From nowhere, he produced a stunning 30-yard volley that brought Benfica level. Now Arsenal had a dilemma. Did they push forward to make the most of home advantage and leave themselves open to the counter? Or did they sit back and take their chance during extra-time? They opted for aggression and paid the price in the additional half-hour. Valery Kulkov and Isaias did the damage, and the European dream had survived just two rounds. And the man who masterminded Arsenal's downfall? One Sven Goran Eriksson, a name which England fans would become familiar with in the years to come.

The League Cup quest had ended at Coventry the previous month and, after the faltering start, a second league title in two seasons looked a distant hope. That left the FA Cup. The Christmas programme was a disappointing one with one point taken from three games and to make matters worse the free-scoring Wright (he had hit all four in a 4–2 win against Everton) was suspended from the FA Cup third round clash at Wrexham. North Wales can be a cold, damp place in the first week in January and Wrexham fancied their chances of an upset. Arsenal were prepared, however, and Graham, as always, reasoned that if his men matched the spirit of the opposition then they could make their superior ability count. All was going to plan. Arsenal did not seem in the least bit intimidated at the Racecourse Ground and were ahead through Alan Smith just before half-time.

That should have been the end of Wrexham's resistance and it looked that way as Arsenal led with just eight minutes left, but then Mickey Thomas decided to make his presence felt. At 37, he was very much the veteran, but he showed he still had the appetite for it when he brought Wrexham level with a free-kick from 25-yards out. Another highly experienced man, Gordon Davies, barely gave Arsenal time to catch breath when he crossed for Steve Watkin to hook home a second for Wrexham. Arsenal poured forward in search of a leveller, but time was not their friend. Arsenal were out – out of the FA Cup, out of the League Cup, out of the title race and out of Europe. Graham emerged from the visitor's dressing room to say, 'This is the lowest point of my career.' Arsenal ended the 1991/92 season in a respectable fourth place, but there was no glory and no trophies.

Things weren't going much better on the international front for England. Under Graham Taylor's management England went out of the European Championships at the group stage, drawing with France and Denmark and losing to Sweden, but behind the scenes plans were being made for an event that was to change the face of football in this country forever – the arrival of the Premiership. The voice of Arsenal vice-chairman David Dein was one of the loudest in support of the new-look top flight. It gave clubs more access to television money and marketing, and he could see the potential in the project and backed the idea to the hilt. A new era was beginning.

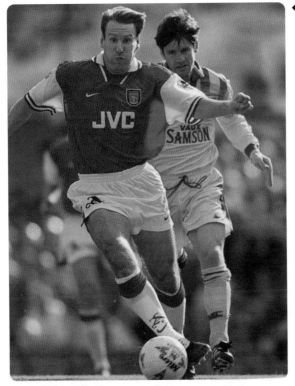

◄ **Paul Merson** was one of the stars of George Graham's reign. He was a skilful, right-footed midfielder who scored some spectacular goals, with measured chips as his trademark.

◄ **Supersub Perry Groves** spent six years at Highbury. The tricky winger made 120 appearances for the Gunners, 83 of which were as a substitute. His pace and energy, combined with a huge throw-in made him a cult figure on the North Bank.

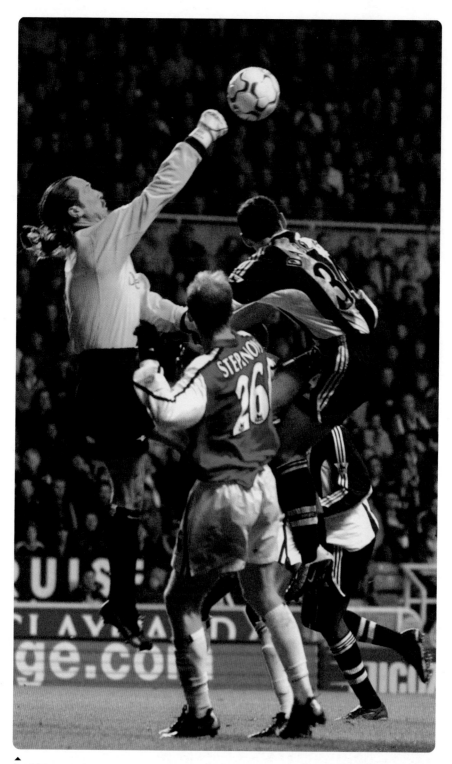

David Seaman is rightly regarded as the greatest ever Arsenal goalkeeper. He was at the heart of the Club's successes under George Graham and Arsène Wenger, making more appearances and winning more honours than any other Gunners custodian.

▲ **Michael Thomas** scores the goal that seals the 1988/89 championship in the dying seconds of the final match of the season against Liverpool at Anfield. It was one of the greatest moments in the Club's history.

▲ **The view from the new all-seated North Bank** for the opening match of the 1993/94 season against Coventry, a match that Arsenal lost 3-0.

Ian Wright remains one of the Club's greatest ever goalscorers. His 185 strikes in 288 appearances stood as a record until he was overtaken by Thierry Henry in 2005.

Alan Smith celebrates winning the league championship in 1990/91 in the Highbury dressing room with David Rocastle. Smith top-scored that season with 22 league goals.

Bruce Rioch was appointed Arsenal manager in June 1995. One of the first players he brought to the Club was Dutch forward Dennis Bergkamp in a big money transfer from Inter Milan.

◀ While Rioch only lasted a season, Bergkamp went on to become a Club legend, showing some of the greatest skills ever seen at Highbury during an 11-year career which included over 400 appearances and 120 goals.

Arsène who? said many of the newspapers when the Frenchman was appointed manager of Arsenal in September 1996. He is now rightly regarded as one of the finest mangers in the world.

One of the first members of the French Invasion that followed Wenger's appointment was Emmanuel Petit who arrived from Monaco. The powerful midfielder was to blend perfectly into the Arsenal midfield alongside lanky youngster Patrick Vieira.

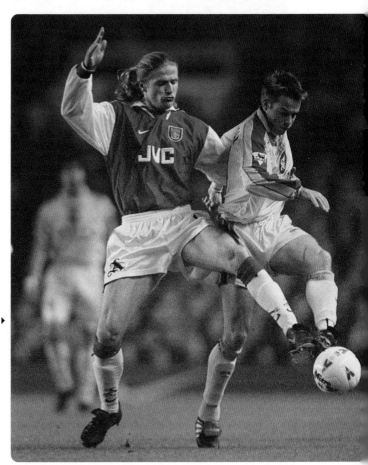

◄ **Nicolas Anelka** arrived at Highbury as a gangling 17-year-old in November 1996. He broke into the first team in 1997/98 when Ian Wright suffered a long-term injury. He was in superb form for much of the campaign as the Club won the Double. His run continued the following season although Arsenal narrowly failed to defend their title. He left in the summer of 1999 when he was transferred to Real Madrid despite pleas from the manger to stay.

Marc Overmars steers the ball underneath Newcastle keeper Shay Given to give Arsenal the lead during the 1998 FA Cup Final.

▼

Patrick Vieira was one of Arsenal's biggest stars during his nine trophy laden years at the Club. He possessed stamina and strength to go with composure and a superb passing ability. ▶

Tony Adams displays the Premiership trophy and the FA Cup during the team's parade through the streets of Islington after sealing the Double at the end of the 1997/98 season. ▼

Graham's response to the previous season's failures in both the league and the cups was to bring in John Jensen from Danish club Brondby for £1.7 million. Jensen had been one of the stars of the Denmark team that was 'dragged off the beaches' to take part in the European Champions to replace Yugoslavia, who were denied participation because of the problems in the Balkans. Denmark stunned Europe by beating the Germans in the final and Jensen scored one of the goals. Graham liked his hard-working style and, although David Rocastle was sold to Leeds, with the Dane's arrival and an ever-improving youngster called Ray Parlour coming through the ranks Graham was not short of midfield personnel. Parlour had played a dozen matches the previous season, but this would be the campaign in which he established himself as a first-team regular.

Up for the cups

Changes were afoot at Highbury at the start of the 1992/93 season as the North Bank was being re-developed and a huge mural was constructed, filled with the painted faces of fans. The idea was to camouflage the cranes and scaffolding that were needed to rebuild the stand, and it was certainly pleasing on the eye. Less pleasing was the team's start in the league – a 4–2 home defeat by Norwich and an away defeat at Blackburn. These were followed by victories away at Liverpool and at home to Oldham. It was the kind of inconsistency that would encapsulate Arsenal's season, but which made them such dangerous opponents in the cup competitions.

In the League Cup the first round was, as always, a two-legged affair and at Highbury Millwall were leading until the much under-rated Kevin Campbell came off the bench to equalize. The second leg ended with the same scoreline and again Campbell was the scorer. Arsenal held their nerve in the penalty shoot-out and went through 3–1. Then they needed a replay against Derby. Campbell was once more the hero in the away game, which ended 1–1, and he and Ian Wright scored the goals that took Arsenal through at Highbury. The next round was to be a true test of Arsenal's resolve – away to Scarborough in the first week of January. Naturally, the experiences in the FA Cup during the previous season were brought up, but Graham's response was simple and predictable. 'The team will just have to make sure that it doesn't happen again,' he said. 'It is up to them.' It was an icy, freezing night on the North Yorkshire coast, tailor-made for a giant-killing, but courtesy of a match-winning goal from the most unlikely of sources, Nigel Winterburn, ever-professional Arsenal secured a quarter-final place against Nottingham Forest. Two strikes from Ian Wright and the team were then through to the last four.

The league form was suffering as a result of Arsenal's cup commitments, but Graham was realistic enough to know that something had to give. Relegation was never on the agenda, but neither was the title, so the cups became the priorities. The semi-final of the League Cup was to prove an interesting one for Ian Wright, because Arsenal drew his old club Crystal Palace. The reception he got at Selhurst Park was hostile, but he quietened the crowd in the best way possible – by scoring from the penalty spot. Alan Smith added two more and Arsenal were left to defend at 3–1 lead at home. Wright scored again, Andy Linighan added another and they were on their way to Wembley.

Although Arsenal were favourites for the final against Sheffield Wednesday, they were not without their selection problems. Graham had spent during the season to bring Martin Keown back to Highbury from Everton for £2 million, but he was cup-tied. Alan Smith, such an important part of the Arsenal strategy and such a tremendous foil for the ebullient Wright, was injured, while another key defender, Lee Dixon, was suspended. Graham felt he had little option but to recall Paul Davis, who had only just come back into full training after a hamstring injury. Alongside him was Steve Morrow, essentially a squad player to be used in either emergencies or as a substitute. Neat, tidy and not afraid to tackle, Morrow was the perfect man to have around and he was to have a day to remember.

Wednesday scored first through their American midfield player John Harkes, but after 20 minutes Arsenal were level due to the kind of swerving right-foot drive that was the hallmark of Paul Merson. With 20 minutes left came Morrow's first memorable moment.

Merson, a constant threat to Wednesday, crossed from the left and Carlton Palmer failed to clear. Morrow scored his first senior goal and Arsenal were the victors, but there was to be no lap of honour for the Northern Ireland international. At the final whistle came an example of over-exuberance from captain Tony Adams. He ran straight to Morrow, lifted him on to his shoulders – but then dropped him. Morrow suffered a broken arm and was taken off on a stretcher, in so much distress that he was given oxygen. 'It was a silly, freak accident,' said Graham. 'You can't tell players not to celebrate when they have just won a major cup final, but it took some of the gloss off the victory for me. You couldn't help but feel sorry for Steve.' One cup was safely in the trophy cabinet. Now Graham, a man never satisfied, set his sights on the FA Cup.

One down, one to go

That run had started in, of all places, Yeovil. They were a famous cup-fighting team, one that no one wanted to draw, especially on their own Somerset turf, but there was no need for alarm and it gave Graham the chance to jibe back at the assembled media who had come to the Huish in the hope of another headline-grabbing upset. A hat-trick from Ian Wright saw Arsenal comfortably through to the fourth round and Graham couldn't resist a wry smile as he gave his post-match press conference. 'Sorry, you've had a wasted journey,' he said. (A few days later, Arsenal survived at Scarborough in the League Cup and Graham was at it again, 'So that's two wasted journeys then!' he said.)

However, there was to be more of a scare in round four and Arsenal's resilience would be tested to the full against Leeds. They had gone two goals up at Highbury, but Arsenal refused to submit. By now, Romford-born Parlour was a first-team regular and he led the revival by scoring to reduce the arrears. Lifted by the goal, Paul Merson again gave a glimpse of his class with a stunning shot to ensure a replay at Elland Road. With eight minutes left, they trailed 2–1. Smith had kept Arsenal in the game with his strike and then Ian Wright first forced extra-time and then scored the winner in the additional half-hour. Wright scored two more in the fifth round as Nottingham Forest were beaten at Highbury and the sixth round draw took Arsenal to Ipswich – never an easy ground and after their 1978 FA Cup final win the East Anglian side felt that they had the psychological edge. They couldn't have been more wrong, though. Graham recalled Tony Adams after a two-game absence due to an injury suffered while on a night out and he even scored as Arsenal won 4–2. Wright, an own goal and substitute Kevin Campbell were the other scorers.

Then came the match Arsenal had been waiting for – a semi-final against Tottenham and the chance to exact revenge for 1991. 'It is definitely one for the fans to get excited about,' said Adams, 'and for us it is the chance to make up for what happened two years ago, but more than anything it is about getting to the final and then winning that. We mustn't lose sight of that.' To say that there was ill-feeling going into the game was an understatement. In the league game between the two teams the previous December there was controversy from the start. Arsenal felt they had been denied a clear penalty and after that the match was littered with a series of nasty incidents. Manager Graham was fined £500 pounds for remonstrating with referee Alf Buksh at half-time and Ian Wright was given a three-game ban after a punch at Tottenham midfielder David Howells was missed by the match officials, but picked up by the television cameras. After the match it also emerged that Tottenham full back Justin Edinburgh had indulged in the 'verbals' by calling Adams 'a donkey' whenever their paths had crossed. If ever words came back to haunt someone it was to be in that semi-final.

Arsenal were cool and calm, and there were barely any flashpoint moments save for a cynical foul by Lee Dixon that earned the full back a second yellow card and thus a red. The League Cup final was a week later and the ensuing suspension cost Dixon his place in it. Adams emerged as the match-winner with a header from a Merson free-kick. Two years before, after Tottenham's 3–1 win, it was Paul Gascoigne's 'Let's all get bevvied' gesture to Spurs fans that had captured the attention. Gascoigne had left in 1991 to join Lazio, though, and without him Tottenham lacked the special quality to open up Arsenal's well-organized rearguard, so now it was Merson's turn to encourage the Arsenal faithful to celebrate.

In the final it was to be Sheffield Wednesday again. Obviously, there was no Steve Morrow on the pitch because of his injury, but he had cause to remember the day because he was presented with his League Cup winner's medal ahead of the game. In the League Cup final he was in an ambulance during the medal presentation ceremony, but there were to be no other winners that day. Ian Wright, playing in immense discomfort because of a broken toe, had put Arsenal ahead after 21 minutes and it all seemed to be going Arsenal's way, but with 20 minutes left David Hirst equalized and extra-time brought no outright result. Combat was to be resumed in a replay.

If the first match was tame, the replay was to be one for the brave-hearted. Tony Adams and John Jensen left their calling cards on Hirst and Chris Waddle. Wednesday were in no mood to let those challenges go without retribution and Mark Bright, a tough, abrasive competitor, broke Andy Linighan's nose with his elbow. With honour seemingly satisfied, a football match broke out and it was Wright who put Arsenal ahead after 33 minutes as he accelerated on to a through ball from Smith to score past Chris Woods. However, with 25 minutes left Chris Waddle, jeered throughout for his strong Tottenham connections, equalized with a volley that was deflected past David Seaman.

Into extra-time the final went and there seemed to be every chance of a penalty shoot-out when, in the last minute, Linighan reaped the reward for his bravery in refusing to leave the field despite his painful injury. Arsenal were given a corner and both Adams and Linighan went forward to add their height and muscle to the attack. Graham could be seen waving frantically, aware that if Wednesday cleared the ball and broke away Arsenal would be stretched at the back. He needn't have worried. As the ball came over, Linighan out-jumped Bright and his header squirmed through the grasp of Chris Woods and over the line. It was a moment to savour for Linighan, who had at one time had asked for a transfer from Arsenal because of his lack of first-team football. He had also struggled to win over the Arsenal fans. His name was frequently jeered when it was read out on the PA and Adams said after the final, 'Until now I thought his name was Andy Linighan Boo!'

Graham had now become the first man to win all three major domestic honours both as a player and a manager, and he saw a strange similarity in the scorers of the goals that had won the League Cup and the FA Cup. 'Like Steve Morrow, he [Andy Linighan] has scored a winner in a final and ended up with a broken bone, but I am delighted that our heroes on both occasions have been players who would not normally command such attention. I never thought of taking Andy off because he had a broken nose. In fact, I spent my whole career trying to get one because it adds character to your face!'

David O'Leary makes his final appearance

The season was a fitting climax to the Arsenal career of David O'Leary. He was on the move and his testimonial game against Manchester United, which occurred between the two clashes with Wednesday, drew a crowd of more than 22,000. Graham knew that O'Leary would be leaving and that was his motivation in signing Martin Keown. 'To be honest,' said O'Leary, 'I didn't want my time at Arsenal to end, but I was thrilled to be able to complete 20 years of service at the Club. I would have hated to have been shown the door after 19 years. When I realized that I had worn that red shirt for the last time I will admit there was a tear or two in my eye, but I wouldn't have missed the experience I had at Arsenal for the world and if you're going to go out then the FA Cup final has to be the ideal setting.'

Just before Arsenal took on Burnley in the league in August 1974, Bertie Mee had made something of prophetic announcement. 'Tomorrow,' he said, 'you will see a very special player make his debut.' No name was mentioned, although it was common knowledge that Arsenal had in their ranks a central defender of enormous potential who was so mature for his age that he had played for the reserves at the age of 16.

With his long legs and loping stride, David Anthony O'Leary, who had been born in Stoke Newington, London, a stone's throw from Highbury, in 1958, but had moved to Dublin at the age of three, initially looked a little like Bambi. However, it was soon evident that Mee was right – O'Leary was special. He was a footballing centre back in an era when many thought scars above the eyebrows and a jagged nose were the hallmarks of a 'proper' defender. Indeed, one of the things that was special about O'Leary was that he broke the mould.

Despite his youth, in his first season with Arsenal O'Leary played 30 games and over the next ten years would be an ever-present – he played 558 league games for the Club – except for one season when injury restricted him to 27 matches. His first major honour had come in the 1979 FA Cup final win over Manchester United and he was also part of the Arsenal teams that had lost the 1978 and 1980 finals, and the 1980 European Cup-Winners' Cup final. He also represented his country, the Republic of Ireland, 68 times, playing a significant role in that side's success in the World Cup finals of 1990 in Italy.

O'Leary broke numerous appearance records for Arsenal – he was the youngest person to reach the hundred- and two hundred-match milestones and made his four hundredth appearance when he was only 26 years of age. In November 1989 he passed the all-time record of 621 first-team games set by the late George Armstrong. Although he was not a regular in the 1989 team that won the league, he was still a key part of the squad and played in the dramatic 2–0 win at Anfield that clinched the title in the last game of the season. With the emergence of Tony Adams and the arrival of Martin Keown and Steve Bould, O'Leary had no longer been an automatic selection under George Graham, but he was still very much part of the team. He holds the all-time record for first-team appearances at 722 and played over a thousand games for the Club at all levels.

O'Leary left Arsenal for Leeds in 1993, but suffered a serious heel injury in September 1995, accepted that his career was over and retired. He became assistant manager at Leeds under George Graham in September 1996, taking over the top job two years later, when Graham departed for Tottenham. He had a fair amount of success there, adopting the Arsenal approach and placing a great deal of emphasis on the youth set-up, but was sacked in 2002. A year later he was back in management at Aston Villa, but left the Midlands club in 2006 by mutal agreement.

A European adventure

Having finished tenth in the league the previous season, in 1993/94 a drastic improvement was needed if the Highbury team was to pose a serious threat. The first-day signs were not good as Arsenal were beaten 3-0 at home on a blistering hot afternoon by a Coventry team managed by former Highbury striker Bobby Gould. The memory of the double-cup triumph of just a few months earlier was beginning to fade, but then came a remarkable run that suddenly ignited hopes of winning the Premier League. Arsenal won five successive games and against decent opposition as well. Tottenham at White Hart Lane and Sheffield Wednesday at Hillsborough were victims of the revival, as well as Leeds and Everton at Highbury, but with two of those wins featuring a 1-0 scoreline the song 'One–nil to the Arsenal' began to be heard on the terraces, as well as the 'boring, boring' tag. Graham thought it unfair and reasoned that a team that could field the likes of Paul Merson, Ian Wright and Anders Limpar could not be a solely defensive one, but Arsenal became victims of the old truism – reputations are easy to get and hard to lose. What was clear was that, for all Graham's protestations, Arsenal did lack the style and fluency of a vibrant Manchester United, who were on course for a successive title win.

If Arsenal were to achieve success again it had to be in one or both of the domestic cups or in Europe in the Cup-Winners' Cup. There was, however, to be no glory in the two cups that Arsenal were defending. In the League Cup Arsenal overcame Huddersfield and then Norwich in a replay, before losing at home to Aston Villa. In the FA Cup Arsenal survived a tricky match at Millwall thanks to a goal from Tony Adams, but then came a major upset against Bolton. Adams and Ian Wright scored the goals that gave Arsenal a hard-earned draw in the highly charged atmosphere of Burnden Park, but there was a shock in the replay when, despite a goal from the ever-reliable Alan Smith, Arsenal were beaten 3-1 in extra-time.

Now it really was Europe or bust. Wright and Paul Merson scored the goals that gave Arsenal a surprisingly fragile 2-1 from the home leg of their tie against Danish club Odense. Kevin Campbell scored in the away match and Arsenal were through to meet Standard Liege of Belgium. Standard were a club with a rich European tradition, but they were to be blown away by Arsenal. The home leg was comfortable enough – a 3-0 win with two goals from Ian Wright and another from Paul Merson. 'Very professional,' was Graham's assessment. In the away leg, though, Standard were dismantled in the most clinical fashion as Arsenal won 7-0. The goals came from Adams, Ian Selley, Smith, Merson and substitute Eddie McGoldrick, and Kevin Campbell helped himself to two. Afterwards, Merson was euphoric. 'What can you say about that?' he asked. 'That performance was just cosmic. It was complete, as near as you will get to perfect.'

Now, things were set to get tough, though, and instead of the attacking flair that Arsenal had shown in Liege, they needed resolve against the Italians of Torino. They would also have to do battle without the unpredictable talents of Anders Limpar as the Swedish winger, never short of a word if he felt it was needed, was becoming an increasingly peripheral figure at Arsenal and Graham had accepted a £3 million bid from Everton for him. On the pitch a goalless draw in Italy was achieved without too many alarms, but Graham was aware of the pitfalls in the second leg at Highbury. 'We have to be careful and we cannot afford to go gung-ho,' he said, mindful of how, just two years before, Arsenal had brought a creditable 1-1 draw back from Lisbon only to be eliminated by Benfica. 'We don't want that experience again,' he said.

There was caution right enough, but Arsenal showed they had learned their lesson from the Benfica game. They chose their moment and that moment involved Tony Adams, who scored from a set-piece. Now it was Paris St Germain in the last four. This was a French team that included David Ginola and which was on an unbeaten 35-match run. They were talented and they were confident, but Arsenal were determined. Their focus was on European glory and the performance in Paris was one of sheer professionalism. Arsenal took the lead through an Ian Wright header. PSG equalized, but Arsenal were still in the driving seat. There was to be no rerun of the Benfica scenario, but the second leg did provide Graham with a poser concerning Wright. The striker was all energy and enthusiasm and had been a headache for European defences all season. He was abrasive, gave as good as he got – an attitude created by the tough, no-quarter atmosphere of the non-league football of South London where he had played until he was 20 – and he went into the home game against PSG with a booking to his name, aware that one rash challenge, one flash of temper and he would be out of the final should Arsenal go through. However, Graham had a simple philosophy – play the game in front of you and if there is a problem deal with it afterwards. He wanted Wright's pace and goal threat, and risked playing him.

Ironically, it was Kevin Campbell who made the breakthrough early in the game and Arsenal comfortably held on – but there was a price. It was as though the French were fully aware of the disciplinary tightrope Wright was walking and they did their best to provoke him. He held out, but then his natural competitive streak took over as he chased a ball deep in the PSG half. He could have let the ball run out, but he refused to give it up and went in with a challenge. Replays showed he hardly made any contact, but the PSG defender rolled around in 'agony'. A yellow card was brandished and Wright was out of the final.

Now Graham had a problem, but he knew, if nothing else, he could rely on his defence and he saw nothing wrong in that. He described Tony Adams as 'the heart of Arsenal'. He explained, 'We have always been strong defensively and what's wrong with that? What I won't have is all this talk about us being a long-ball team. Yes, sometimes we by-pass the midfield, but not all the time. I don't know anyone who wants to be successful without playing attractive football and I am no different to anyone else in that respect. We won two championships playing excellent football. We won at Liverpool and then two years later we won the title again by losing only one game. I know we aren't right at the moment, because I know what it takes to win championships. We have a defence as good as any in the country, but we definitely need more quality in midfield, although we've got good forwards.'

However, resources were stretched to the limit as they prepared to take on Parma from Serie A in the Cup-Winners' Cup final in Copenhagen. Parma, while not the most illustrious name in Italian football, had talents to spare and they were the holders of the trophy, having beaten Royal Antwerp the year before. Also, while Arsenal were hit by injuries to key players and by the suspension of Ian Wright, Parma had a true galaxy of stars from which to select their team and they were especially blessed up front. They had Sweden's Tomas Brolin, whose goal had effectively put England out of Euro 92 in Sweden. They had Tino Asprilla, the hugely gifted but totally unpredictable Colombian, who was to join Kevin Keegan's Newcastle. They also had one Gianfranco Zola, who was to become so popular at Chelsea. Arsenal? They were huge outsiders. Already without Wright, Graham had to formulate a strategy without John Jensen, David Hillier and Martin Keown, but the night before the game, after a training session, Merson said, 'There is something about this Club and these players at times like this, you know. Everything is against us here, what with the players we have missing, but the mood is good. I fancy us to surprise a few people.'

What was kept quiet was a rib injury to goalkeeper David Seaman and it was only a pain-killing injection that enabled him to play, but Merson's words were to prove prophetic. Adams and Steve Bould were in commanding form and what Arsenal needed was a break, an opening in which to snatch a goal that they felt they could defend. That chance came in the 21st minute. Lee Dixon played the ball forward from a throw-in and sweeper Minotti made a hash of the clearance. Alan Smith was ready to pounce some 20 yards out and his left-foot volley nestled in the net to give the striker 'an incredible feeling'. Arsenal then sensed that this would be their night. Just a few minutes before Smith's goal, Brolin – later to link up with Graham at Leeds – had hit the post and could only watch as the ball rolled agonisingly across the face of the goal. Parma had the majority of the possession, as they were entitled to do with the players at their disposal, but Arsenal held out with Bould and Adams in a 'they shall not pass' mood. Smith played his part by retaining possession when the ball was played up to him, and Paul Davis and Steve Morrow worked Trojan-like in midfield.

The cup went to Arsenal but it was no surprise to Graham. 'Once we went a goal in front I knew we had a chance because our strength is keeping clean sheets. We had a team of heroes against Parma and none more so than Alan Smith, who worked so tirelessly up front. Parma were fitter than us and they were sharper than us. Their forwards were outstanding, especially Brolin. We are a Club with a marvellous team spirit and everyone – including the guys who couldn't play – were completely involved. You have to remember that ten of the Parma squad will be in the World Cup finals in the USA next month. They were a very hard proposition for us.' Adams is no doubt even today about the scale of that achievement. 'I go to a lot of these forum affairs, you know, like question and answer sessions. When I am asked what was the best defensive display, I can answer that straight away: Parma in Copenhagen. At that time, all the back four and the goalkeeper were at the top of our game. They just could not break us down. As a unit, we were the best.' Parma manager Nevio Scala paid tribute to the winners when he said, 'Tactically and technically, we did not function. Why? Because Arsenal were the better team.'

Shocks and revelations

But if that season ended in glory, the following one of 1994/95 was to be traumatic, both on and off the field. Graham spent the summer boosting his squad with Swedish midfield player Stefan Schwarz, striker John Hartson, winger Chris Kiwomya and Dutch front man Glenn Helder. It was soon apparent, however, that Arsenal lacked the talent to mount a sustained challenge for the league. They opened the programme with five matches without a win – losing to Leeds, Liverpool and Newcastle and drawing with Blackburn and Norwich. The League Cup quest was over in November as Sheffield Wednesday won 2–0 at Hillsborough, while Arsenal went out of the FA Cup at the third round stage with another of those embarrassing defeats against inferior opposition, this time Millwall. Arsenal had been held to a goalless draw away and the replay seemed a mere formality, but they lost 2–0 and yet again it seemed as though Europe would hold out the best chance for glory as Arsenal defended the Cup-Winners' Cup they had won in such heroic fashion in Copenhagen. They got results of

3–1 away and then 3–0 at home against Omonia of Nicosia, but had a scare against Danish club Brondby. Ian Wright and Alan Smith scored the goals that gave Arsenal a slender 2–1 advantage to take to Denmark in early November and strikes from Wright and Ian Selley saw Arsenal scrape through with a 2–2 draw and a 4–3 aggregate win. It wasn't impressive and already there were happenings off the pitch that were to undermine Arsenal's season.

In that same month came the public revelations from striker Paul Merson that he had gambling, drugs and alcohol problems. He went into rehabilitation and was banned by the FA for two months. 'We stood by Paul because it was the right thing to do,' said Graham. A tearful Merson made the confession about his addictions at a press conference and then went straight to a clinic in Hampshire to deal with his problems. Arsenal, meanwhile, would have to get by without the talents of Merson on the pitch and his departure was a considerable loss.

However, before the team resumed their European campaign, there was another headline-grabbing development at Arsenal. On 21 February 1995 George Graham was sacked.

It would certainly be a great shame if George Graham was only remembered for the controversial circumstances in which he left the Club. He revived Arsenal at a time when they lacked direction and credibility. He brought honours on an almost annual basis and won two league titles, two League Cups, an FA Cup and a Cup-Winners' Cup. He also brought players of the quality of Ian Wright to Arsenal. 'As time passes, he will become a greater and greater figure in the history of Arsenal,' said Brian Marwood, who was one of Graham's first signings. 'He will be a terribly hard act to follow.'

Houston takes the helm

The man who stepped into Graham's shoes was Stewart Houston, Graham's assistant, who was asked to take over for the rest of the season. He was convinced that if he retained the Cup-Winners' Cup he would have the chance to manage the Club on a permanent basis, but his plans were to be scuppered by a freak goal. His first European tie was against Auxerre, known as the academy team in France. They produced top-class players at a prolific rate and the club was run by one of the shrewdest men in European football, Guy Roux. Houston's hopes of a winning start appeared to be dashed in his first European match as, courtesy of a penalty from Ian Wright, Arsenal were held to a 1–1 draw at Highbury, but Houston was still confident Arsenal could progress as he could now call on the rehabilitated Merson to help the cause. His confidence proved to be well-founded as Arsenal won 1–0 in France, thanks to a strike from Ian Wright.

Now came some real drama in the semi-final against Sampdoria of Italy. Over the years, European football has been littered with sterile, boring tussles in which the result has been more important than the performance. Entertainment has often been way down on the list of priorities, but the two clashes between Arsenal and Sampdoria would break that mould. The Sampdoria manager was the same Sven Goran Eriksson who had been in charge of the Benfica team that beat Arsenal four years earlier in the European Cup. He had also been in charge of the Gothenburg team that won a league title and the UEFA Cup, he had won three league championships with Benfica and taken Roma to a European final. In other words, his track record was excellent.

For the first leg at Highbury, Sampdoria were without two of their leading lights, David Platt and Ruud Gullit, but the team still came to attack with Eriksson mindful of the value of away goals in European competitions. He also had a team packed with experience and believed he could get the result that would secure Sampdoria's place in the final, but it was Arsenal who thought they had struck first as Tony Adams diverted the ball into the net following a flick-on by Steve Bould. Unfortunately this was ruled out for a foul by Ian Wright on Walter Zenga in the Sampdoria goal, but Arsenal – and Bould – were not to be denied and ten minutes from half-time they did take the lead with Bould's first goal of the season, which the central defender calmly tucked away after Zenga had saved from David Hillier. Over the years Bould's goals have been like London buses – you wait ages for one and then two come along together. In the 40th minute he scored another with a near-post header that deceived Zenga. However, at half-time Sampdoria re-grouped. 'I told them to keep calm, to keep their nerve,' said Eriksson. They did and scored when Yugoslavian striker Vladimir Jugovic drove the ball past David Seaman, but the two-goal advantage was restored when Paul Merson threaded a superb pass through for Ian Wright to flick the ball past Zenga. At 3–1 Arsenal looked assured of a place in the final, but Jugovic hadn't finished yet and when he scored his second 15 minutes from time the pendulum swung back into Sampdoria's favour.

Arsenal had no time to dwell on whether that would be enough, though. The internal turmoil at Highbury had brought inconsistency on the pitch and going into Easter there were nine teams who were candidates for relegation. The Premier League was being reduced to 18 clubs and Arsenal were in danger of being one of the four who would go down that season. Two convincing wins against Ipswich, 4–1, and Aston Villa, 4–0, eased those fears and made the mood for the second leg of the semi-final in Genoa a more relaxed one.

This time they were confronted by a much more powerful Sampdoria line-up and Martin Keown was ordered to do a man-marking job on the talented Jugovic, but it was Roberto Mancini who was to cause Arsenal the first major problem when he lobbed the ball over Seaman to put Eriksson's men ahead. On the hour, Arsenal were level on the night and back in front in the tie when Ian Wright prodded home the equalizer after a Paul Merson corner was flicked on by John Hartson. Ten minutes from time, Wright, who been on the receiving end of several fearsome tackles was taken off, but he had hardly got comfortable on the bench when the Italians went ahead through Claudio Bellucci. Arsenal were forced to attack and almost inevitably fell victim to a sucker punch when Attilio Lombardo accelerated clear on the counter to score Sampdoria's third. The resolve that had been instilled into Arsenal by Graham resurfaced, though, and it was one of his close season signings who came to the rescue with only three minutes left. Stefan Schwarz had not made any significant contribution to Arsenal's season, but he made amends when he drove a 35-yard free-kick goalwards and, although Zenga got a hand to the ball, it crept into the net.

Extra-time could not separate the teams and they faced the drama of a penalty shoot-out. Seaman saved from Sinisa Mihajlovic and Jugovic, while Dixon scored for Arsenal and Eddie McGoldrick missed. Hartson was successful for Arsenal and Aspero scored for Sampdoria. Tony Adams scored, taking it to 3–1 and Sampdoria made it 3–2. If Paul Merson scored, Arsenal would be in the final, but he missed and this gave Seaman his moment. Lombardo looked confident enough as he shaped to take the kick that would keep his team in with a chance, but not as confident as Seaman who saved the effort and Arsenal were through.

Another European cup final

There had been talk ahead of the semi-finals of an all-London final. Chelsea, who qualified as losing FA Cup finalists as Manchester United had done the Double, were playing the modest Spanish team of Real Zaragoza, but Zaragoza proved a more formidable unit than Chelsea had anticipated and won 4–3 on aggregate. If Chelsea had qualified the final would have been at Wembley. Instead it was staged in Paris, with Arsenal the hot favourites, but in the Zaragoza ranks was one player who would need no motivation – Nayim. The Moroccan-born midfield player had been at Tottenham after Terry Venables signed him from Barcelona. While not a failure, he had struggled to establish a regular place in the starting line-up and had moved back to Spain. Ahead of the final he was aware that Arsenal were fancied to win, but he also had a warning for them. 'Not many people gave us a chance against Chelsea, but we won that match. I think we will be able to do the same against Arsenal. We may not have many players who are world famous or anything like that, but we are a close team and we have a fantastic spirit. That has got us to the final and now we intend to win it,' he said. Nayim was especially glowing in his assessment of Zaragoza's Juan Esnaider. 'He is quick, he is fast and he has a good goal-scoring record. Arsenal need to be ready for him.' Those were wise words.

The Zaragoza supporters were outnumbered among the 48,000 fans who crowded into the Parc des Princes, but that suited the Spaniards, because it meant there was more pressure on Arsenal. The game was goalless after 90 minutes and then Nayim's forecast became a reality as Esnaider put Zaragoza ahead. In doing so he became the first player to score in every round of a European competition, but John Hartson bundled home an equalizer and the penalty scenario that Arsenal encountered in the semi-final appeared set for a repeat. Then came an extraordinary moment for Nayim and for David Seaman in the Arsenal goal. Nayim had been singled out as the playmaker, the man that made Zaragoza tick, and Houston had deployed first Martin Keown and then David Hillier to stifle him. However, as fatigue set in, so spaces appeared. Arsenal looked set to accept penalties, boosted by their success again Sampdoria in the semi-final. Zaragoza, though, had one last attack in them – or rather one last shot.

Nayim from the halfway line

Nayim collected the ball just inside the Arsenal half. He looked up in the hope of seeing a team-mate making a forward run so that he could exert one last moment of pressure on the Arsenal defence, but there was no one. Instead Nayim decided to hit and hope. At the very least it would eat up time and gain ground. At best, it might trouble Seaman. It was to be the latter. The ball went high into the Parisian sky and somehow arced over the stranded Arsenal goalkeeper. A matter of inches either way and it would have drifted away for a goal-kick or Seaman would have saved it, but it was perfect. The Zaragoza fans behind the goal were silent, as though they couldn't believe what they had seen, but suddenly there was an explosion of noise as they realized they had seen a goal scored from 50 yards.

Seaman, ever the professional, blamed himself afterwards. Nayim? At first it seemed as though he has been swallowed up by the pitch as the bodies of his team-mates piled on to him. Later, as he spoke about the goal, there seemed to two distinct versions. At first, he seemed to suggest it was an accident. 'I was just killing time, keeping the ball out of our half,' he explained. 'I cannot say I meant to shoot.' Later, as the enormity of the moment sunk in, there was an adjustment of thought. 'I saw Seaman just a little off his line and decided to try my luck,' he said. 'I had seen Esnaider, but thought he could have been offside. I was quite clear in what I was trying and I was really concentrating.' He had support form the man who had taken him to Tottenham, Terry Venables. 'I have seen him trying the same thing in training and during a match. He and Paul Gascoigne were always trying to outdo each other. It was the spin he put on the ball that beat David. It wasn't just a lob.' In fact, the truth was probably a mixture of both. Seaman was not to blame. No one could have anticipated a shot of that accuracy from that distance, but neither was it a hit-and-hope effort – that was not Nayim's style.

In the aftermath of the defeat it emerged that the most significant casualty was Stewart Houston. If Arsenal had won he would have had a chance of being given the job on a full-time basis, but the setback prompted the Arsenal board to search for a new man. That would turn out to be Bruce Rioch, who, it has to be said, had one of the most strange and eventful reigns as Arsenal manager.

Chapter Eleven

LIFE AS AN ARSENAL PLAYER

That's what I've always loved about Arsenal – they do things properly

At this point in the story of Arsenal Football Club it is perhaps appropriate to pause for a moment, to reflect on what playing for the team in modern times is actually like, and if there is one player whose career epitomizes the glories and the setbacks, the emotional highs and lows of life at Highbury during the Club's most formative era, it is Tony Adams. He is a product not only of the Arsenal system that has been responsible for so many exceptional talents over the years, but he has also experienced the dark side of being a modern footballer and been a member of that exclusive club who have, many believe, too much money and too much time on their hands in which to spend it. Adams is a recovering alcoholic. He has made no secret of that fact and has not shied away from describing the turmoil that it has caused in his life. He knows the grief he inflicted on those around him when the booze had such a grip on him and he now works to help others cursed with the same addiction. He has been open and he has been brave. His ability has never been in question and neither has his courage. 'During Euro 96,' says physiotherapist Gary Lewin, 'Tony needed six injections to enable him to play. Six! But that's him. Brave... very, very brave.' After the 1998 World Cup in France Adams decided he would no longer take the anti-inflammatory drugs that he used so regularly to get himself out on the field and yet he still played on for another four years.

In his two decades at the Club Adams formed an extraordinary bond with the fans and to this day he is an iconic figure to them. He never played for another club, nor did he want to. Sir Alex Ferguson tried on more than one occasion to prize Adams away from Highbury, but each time he received the same negative response. Adams is the link between the past and the present, the common factor between the days of Terry Neill and the modern era of Arsène Wenger. He is Arsenal through and through, and no one is more qualified to talk about what it means to play for Arsenal.

The start of a great career

The steps that lead up to the main entrance at Highbury have witnessed the arrivals and departures of some of the most famous names in football. Tony Adams walked up them for the first time when he was 13. In the years to come, during the days when his life was ruled by alcohol, those steps would have another use. 'After a night's drinking on the Holloway Road that's where my drinking buddies would dump me. They'd just leave me there,' he says.

Chief scout Steve Rowley had spotted Adams playing schoolboy football in Dagenham and had immediately recommended that the Club take a look at him. Adams duly arrived on the appointed evening with his father, Alex. 'The problem was,' recalls Adams,' that there had just been a lot of re-organization at the Club and no one knew who one another was. There was Tommy Coleman and Terry Burton as the coaches, but everyone was new. My dad said to the commissionaire guy that we had been sent by Steve Rowley and he had never heard of him. Terry spoke to Tommy and neither of them knew who Steve Rowley was either. That could have been it for me, an Arsenal career over before it had started, but we were just walking out when Terry Burton said that as we were at the Club we might as well have a bash and see what I could do. Like a lot of young players I had been doing the rounds – my local club West Ham, Tottenham, Leyton Orient and Fulham – but Arsenal was different. I loved it. Myself and my dad, we both loved it. It was all done with small numbers and that meant the players got more attention. It was intimate, more selective. At West Ham, there was an ex-player looking after 50 kids, so it was chaotic and I didn't feel I was learning.'

Arsenal liked what they had seen. The caretaker manager Steve Burtenshaw sent Adams' mother some flowers and then asked the young defender to sign. 'That's what I've always loved about Arsenal – they do things properly.' Adams senior was also keen for his son to join Arsenal. 'My dad, who was in the building trade, said to me that it was like him being asked which asphalting firm he wanted to join. He would always say the best one and that is how he regarded Arsenal – the best. That was my mind made up.'

Adams is full of praise for Steve Rowley, the scout who first sent him to Highbury. 'As far I'm concerned Steve Rowley is in a different class as a scout. I was talking to a mate of mine and said the book I want to read is not the story of Reggie and Ronnie Kray. No, the one I want to read is by their driver. It would give their story from a totally different perspective. Steve Rowley is, for me, the story of Arsenal Football Club. If there has been one major, influential individual at Arsenal over the last 20 years it's Steve Rowley.'

Adams made his first-team debut in November 1983 under the management of Terry Neill, but within a month Neill had left and he played with Don Howe in charge for two years. Then came George Graham – 'My third manager in three years.' says Adams. However, Adams is appreciative of the work that Howe did and believes it should have received more recognition. 'He brought some good players in, players like Paul Mariner,' he says. 'Many people thought he was past his best, but to me he was a tremendous signing. He was a great professional and I learned from him. He was a striker, but he was used as a central defender against Tottenham in one game... ahead of me! And he was outstanding.'

Trophies and titles under Graham

It was under Graham, though, that Adams flourished. 'Don Howe was a bit unlucky, because there were a whole group of really good young players coming through just as Don went and George arrived that was fantastic – people like Michael Thomas, Martin Keown, David Rocastle. We were all hungry and ambitious. George recognised the talent that was there and let it happen. Yes, he could have gone with the old faithfuls, like Kenny Sansom and Tony Woodcock, but George didn't do that.'

League titles in 1989 and 1991 were proof that the Graham methods were working. 'In fact, we should have done the Double in 1991 and the fact we didn't was down to Paul Gascoigne in that FA Cup semi-final at Wembley,' says Adams. 'That squad was terrific that season. We could have done it all round the world that year, we were that good, but I think George came into his own in 1994. Let's face it, we were a very average team at that time and yet we won the European Cup-Winners' Cup. If we had played that season the way, say, that Arsène Wenger likes to play and really opened up, we would have won nothing with those players. If I had done overlaps like Arsène wanted me to do in 1998 and scored my share of goals and, you know, just gone out and played, we would not have won the Cup-Winners' Cup. No chance.'

However, while Adams was basking in the glory of season after season of trophies and titles, he was also developing a heavy dependency on drink. He doesn't blame anyone else for his alcoholism – 'Who else is there to blame?' he says – and when asked whether Graham could have done more when the signs of his addiction began to manifest themselves he replies, 'No, there is nothing he could have done. Nothing. Alcoholics are very clever, you know. They learn how to disguise things, how to keep it quiet.'

Adams' admiration and respect for Graham has never diminished over the years. 'He was a great, great manager,' he says. 'He worked with different styles and he was tough. There is something about the Scots as well – they have that grit and determination. He had his personal problems domestically at the time, but he never, never let them affect his work with the players at Arsenal, and it would have been easy to let that happen. And if you look at his record, with the finances he worked with compared to others, he did magnificently. He had good fortune with the players he had coming through, but he also brought some very good players to the Club. Some didn't work out, but for every Stefan Schwarz there is an Ian Wright, an Alan Smith, an Anders Limpar, a Steve Bould and a Lee Dixon. And look at the way he brought Martin Keown back to the Club. They didn't like each other, Martin and George, but George knew we needed him and paid £2 million to bring him back to Arsenal from Everton. He made us good as a team. We worked hard, training was detailed, and he was professional and organized. What more can I say?'

Graham also entrusted the captaincy to Adams. 'He believed in me. He saw something in me and he knew how to use me and to treat me. He was great at man-management. I had been called up by England under Bobby Robson and I wasn't comfortable playing for him. He didn't know me as well as George and when I got back to Arsenal George would say, "Don't bother going to England. You don't want to do that. Stay here. We love you." He would point to something someone had written, someone like Johnny Giles, and say, "He says your rubbish, that you can't play. Well, we will prove him wrong." It was that kind of psychology and it was like a red rag to a bull... I think he could have told me to do anything at that stage.'

Difficult times under Rioch

If Adams does have sympathy for one of his managers it's Bruce Rioch. George Graham had left the Club in the February of 1995 and after the defeat in the Cup-Winners' Cup final against Real Zaragoza Stewart

Houston was out of the running to take over. Rioch was given the job and walked into a minefield of problems. 'The timing wasn't great for Bruce,' says Adams. 'For a start he lost his skipper for six months. I had gone AWOL and that's never a good thing... I had several injuries, which were all alcohol-induced, and I couldn't get on to the playing field. The manager must have been pulling his hair out. He brought Dennis Bergkamp and David Platt to the Club, though, and that was a great thing for Arsenal... but he walked into the Club and took over a squad where quite a few people had their problems. I remember him saying after a pre-season game at Ipswich, "I feel like Marjorie Proops here!"'

As for the lack of success during the season that Rioch was in charge, Adams refuses to blame the disciplinarian approach the manager was reputed to have brought into the dressing room. 'No, it had nothing to do with the image of an "up against the wall" kind of manager. I defy anyone to have come in at that period and made a success of it... There were so many things happening. When we went to Hong Kong I remember knocking on the chairman's door at the hotel to tell him Ray Parlour was in prison! That was the kind of thing happening and Bruce must have thought what the hell was going on, but I reckon he is a good manager.'

As an example of Rioch's managerial capability Adams talks about a game against Leeds, which Arsenal won 3–0, despite the fact that several members of the team had been out drinking before the match. He says, 'Bruce gave the most fantastic pre-match talk. It was brilliant. There has never been a more powerful speech than the one before that game. It moved me – and not a lot of managers have done that I must admit. We were tremendous, but it was almost impossible to have that same impact again. He did some other things that were unusual, too. He would sometimes let us have a glass of wine the night before a game. Some of the lads took a glass. Me and Steve Bould took the crate up to our room! Personally, I think it was an impossible situation for him and it didn't matter who you were – Fabio Capello, George Graham or Arsène Wenger – you would have struggled that season.'

Rioch duly left after an issue with his contract remained unresolved and in came Arsène Wenger. So how did Wenger succeed where Rioch hadn't? Adams believes the answer is simple. 'For a start I was three months into being sober. It helps when your captain is in good shape. And he knew the French market, because he immediately brought over three top, top French players – Patrick Vieira, Remi Garde and Gilles Grimandi. They came in and then we were ready to go again.'

As it turned out, Adams was close to severing the bond that had tied him so tightly to Arsenal since he was just into his teens. 'For the only time in all my years at Arsenal I thought about leaving... I wanted to know if the Club was moving forward or not.' The re-assurance came from chairman Peter Hill-Wood. 'I was driving through Wandsworth when my mobile rang. The voice said, "Tony, chairman here in New York." I thought it was a wind-up, someone having a joke by impersonating him. I told him to clear off, or words to that effect, and asked who it really was on the other end of the line. "No, no, no Tony. It is the chairman here. I hear the s**t has hit the fan back there, but don't worry. Hold the fort. A good man is on his way and he will be with you shortly."'

A lesson in French philosophy from Wenger

That man, as Hill-Wood told Adams when he returned from the States, was Arsène Wenger and he would be coming to Highbury just as soon as he'd completed his contract in Japan. However, the first meeting between Adams and Wenger was not exactly cordial. It was in the away leg of a UEFA Cup match in Germany against Borussia Moenchengladbach. Arsenal had lost the first leg 3–2 at home, but had not given up hope of getting through. Pat Rice had been running the team until Wenger arrived, but at half-time in Germany Wenger made his presence felt, much to the annoyance of Adams. 'He came swanning into the dressing room and changed the whole tactics around,' says Adams. 'We had been playing three at the back under Bruce Rioch and with that system had finished fourth in the league and been in the semi-finals of the League Cup – hardly a disaster – and we had got used to playing that way. Suddenly he came in and changed everything around and took me off as well. I just went mad. We lost the game and went out of Europe.'

Adams saw Wenger later at the Club and pointed out in no uncertain terms that Wenger had probably cost him his last chance of winning again in Europe. 'I went ballistic,' admits Adams, 'but he said he heard what I said and would take note – very calm, very assured.' Adams had been sober for three months – 'I couldn't go out on the bevvy like I had done before' – and was also in therapy, managing to stop himself from hitting Wenger as he might have done in the past, so he sat down with Wenger and they talked it through. 'Again he stayed calm and just said, "OK, we play three at the back, no problem," and we finished that season off with three at the back and ended up fourth in the league. We then started to see the quality of player that he was bringing in and I could see the Club was moving forward.'

Wenger knew that winning the confidence of the senior professionals would be difficult. His new dietary programme and physiology-based methods had an impact on the fitness of the players and they respected him because he delivered the results, but his French accent did leave him open to being sent up occasionally by the squad. 'We were at Crystal Palace,' says Adams, 'and we had gone out, but there was a bomb scare. Arsène had come out of the toilet and asked what we were still doing in the room. Ray said in a Clouseau-like voice, "It is a bomb." "A bomb?" said Arsène. "Yes," said Ray in his phoney French accent. Arsène then said, "Raymond – a bomb? Are you taking the mickey out of me?" Honestly it was gold, pure gold.'

Adams is quick to acknowledge, though, that Wenger knows his football. 'Arsène is a winner, no question about that, and he's got the percentages right. Look at the players he's brought to the Club over the years – Marc Overmars, Emmanuel Petit, Thierry Henry, Patrick Vieira, Nicolas Anelka and Robert Pires, and he brought the likes of Ashley Cole through.'

After he had retired from playing, Adams tried his luck in management at Wycombe Wanderers. Although he has no regrets about the experience, it didn't turn out as he wanted – 'I couldn't turn Wycombe into Arsenal,' he says. The quest to be a successful coach has subsequently taken him on a tour of Europe to watch the best in action. He was youth team coach at Feyenoord for a spell and now he's back in the Premier League with Portsmouth, where manager

Harry Redknapp would be the first to acknowledge the contribution Adams has made to Pompey's achievements. However, while Adams knows that he will give any club he's working for one hundred per cent, his heart will always be at Arsenal, where to this day he is called 'Skipper'.

Chapter Twelve

RIOCH AND INTERNATIONAL ARSENAL

Although his tenure as manager was brief, Bruce Rioch's legacy to Arsenal was Dennis Bergkamp

Bruce Rioch came from a military background and was known as a disciplinarian. He was a combative midfield player with Derby County and Everton, and also played for Scotland. Anyone who came face to face with him on the field will tell you, 'Bruce Rioch was a hard man. You didn't mess with him.' Prone to attacks of temper, early in his managerial career he had to leave Torquay when, in the heat of the moment, he kicked out at one of the players and during his time at Arsenal he was involved in more than one contretemps on the touchline, but there were definitely two sides to Rioch. He could also be amenable and approachable, and his respect for the Club he had joined was always evident when he called them 'The Arsenal' – never just 'Arsenal'. He was desperate to be successful and wanted to make full use of the resources he had at his disposal, which were substantial compared to those he had had at Bolton. He looked for positive, attacking football from his teams and loved the game to be played the right way. In fact, he was clear about that during the six-hour meeting he held with his coaching staff just after his arrived at Arsenal.

Inspired signings

A close examination of the squad left him in no doubt where the priority lay. 'They told me we probably had just one 20-goal a season man and that was Ian Wright. We had to remedy that,' he said, so he moved quickly and positively to sign two high-profile names. In came Dennis Bergkamp from Inter Milan for £7.5 million and David Platt from Sampdoria for £4.75 million. The capture of Bergkamp was a masterstroke, while the presence of Platt gave Arsenal an injection of much-needed experience and an attacking midfield player with an impressive goalscoring record. Bergkamp, in particular, became a Highbury hero and his arrival didn't only impress the fans. When Ian Wright heard on the radio that Arsenal had bought Bergkamp, he didn't believe it and drove straight to Highbury to meet the player. Bergkamp immediately felt at home and together they would form what Arsène Wenger called the 'fire and ice' partnership.

Bergkamp had had a miserable time in Milan and was clearly was ill at ease with the Latin football culture. 'They would pay the gardener to take pictures of my wife sunbathing,' he said of his time in Italy. 'There was just no privacy and I am a very private person. I just didn't enjoy my time there at all.' He was also less than happy about his role in the Inter team. They asked him to play as an out-and-out front man, while he preferred to be a 'shadow striker', just behind the striker. There had also been interest in Bergkamp from Real Madrid, but he felt he would adjust more easily and be better suited to life in England, and he was right, because he was to stay for a decade.

'A superb professional,' was the verdict of Club physiotherapist Gary Lewin. 'There was never a moment's bother with him, not one.' And as Paul Merson observed later that season, 'You train, you come off the field and you're having lunch – and Dennis is still out there practising free-kicks. No matter how hard you work, you cannot work as hard as Dennis.' Rioch had successfully brought in a player whom many regard as the best foreign import to the Premier League and Arsenal supporters now had a star who would match the impact that Jurgen Klinsmann had in his brief sojourn at Tottenham. Fans even stole the song with which the White Hart Lane faithful had regaled the German, singing 'There's only one Dennis Bergkamp' to the tune of 'Winter Wonderland' (and singing it about Bergkamp for considerably longer than their Tottenham counterparts could sing it about Klinsmann).

However, along with the arrivals there were the inevitable departures. Kevin Campbell, who had played such a major part in the successes Arsenal had achieved under Graham, left for Nottingham Forest when his contract at Highbury expired. He was followed by Stefan Schwarz. The Swede had produced impressive performances during his year at the Club, but his family could not settle in London and he moved to Fiorentina in Italy. It was a serious blow for Rioch when striker Alan Smith announced that his persistent knee problems were showing no signs of improvement and that he was being forced to quit, and there were other injury problems to key players that made Ricoh's tenure at Highbury a difficult one. Platt, in particular, was dogged by cartilage problems that restricted him to 29 games and just five goals. Wright was also injured and never seemed totally at ease with the Rioch style of management. In fact, in February 1996 he even asked for a transfer, although he later withdrew the request saying, 'To be honest, I just want to spend the rest of my career here at Highbury.'

A difficult situation for Rioch

On the field there was a bright enough start. Arsenal didn't lose in the league until the game against Chelsea at the end of September and Bergkamp got on to the score sheet at the seventh time of asking when he scored twice in the 4–2 win against Southampton at Highbury. The FA Cup run didn't survive beyond the third round as Sheffield United drew 1–1 at Highbury and then won the replay 1–0 at Bramall Lane. It was after that match that Platt's knee problem ruled him out for two months. Fortunately the League Cup threatened to be more productive, though

The run started in comfortable enough fashion with an 8–9 aggregate win over Hartlepool in which Bergkamp scored a hat-trick at Highbury. Then came a 3–0 win at Barnsley, which proved easy, despite the Yorkshire team's reputation as dour cup fighters. At the end of November Sheffield Wednesday were beaten at Highbury, thanks to goals from Ian Wright and John Hartson, and that meant a January quarter-final against a Newcastle team that were playing stylish, gung-ho football under Kevin Keegan. This would be a major test for Arsenal, no question. It was a magnificent atmosphere at Highbury that night, Wright was at his effervescent best and Arsenal won 2–1, but a touchline skirmish between Lee Dixon and David Ginola sparked a bitter row between Rioch and Newcastle assistant manager Terry McDermott, which lead to an FA inquiry and a rap on the knuckles for Rioch. In the semi-final clash with Aston Villa Bergkamp, at his sublime best and giving one of his most memorable performances in a red shirt, gave Arsenal a 2–0 lead in the first leg at Highbury. However, just when Arsenal looked assured and comfortable, two alarming defensive lapses allowed Dwight Yorke to pull Aston Villa level. Now all Villa needed was a 0–0 or 1–1 draw at Villa Park and they were through to the final. After extra-time it was 0–0 (away goals counted double after normal time) and Arsenal were out.

The season was far from over, however, and there was a dramatic last day finale to the league programme. The last match was at Highbury against a Bolton team that Rioch had left a year before and which had already been relegated in his absence. In the match at

Burnden Park the previous October, Arsenal had pummeled Bolton, but lost 1–0. Highbury appeared to be a case of deja-vu. Bolton, free of any pressure, were 1–0 up, there were only eight minutes left and Arsenal looked as though they would be deprived of a European place. Then Rioch's signings of the previous summer made their presence felt. David Platt was now fit again and equalized to give Arsenal hope of the win they needed to secure the fifth place finish that would guarantee UEFA Cup football the following season. The Platt goal lifted both the crowd and the team, and within two minutes they were ahead when Dennis Bergkamp hammered in the winner. At the final whistle, Rioch was both joyous and phlegmatic. 'That's what I bought them for!' he said.

However, the goals were not enough to keep Rioch in a job as the board finally lost patience with his procrastination over his contract. Since the start of the season, and at every subsequent monthly board meeting, Rioch had persistently rejected overtures to sign. The situation didn't change in the close season and at a meeting before the start of the following season Bruce found something else to query. 'It was all becoming too much and we decided that was enough, and we decided to look for a new manager,' explains chairman Peter Hill-Wood. Although he hadn't actually signed it, Rioch had originally verbally agreed a two-year contract and Arsenal decided that he should be given a year's salary as severance pay. 'We thought that was the right thing to do. We couldn't, as a Club, let that situation go on. We needed him to make a commitment,' says Hill-Wood.

Rioch had been the full-time manager of Arsenal for only 14 months, the shortest tenure of any Arsenal manager in the 20th century. Tony Adams, who was the team captain at the time, has argued that Rioch was unfortunate and that circumstances conspired against him. He lost key players to major injuries at the wrong time. Steve Bould, for example, described by Rioch as a 'colossus', missed the last four months of the season with a groin injury. The emerging Ray Parlour was out for two lengthy spells and Platt was also cursed with the scourge of injury. The season had not been a disaster, but it could – and perhaps should – have been better. Rioch's philosophy of bright and inventive football, characterized by the superb Bergkamp, had won over the fans, but the breaks did not fall his way. In contrast to Rioch's brief stay, his successor was to last more than a decade and revolutionize not only football at Arsenal, but also, perhaps, football in this country. Arsène Wenger was on his way.

Chapter Thirteen

ARSÈNE WHO?

> He is a very impressive
> individual, and after meeting
> him and talking to him there
> was absolutely no doubt
> in my mind that he was the
> man to take us forward

After the departure of Rioch speculation was rife about who would become the next manager of Arsenal. The first name in the frame was Johann Cruyff, who was out of work after leaving Barcelona, but when the Dutchman wasn't appointed immediately he was quickly ruled out of the race. After all, why should there be any hesitation. Cruyff was unemployed, so there was no compensation issue to be sorted out. In fact, the clues had been there since Glenn Hoddle took the job as England manager. Hoddle had been asked for his advice about who should fill the role of FA technical director, to oversee the development of football in a country that, for all the talent that it had produced over the decades, had just one World Cup to its name. His recommendation was Arsène Wenger. Hoddle knew Wenger because he had played under him at AS Monaco in France and had become very interested in the Frenchman's new, scientific approach to the game, an approach that was very different to the one Hoddle had been used to at Tottenham. Hoddle's suggestion of Wenger for the FA position went no further than that. However, David Dein, the Arsenal vice-chairman, had also identified Wenger as a candidate for the Arsenal job.

Dein and chairman Peter Hill-Wood had met with Wenger at an Italian restaurant in Chelsea to talk about the prospect of Wenger taking over at Highbury. Dein had known Wenger as a close friend for years and was convinced that his encyclopedic knowledge of the game would be a huge asset to the Club. Hill-Wood openly admits that he had reservations about the appointment. 'I wasn't sure that English football and Arsenal were ready to have a manager from the continent,' he says, 'but then I met him and we talked for hours. His English was impeccable and his knowledge of not only football, but also world affairs, was remarkable. Whatever subject we broached, he was able to voice an educated opinion. He is a very impressive individual, and after meeting him and talking to him there was absolutely no doubt in my mind that he was the man to take us forward – no doubt at all. It was perhaps the best decision we have ever made because the Club has gone from strength to strength.'

Wenger has subsequently revealed that he was also courted by clubs in both Germany and France, but wanted to come to England and Arsenal in particular. 'Certainly there was no hesitation when I got the chance to manage Arsenal. They came to see me and within half an hour the deal had been settled – my salary, the length of contract, everything... If I was in their position maybe I would have shown a little apprehension. If there was a little concern on their part, I could have understood that as there is no history of success with French managers in this country. It is still a bit of a puzzle to me even now, because of that, why Arsenal, a traditional English club, would want me and why they would make that move, but I am very glad they did.'

So Wenger agreed to take the job, but stressed that he could not start until October. Disillusioned with the corruption within French football, he had gone to work in Japan with the Nagoya team Grampus Eight, and had found the honesty and integrity of Japanese football refreshing after the intrigue and cut-throat world of European football. He insisted that, although he would take the job at Arsenal, he had to fulfill his contractual obligations in Japan. Arsenal agreed. However, Wenger already knew the first two players he wanted to bring in to bolster that team that he had seen playing on the many videos Dein had given him.

Wenger makes his first purchases

Wenger knew all about Patrick Vieira, who was being given limited first-team opportunities at AC Milan. Wenger reckoned he would be perfect for the English game, but that Arsenal had to move quickly, because Ajax of Amsterdam were also keen. Wenger won the day. He also realised, though, that there were no other French players at Arsenal at the time and that Vieira would feel lonely and isolated at a new club in a new country. Consequently, Wenger recommended that Arsenal sign the highly experienced and hugely dependable Remi Garde, who was on a free transfer under the Bosman ruling. However, Garde wasn't at Arsenal just to make Vieira feel at home. He had a decent pedigree of his own, having played for Lyon and Strasbourg, and was comfortable as either a midfield player or a sweeper – so comfortable that he had played six times for France.

Wenger was already putting into place the squad he wanted to take over when he did arrive, but there was a vacancy to be filled until then and, for the second time, Stewart Houston was asked to be caretaker, with Pat Rice as his assistant. Houston had done the job the previous year, after George Graham's departure, and had taken Arsenal to the Cup-Winners' Cup final. Under Rioch he had reverted to assistant again and after Rioch left Arsenal turned to him once more.

There were other changes in the backroom staff during the close season. Tom Walley was made youth team coach and Liam Brady, a true Highbury hero, was put in charge of youth development, a job that was to have growing importance over the years as Arsenal expanded their academy. On the playing front, John Jensen moved back to Brondby, the Danish club from where Arsenal had signed him.

As the new season began, Houston had three players – Tony Adams, David Seaman and David Platt – who had played a significant role for England in that summer's Euro 96 tournament and Dennis Bergkamp who had also played for Holland. Adams had come back with a knee injury that was to keep him out until September and Ian Wright was missing from the starting line-up for the first four games of the season. So, given these circumstances, and especially the turmoil at Highbury caused by the late exit of Bruce Rioch, the 1996/97 league campaign opened well, with a convincing 2–0 win over West Ham with John Hartson and Dennis Bergkamp scoring the goals. In fact, the team lost only once in the 11 league games prior to Wenger's arrival and that was a 2–0 defeat at Liverpool.

In mid-September, however, Houston resigned. George Graham had served the year's ban imposed by the FA following an inquiry into a number of transfers and had taken over at Leeds. Graham and Houston had developed a close working relationship in their time together at Arsenal, and Graham wanted to recreate that at Elland Road. It was now evident to Houston that he would never get the number one job at Arsenal and he wanted the chance to manage a club on a long-term basis, so he left Arsenal, turned down Leeds and went to take over Queens Park Rangers, where he made former Arsenal manager Rioch his assistant. The last thing Peter Hill-Wood and his Arsenal board needed at that moment was more uncertainty and change, and Grampus were contacted with a view to letting Wenger leave before the end of his contract. The Japanese were sympathetic and Wenger was now set to arrive at the end of September rather than in mid-October. In the meantime, Pat Rice was at the helm and, with the new direction, Arsenal swamped Sheffield Wednesday 4–1. Wright scored a hat-trick and scored again as Arsenal won 2–0 at Middlesbrough. After the second leg of the

UEFA Cup tie in Germany against Borussia Moenchengladbach, which Arsenal lost 3–2, meaning they were out of the competition, Wenger came in to take charge of the match away to Blackburn on 12 October, which Arsenal won 2–0. Arsenal finished that season in second place.

Later Wenger admitted that he was just a little fearful about how he would be viewed when he took over at Arsenal. 'There was a lot of interest when I arrived, yes,' he said. 'I was confident I could win people over, but I also knew it would be hard, because I saw that nobody knew me and nobody had any idea what I had done before. I had to start from scratch and when that happens you know you must have a good start or you will have no credit at all. I could have had a comfortable life if I had stayed in Japan. I could have stayed five, six, seven years, as long as I wanted, but I always wanted to work in England and when the chance came I took it.'

Adjusting to a new way of life

The new Arsenal manager was immediately impressed by the passion of the fans in England – no matter which division their teams played in. On the face of it pop star Robbie Williams and a London taxi driver would have little in common, but both made an impression on Wenger. 'Robbie Williams, he makes no secret of the fact that he supports Port Vale and they are the football club he loves above all others. In France that would never happen. A celebrity over there would be associated with one of the more glamorous clubs, like Paris St Germain, not a lower league club like Port Vale. The taxi driver? Soon after I arrived at the Club I took a cab to go into central London. The driver recognised me, and after I confirmed who I was he told me that he supported Leyton Orient and that I should go down and watch them, because they had some very good young players. Again that would not happen in France. I don't think there is another country in Europe with the passion for their clubs that the English fans have.'

Just how Wenger was to change the whole dynamic of Arsenal was evident to chief scout Steve Rowley during his first meeting with the new manager. 'He introduced himself and began asking about how I went about the job. Then he hit me with a question that really stunned me. He asked me if I had my passport with me,' said Rowley. I said I hadn't, because there was no call for it travelling to places like Manchester and Birmingham. He told me that in future I was to have my passport with me at all times. I knew what he meant a few days later. He sent me to Brazil to watch some young players and to meet a scout out there that he knew. It was such a change to what I had been used to over the years. Suddenly I was at youth tournaments not only all over Europe, but also all over the world.'

Rowley was to get an insight into the global, not just European, knowledge that Wenger has of the game when he was sent by the manager to cover the 1997 World Youth Championships for under-20 players in Malaysia. Late at night the phone went in his hotel room. 'It was the gaffer on the other end of the line,' said Rowley. 'He was asking if I had seen any good young players in the tournament. I had been to three or four games and said there had been no one exceptional. Then I remembered. "There was one player," I said, but I was stuck. He had caught me off guard and I was scrambling around for the paper on which I had written his name. "It was, it was... Bonaventure something, err..." And straightaway he said, "That would be Bonaventure Kalou. He plays for the Ivory Coast and he is 17, but I shouldn't worry about him. He does not have a passport that will enable us to play him." I was dumbstruck that he knew so much, but as the years have gone on I have seen just how many contacts he has. It is a worldwide network and if there is a good young player out there, he will know about him.

'He has changed the way the whole scouting system works, not just at Arsenal, but all over the country people have copied him. Obviously, he is very strong in France and we have a great man there in Gilles Grimandi. He was signed by the gaffer and played for us for a good few years, so he knows what kind of player is needed. He will contact me or the gaffer and identify a player he believes is worth watching. That was the case recently with Bacary Sagna. Gilles knows that in English football a defender has to do just that – defend. It's a very physical game in this country compared to football on the continent and you always have to be aware of that. Gilles saw Sagna, I went to see Sagna and we checked him out thoroughly, home and away. I was also tipped off by one of the gaffer's contacts about Gael Clichy. He was playing down in Nice. I saw him in the warm-up and could see he was class. What the gaffer has done is basically have a scout in every country. That's how we get to know about the likes of Cesc Fabregas, Robin van Persie and Johan Djourou. Our scouts abroad are top class. They know the type of player that Arsenal want.'

After his arrival Wenger spoke to the coaching staff at the old training base in London Colney, including Bob Wilson, the goalkeeping coach. Wenger would have been happy to have had Stewart Houston stay on as his assistant, but Houston preferred to move to Queens Park Rangers, which Wenger understood, so he asked David Dein whether there was anyone else who could do the job. 'He [Dein] said immediately that Pat Rice could do it,' says Wenger. 'I asked to talk to Pat on the phone and I felt straightaway that we would get on. I could see how much the Club meant to him and I felt it would work between us.'

While keen to work with existing staff, Wenger also brought in some of his own people and early in 1997 coach Boro Primorac arrived. The Bosnian had won 18 caps for the former Yugoslavia, and had become a close friend and trusted confidant of Wenger when they met in the South of France. 'We are on the same wavelength and we worked very well together in Japan. I make a sign and he knows exactly what I mean. It is a kind of telepathy. He knows me by heart and he helps to work on technique with the players.'

Winning over the players

Wenger's first talk to the players could have been daunting and, by his own admission, he kept it short and sweet. 'I didn't say very much, because I was very keen to see what they were like in a real game with me in charge. I just said I am the new manager and I hope we will do well together. I suggested we go out and practice, because that would give me the opportunity to see the real level of the team. I saw players with big personalities and a unique amount of experience. Look who I had – David Seaman in goal, Lee Dixon, Nigel Winterburn, Martin Keown, Steve Bould and Tony Adams at the back, with David Platt, Dennis Bergkamp and Ian Wright... Yes, there was a bit of suspicion about me. I think that for a long time they were testing me. There were frequent questions – about tactics, what did I think about this or that – but I think that is the case with any new manager.' Wenger also realized the importance of winning over Tony Adams, the captain and the leader. 'He was fighting his battle with drink and was in some turmoil. He needed a lot of strength and I felt it took a lot out of him to keep his motivation. In the past Tony had sometimes played when he was drunk, but he was never a problem to me – never.'

If it works...

As with any group, Wenger knew he had to establish his authority in the dressing room. 'It is like politics,' he said. 'It could have been you against all of them, but I was not scared that they were testing me out, not at all, because when you want to lead a group you need to show that you can do it. What impressed me most of all at first was that I had in that squad players with real guts, players who were winners and proven winners. During the week I would keep thinking about their ages, that these guys were old, but by the time you got to the game on Saturday I knew I had lions out there. They stood up to be counted and the tougher it was, the better. You see a little guy like Nigel Winterburn and in the week in training, yes, he sometimes did look his age, but when the competition started, he was a lion.'

Wenger resisted the temptation to break up his defensive unit just because they were old. 'I kept them together because, basically, I had a good relationship with them. I felt as well that I could really win things with these guys, because they are winners by nature. I also knew that with eight players of more than 30 years of age it would be nearly impossible to dismantle a team like that and re-create a completely new team. I also found out that between those defenders there was a fantastic bond. Put it this way – if you killed one, you killed them all. Single one out and the rest would come to his defence. That is how close they were. It also helped that Patrick Vieira settled in so well and so quickly. Remi Garde being there was a help, no question. He was mature, he was intelligent and a very decent player. He made Patrick aware that he was not on his own... People said straightaway about Patrick that this guy is special and the fact that no one even knew about him made it better. That added to my credibility.'

During his first close season in charge, though, Wenger was constantly thinking about how he could improve his team even further. 'I signed Marc Overmars and Emmanuel Petit. Both did wonderfully for us. Manu and Patrick were terrific in central midfield, maybe the best in the country as a partnership – right foot and left foot, both strong, both powerful and both tremendous players. It was a source of great pride to me that they were both on the field when France won the World Cup in 1998 and that Patrick passed the ball for Manu to score. Maybe coming to Arsenal really helped someone like Manu, as he had not been the French team five years before.'

At first the wider English footballing community didn't take too much notice of the new Arsenal manager. 'That only happened after we won the League and FA Cup Double in 1998,' says Wenger. 'Coming from France and to win the Double in England, that is not an easy thing to achieve. I think from that point on, yes, I was taken a bit more seriously by everyone in England. At first I got the impression that they didn't think I would last in the job, that I would soon be gone, but now they think differently.'

The Wenger transfer credo is a simple one: 'We don't buy world-class players, we make them into world-class players.' This is a policy to which Wenger has adhered over the years. He has tended to baulk at bringing established, high-profile names to Arsenal and the players he has bought tend to have experienced problems at their previous clubs. Like Thierry Henry, for instance. He moved from Monaco to Juventus after the French World Cup triumph, but never reached the heights that tempted the Italian giants to invest £12 million in his talents. Speaking about Henry before Arsenal played Roma in a Champions League, clash

Fabio Capello, the present England manager, said, 'The problem with Thierry was that he was very young and had come from a club that does not have huge crowds. He left a club where he knew everybody and came to a club where everybody thought they knew him. That is a huge change and I don't think Thierry really made the adjustment.' Wenger took Henry and transformed him from a disaffected winger into a striker who is now rated as world class.

However, Wenger does admit that there have been one or two who have got away, players whom he could have signed, but, for a number of reasons, didn't. 'I could have got Claude Makelele for £1.3 million, I could also have got Cristiano Ronaldo, but it is impossible to spend ten years of your life at a club and not miss players. That is part of your life and, of course, there are other managers who are competing with you as well, don't forget that.' It is fair to say, though, that when it comes to auditing the transfer account, Wenger is massively in credit at Arsenal.

The man himself

Wenger's public image is that of a calm professor, who is impossible to ruffle, or so it would seem. 'I have seen Arsène lose it once or twice,' said a member of staff who works closely with Wenger, 'but that's losing it by his standards. Arsène losing it once is what George Graham used to be like on a daily basis!' Wenger does recall steaming into his team on one famous – or rather infamous – occasion. In 2001 Arsenal were not only trailing Manchester United at Old Trafford they were being thrashed 5–1. 'I admit I lost my temper that day,' he has revealed, 'and that has happened a few times, but not very often. On most occasions I don't really show my feelings, because it is better to keep them hidden. You put so much energy into preparing a team and making sure everybody is on board with what you are trying to achieve, and when it doesn't work out there is a massive disappointment. You then have to try to re-build the confidence of the players, not destroy it. Our job would be marvellous without defeats!'

When it comes to adding up his successes and failures, Wenger believes that if there is a season which still haunts him it is 1998/99, when Arsenal won nothing and Manchester United won the famous Treble of the Premier League, FA Cup and Champions League. In the first two competitions it was Arsenal who were denied – in extra-time in an FA Cup semi-final replay at Villa and by just one point in the league. 'That has left a big scar, because Manchester United became superheroes, because they won everything and we felt we could have done that as well. Maybe in the Champions League we were not ready, were not there, but we could have won the other two and we were close to that.'

That said, his record at Arsenal is an extremely impressive one as he has striven to combine the two great loves of his football life – winning football and football that is also attractive on the eye. That hasn't gone unnoticed elsewhere and Wenger has had opportunities to leave Arsenal to take over other clubs or indeed national sides. France and Germany have both made it known that they would like Wenger to take over their national squads, while Real Madrid have been desperate to entice him to the Bernabeu. 'Real wanted me to take over and they wanted me in complete charge. There were big offers from other clubs, but Real were the only ones who could have tempted me. However, at the end of the day I rejected every approach. Why? Because I have a good team here and I always felt that I had not finished the job that I set out to do at Arsenal, to put this Club at a level where it has never been.'

Standards, of course, have now been set by Wenger – first at Highbury and now at Emirates – but three seasons in a row have ended without silverware for Arsenal. Wenger, however, is not despondent. 'It is true, no trophy and I have to accept that,' he said, 'but then it depends on what kind of trophy you are talking about. The League Cup, for instance. I mean if people asked me what I would rather happen – win the League Cup or be in the final of the Champions League in 2006? Well, for me there is no choice. We were very close last season to the league and I still believe we were unfortunate to go out of the Champions League against Liverpool. Decisions did not go our way in the two games against them, but I still feel we have quality at the Club and we will win trophies, big trophies, in the seasons to come.

'I have always recognized that life is made up of successes and failures. It is difficult to be on top for a long period and I am grateful to this Club for giving me the chance to show that I can survive for a long time at the top level. That demands a lot of dedication. I enjoy giving that dedication. Of course, there are difficult moments, there are bound to be, times when you feel really, really terrible, but then when things go well, that makes it worth it.'

Chapter Fourteen

ARSÈNE'S ARSENAL

Every individual has only one
agreement with the Club –
to win trophies

rsène Wenger sensed there was a remarkable spirit among the
players he had taken over at Arsenal, but just how remarkable
was evident in a Premier League game at Newcastle on 30
November 1996. Newcastle were the league leaders. They were the
people's team, everybody's second favourites, and played with the style
they had adopted under Kevin Keegan, re-enforced by the arch
goalscorer Alan Shearer. Lee Dixon had stunned the St James' crowd
with a goal in the 12th minute, but ten minutes later Shearer had put
Newcastle level. Then came a flashpoint. They had been team-mates
over the summer in Terry Venables' England side that reached the semi-
finals of Euro 96, but back in club football Shearer and Tony Adams
were the fiercest of rivals. A minute after he had scored, Shearer was
accelerating towards the Arsenal goal when he was brought down
by Adams. That meant a red card for the Arsenal captain and now
Wenger's men were going to have to show the grit that he has sensed

on the training ground, but wanted to see manifest itself on the pitch. The Newcastle crowd smelt blood and assumed victory was theirs for the taking, but Arsenal dug deep, re-organized and then won the game with a breakaway goal from Ian Wright. Not only did Arsenal win, but they were now top of the table and Wenger was suitably impressed. 'There is something special about this team,' he said afterwards. 'They have a good camaraderie, because they have been together so long.'

Southampton were duly beaten at home with goals from Merson and Wright, but Arsenal could only manage a 2–2 draw at Derby with goals from Adams and John Hartson. Then came a defeat at Nottingham Forest and draws with Sheffield Wednesday and Aston Villa. Arsenal had dropped to third, but there was still the FA Cup to come. A Hartson goal enabled Arsenal to take a 1–1 draw to Roker Park and that was the night when Wenger saw the best of Dennis Bergkamp. Stephen Hughes scored one goal, but it was a stunning effort from the mercurial Dutchman that clinched a fourth round place. Up next was a tie with history attached, as Arsenal were drawn at home to Leeds, who were now managed by George Graham, the man who had been forced to leave Arsenal in the wake of the transfer scandal that had emerged two years earlier. It would be a fascinating duel. For public consumption Graham insisted that the match was nothing special, but few were convinced and there was no mistaking the grin of satisfaction as a Rod Wallace goal and a magnificent performance from goalkeeper Nigel Martyn put Leeds through.

That left Arsenal with just the push for a European place to motivate them for the rest of the season, but Wenger was already drawing up his plans about how to bolster his squad for the next campaign. The title quest, Wenger conceded, was over by February after a drab goalless draw against Tottenham and a 2–1 defeat by Manchester United at Highbury. However, a glimpse of the future was evident in March when an unknown from Paris St Germain arrived at Arsenal. His name was Nicolas Anelka. He was only 17 years of age and cost a mere £500,000, but he had talent, so much talent that Wenger gave him some substitute appearances during the run-in to the league programme. He was also to prove one of the most single-minded and difficult players that Wenger has had to handle in his time at the Club – and one of the most shrewd investments ever made in football.

Arsenal's results in the last six weeks of the season highlighted to Wenger just where the problem lay for his team. True, they did lose at home to Wimbledon, but that could happen to any of the top teams if it was the Crazy Gang's day. More significant, though, were the defeats to Newcastle and Liverpool at home. The one against the Merseysiders had more than a hint of controversy about it as Robbie Fowler was sent tumbling under a challenge by David Seaman. The England goalkeeper immediately protested his innocence and Fowler himself gestured to referee Gerald Ashby that he had not been touched and that his momentum had caused him to fall. Ashby was unmoved. Fowler took the kick, Seaman saved it, but Jason McAteer fired home the rebound.

On the last day of the season Arsenal could, in theory, still qualify for the Champions League by taking the runners-up spot behind champions-elect Manchester United. Arsenal and Newcastle went into their matches with the same points total and the same goal difference. Arsenal won 3–1 at Derby, but Newcastle hit five. It was to be the UEFA Cup for Arsenal and Wenger was left thinking about what might have been had his men avoided defeat against Newcastle in the last but one game of the season. In 1996/97 Arsenal had lost at home to their three immediate rivals – Manchester United, Liverpool and Newcastle – and that told Wenger that in the tough, tight games Arsenal were left wanting. Not for effort, character or commitment – Wenger had seen evidence a-plenty that Arsenal would never be short of those qualities – but they needed more 'players who could make a difference,' as he puts it. Wenger was determined that in the years to come there would be no repeat of this season.

Wenger strengthens the squad

The arrival of new faces had already started with Anelka. He turned 18 soon after his transfer to Arsenal and he was a young man in a hurry. It was a brave decision for him to move to Arsenal. He knew no one and, although compatriots Patrick Vieira and Remi Garde were already established at the Club, he had no contemporaries. He was homesick and was forever on his mobile phone to friends back in Paris, but he wanted the chance of first-team football and he wanted to make it work at Arsenal. Come the close season, though, Wenger acted by bringing in more talent. The infusion of television money had made the Premier League arguably the wealthiest of its kind in the world and the financial constraints which managers of other generations had been forced to operate under had now been lifted. Football was changing, with legal issues becoming as much a part of the game as tactics and strategy.

The first major breakthrough in the courts had been the Bosman ruling, which meant players could leave on a free transfer once they had fulfilled their contract to a club. Arsenal have both benefited and suffered from that ruling. They signed Sol Campbell on a free transfer from Tottenham in one of the most controversial transfers in modern history (his market value would have been around £20 million), but in summer 2008 they also lost Mathieu Flamini, who decided not to renew his deal at Arsenal and moved to AC Milan. Eventually, UEFA would be forced to drop the 'four-foreigner rule' in European competitions whereby a club could only field four players whose home association was not that of the club where they were playing, as EU employment law dictated that such a restriction was illegal. EU law also meant was that there could be no limit on foreign players in any team if they were from European Union countries. The whole landscape of football in England was about to change and there would be a time when Arsenal would field a team with no English, or indeed British, players.

Back at Arsenal, Wenger was making adjustments to his squad. Out went Paul Merson, a decision that surprised and indeed upset many Arsenal fans who had seen the homegrown Merson become a key player at the Club. Like Charlie George of a previous era, they felt they could identify with him, but Wenger felt otherwise and Merson moved to Middlesbrough. For all his benign image, there is a ruthless streak in Wenger that has come to the fore on many occasions in his 12 years at the Club. Wenger wanted a wide player and set his sights on Marc Overmars.

Nicknamed the 'Flying Dutchman', Overmars had been a sensation at Ajax, but had suffered a serious knee problem and many top clubs were guarded about taking a risk on him, although Real Betis of Spain were also interested. Overmars, perhaps influenced by the success that his compatriot Dennis Bergkamp had enjoyed at Highbury, opted for Arsenal. Wenger revealed that he had not been put off by talk that Overmars was never regain full fitness. 'When I did my homework on him, I discovered he was upset at the rumours that he was not fit and that he could not play again to his true ability. That was a good sign for me – a player who is hurt and who has something to prove.'

That was just the start of Wenger's transfer spree. In Monaco there were two players that he rated highly – Emmanuel Petit and Gilles Grimandi. Petit was to form one half of a tremendous central midfield axis at Arsenal as Wenger paired him with Patrick Vieira. He could play left back, central defence or midfield. He was strong and could pass a ball. Tottenham manager Gerry Francis was also interested in signing Petit, but once the Frenchman knew that Arsenal were keen, there was only one choice for him. Grimandi was also to become a valued member of the Arsenal squad. Described by Wenger as 'a great professional,' he was happy to play wherever he was asked to and Wenger values Grimandi's opinion so highly that he is now Arsenal's chief scout in France. Wenger had sent Boro Primorac to watch the famous Toulon under-21 tournament in the South of France and the Bosnian had come back with glowing reports of a young Portuguese winger by the name of Luis Boa-Morte. He was signed from Sporting Lisbon and Wenger then returned to Monaco to sign Christopher Wreh. As for English talent, Steve Rowley had been hugely impressed by the emergence of a young central defender at Luton called Matthew Upson and he also joined the Club.

The season opens and Wright goes for a record

Now Wenger was ready for the assault and leading that charge was Ian Wright. In his sights was the Club's goalscoring record, set by Cliff Bastin at 178 goals, and he made inroads into this by scoring the Arsenal goal in a 1–1 draw at Leeds on the opening day of the 1997/98 season. Two more followed in midweek as Coventry were brushed aside and now he needed just two more to break the record. It was Bergkamp, not Wright, who stole the show at Southampton, though, when he scored two and Marc Overmars another in a 3–1 win. Bergkamp was at his best again as he bagged a hat-trick at Leicester in a 3–3 draw and then came Tottenham at Highbury. The pre-match talk was that this was the perfect day in the perfect arena for Wright to at least equal the Bastin record against the oldest enemy in Arsenal's history. 'I'm not so sure about that,' said Wright, aware that Tottenham would now have extra motivation to keep him off the scoresheet. 'I am sure the likes of John Scales will have something to say about it.' Scales did, as did Ian Walker in the Tottenham goal. He saved superbly from Anelka and Tottenham emerged with a creditable draw. But Wright didn't have to wait long, only two weeks in fact until Bolton Wanderers came to Highbury and were beaten 4–1, with Wright scoring a hat-trick. The record was his at 179 goals.

However, three days later came an uncanny echo of the experiences of the Double-winning side of 1971. Over 25 years previously Arsenal had lost to Cologne in what was then called the Fairs Cup, but manager Bertie Mee wasn't too dejected. 'With the programme of matches to come, ' said Mee, 'maybe this will be a blessing in disguise.' Wenger must have felt much the same way when Arsenal went to Greece to play PAOK Salonika, who, to be honest, were probably not the best team in Salonika, never mind Greece. Unfortunately Arsenal had to go without the player who had been in such irresistible form, Dennis Bergkamp, who had refused to fly ever since an unnerving experience with the Dutch World Cup squad in the USA four years earlier. Although he made it clear that he was more than willing to make any journey by car, he had it written into his contracts at Ajax, Inter Milan and Arsenal that he would not be obliged to travel by plane at any time. Without him Arsenal lost the first leg 1–0. Anelka was drafted in, but a number of chances were squandered and Greek international Fratzekos beat Seaman with one of the few openings that PAOK created. 'They were more consistent than us overall,' admitted Wenger after the game. 'The atmosphere was not an excuse and neither was the absence of Dennis Bergkamp. Now we have to win by two goals and that will not be easy.' In the second leg they could manage only a 1-1 draw, despite a virtuoso performance from Bergkamp. Indeed, he scored to put Arsenal ahead, but a late strike gave the Greeks a vital away goal and Arsenal were out of Europe at the first hurdle.

Refocussing on domestic competitions

When the League Cup campaign started Wenger made it clear that the competition was fourth on Arsenal's list of priorities and he was going to use the competition to bring back first-team squad players who had been out through injury, suspension or because someone else was in better form, and to give youngsters an opportunity to taste first-team football. That meant players like young Austrian goalkeeper Alex Manninger, who had been signed from Salzburg as the long-term successor to David Seaman, had a chance to play. Birmingham. Coventry and West Ham (where Seaman did play) were all duly dispatched to secure a semi-final with Chelsea. The West London rivals did not share Wenger's 'mix-and-match' approach and were at full strength in both ties. Arsenal took a 2-1 lead to Stamford Bridge after Stephen Hughes and Marc Overmars scored, but when Patrick Vieira was sent off early in the second half of the second leg it looked unlikely that Arsenal would go through and, despite a rare goal from Gilles Grimandi, they lost 3-1.

Back in the league, Arsenal were serving notice that they were intent on bringing the title back to North London and successive derby wins against Chelsea at Stamford Bridge, where Nigel Winterburn had hit a spectacular winner, and West Ham at Highbury were proof that they had the heart for the battle. Against West Ham Overmars scored twice and Ian Wright added to his ever-growing tally, but Bergkmap was once again at his supreme best and finally got the goal his performance warranted. Bergkamp had scored eight goals from nine games and was in inspired form.

For some reason, Arsenal then hit a trough during which their league form fell away alarmingly. Goalless draws at Crystal Palace and at home to Aston Villa were frustrating enough, but then came their first league defeat of the season. Derby County had just moved to Pride Park and were convincing 3–0 winners. Wenger was flummoxed as to what had gone wrong. Even worse, Manchester United were the next opponents at Highbury and Wenger had to break up his central midfield because Emmanuel Petit was not available and Dennis Bergkamp was also out, both because of suspension. The occasion lifted Arsenal, though, and within 30 minutes they were two goals up. Nicolas Anelka had been brought in as a replacement for Bergkamp and justified the trust placed in him by scoring the first goal, before the dynamic Vieira fired home the second. That's when the man that Arsenal fans love to hate made his telling contribution. Teddy Sheringham may have moved to Manchester United during the close season, but to the Arsenal faithful he would always be associated with Tottenham. Sheringham brought United back into the game with two goals before half-time and Arsenal's confidence seemed to falter, but David Platt had other ideas and in the second half, after Arsenal had recovered their composure, he headed in the winner.

That should have been the catalyst for Arsenal to surge up the league, but in fact they lost their next two matches, at Sheffield Wednesday and then at home to Liverpool. Ian Wright scored the goal that earned them a 1–0 win at Newcastle, but then came a shock 3–1 home defeat to Blackburn. Three losses out of four was not title-winning form and Arsenal seemed to be falling further and further behind Manchester United. At the turn of the year they were in sixth place and 12 points behind United. Worse was to come in a 2–2 draw with Coventry, when Patrick Vieira was sent off, and it seemed that, after such a promising start, Arsenal's season was beginning to taper off.

Wenger has said, 'I have always loved the FA Cup as a competition, since I was a kid growing up in Strasbourg. The FA Cup final was, really, the only live game that was shown in France back then and we all gathered around the television to watch it.' However, this season the road to Wembley got off to an inauspicious start. Lowly Port Vale in the third round at Highbury had all the makings of an easy passage into the next stage, but Vale held out for a goalless draw, and in the replay at Vale Park extra-time couldn't divide the teams and it finished 1–1, with Bergkamp once again the scorer of a vital goal. David Seaman emerged as the hero, though, as Arsenal won the penalty shoot-out. Arsenal moved into the fifth round after Ray Parlour and Marc Overmars scored to knock out Middlesbrough, and then came Crystal Palace at home in the fifth round. As was the norm for that season, Arsenal would do it the hard way with a goalless draw at Highbury and a 2–1 win at Selhurst Park with goals from Anelka and Bergkamp.

Another derby game followed – a sixth-round tie at home to West Ham. Arsenal had drawn 0–0 in the league at Upton Park a week earlier as they attempted to claw back United's still formidable lead. That draw brought it to 11 points at the turn of March and many regarded the title race as over. 'It will be difficult,' said a stubborn Wenger, 'but it is not over yet. It was a good point at West Ham, but from now on draws are not good enough.' Wenger's cause was not helped by the continued absence of Seaman with a finger injury or by yet another match being added to an already crowded fixture list when Bergkamp's penalty meant the FA Cup match at Highbury finished 1–1. Before that could be decided they were two vital league games, against Wimbledon in their adopted home of Selhurst Park and the clash with Manchester United at Old Trafford. Wins were needed in both games; defeats were not an option. Christopher Wreh proved to be the hero against Wimbledon and Wenger said, 'I am very pleased for Christopher. We have not had the chance to see the best of him and it has been a difficult year for him.'

A turning point

Now the scene was set for the showdown with United. Alex Manninger, who had excelled in the absence of Seaman, was a slight concern due to a knee problem, but was passed fit and Arsenal had been boosted when United dropped two points at West Ham while they were beating Wimbledon. Arsenal were nine points behind, but had three games in hand and what had seemed impossible was now merely improbable 'There is a bit more pressure on United now,' said Wenger, 'but not enough. Even if we go there and win we still have to win our games in hand, but I hear the bookmakers are taking bets again!' That was for public consumption. Deep down, Wenger knew the momentum was with Arsenal – a win and the psychological lift would be huge.

It was a Saturday game with an early kick-off. The Old Trafford crowd was tense, conscious that if there was one slip up, one lapse in concentration, Arsenal had the players to punish United. And so it proved. With 20 minutes left Wenger took off Wreh and sent on Anelka. His natural pace was bound to be a concern for the United defence, but, with just 12 minutes left, it was his awareness that set up the crucial goal as the lightning-quick Overmars picked up his downfield clearance, accelerated into the area and slid the ball under Peter Schmeichel's legs. The race was back on – not that the ever-cautious Wenger would admit it, saying, 'United still have a slight advantage, because we have still to get the points from the games that we have. That won't be easy.'

Next up was the FA Cup replay at West Ham. Seaman was injured, as were Ian Wright and Ray Parlour, and just to compound Arsenal's problems Bergkamp, with a flash of the temper to which he was occasionally prone, was sent off after just half an hour for a clear elbow in the face of West Ham's Steve Lomas. However, Arsenal responded by taking the game to West Ham. The Hammers' goalkeeper Bernard Lama kept Arsenal at bay for a while, but he could do nothing about the effort from Anelka that curled past him into the net on the stroke of half-time. Arsenal stood firm in the second half. Former Arsenal player John Hartson clearly felt he had a point to prove and even though Martin Keown successfully contained the Welshman for most of the game, he managed to snatch an equalizer with five minutes left. The match went into extra-time and then penalties. Arsenal's nerve held, West Ham's did not. It was as simple as that. Manninger saved from Eyal Berkovic, while both Hartson and Samassi Abou hit the woodwork. It rounded off a significant week's work for Wenger and his men.

There were still stern tests to come, though. On the last day of March Arsenal went to the Reebok Stadium to face Bolton. Wright was injured, Bergkamp was suspended and to take his place Wenger called up Wreh, who formed a hugely inexperienced strike force with Nicolas Anelka. Early in the second half Wreh struck a vital goal and Arsenal held out, despite losing Keown to a second yellow card in the second half. Wenger said, 'The message to Manchester United is that we go from game to game looking for a win. Now it is down to the most consistent team.' After the sheer intensity of the league, the FA Cup semi-final came as something of a relief for Wenger and his men. Their opponents at Villa Park were Wolverhampton Wanderers of the First Division and, in truth, their effort was tame one. Just as Bergkamp had launched the season with a salvo of goals, so Wreh was contributing his share of crucial strikes in the finale. His goal separated the teams, but there could and should have been more. Now it was back to the league with an FA Cup final place against Newcastle assured.

Under George Graham, the anthem 'One-nil to the Arsenal' was adopted to the tune of the Village People hit 'Go West'. In an echo of that bygone era, as this season reached its climax and Arsenal prepared to take on Newcastle, they did so, ironically, on the back of five successive 1-0 victories. Two goals from the ever-improving Anelka and another from Vieira clinched a 3-1 win. The victory at Old Trafford and the passage past Wolves had clearly given Arsenal new-found confidence. On Easter Monday they travelled to Blackburn. Rovers, the last team to beat Arsenal in the league, and revenge was to be sweet. Dennis Bergkamp was now back to add his venom to an already potent attack and inside the first 15 minutes Arsenal were three goals up. Bergkamp took all of 75 seconds to convert a chance laid on by Anelka, Ray Parlour got in on the act with two goals and there was another from Anelka. Game over, as they say.

Favourites for the title

After the win, which meant Arsenal were now favourites for the title, Wenger was his usual deadpan self. 'We didn't listen to anyone when people said we didn't have a chance of the league and we won't listen to them now just because we are favourites. In the dressing room, yes, the players are happy enough, but no one down there is going crazy. We have won nothing yet.' Many believed it would be Arsenal who would wobble when the screws were turned, that Manchester United's greater experience would tell at what they call the business end of the season.

In fact, the opposite was true. A place at the top of the league beckoned if Arsenal beat Wimbledon and United failed to beat Newcastle at Old Trafford. United were held to a draw, while Arsenal romped to a 5–0 win. Emmanuel Petit, Gilles Grimandi, Marc Overmars and Christopher Wreh were the scorers and confidence was high at Arsenal.

Now it was away to Barnsley on the dusty, bumpy pitch at Oakwell, but the Dutch duo of Bergkamp and Overmars were on target. Petit used the game to state his case for a World Cup call-up. 'You know, a lot of people over in France, they think this league is easy,' he said. 'I just invite them to come over and see it for themselves. The national team basically ignores French players in England and for me that is a mistake.' Next up were Derby, who came to Highbury determined not to give away an easy win. 'That is what makes this league the most fair league in the world,' Wenger would say later. 'Every team gives their best every time. You cannot take one game for granted – not one.' Arsenal had discovered that earlier in the season when they had played Derby at Pride Park and been soundly beaten 3–0. The Midlands team were anything but a walkover this time around. They defended resolutely and it needed a stunning drive from Petit to break the deadlock. 'Now tell me this league is easy!' was his post-match reaction. Aime Jacquet must have been listening, because later that summer Petit played a major role for his country in the World Cup and scored the final goal of the tournament to seal a 3–0 win for France over Brazil.

Now Arsenal needed just one win from their last three games to be champions. That win came against Everton at Highbury and it was a convincing 4–0. An own-goal from Slaven Bilic, signed by Everton from West Ham, opened the scoring. Then it was time for a piece of Overmars magic as he waltzed around three defenders and slid the ball in. Overmars then added a third before the 'Skipper' himself got into the action, bursting from defence and drilling the ball into the net. That was it. The title had come back to Arsenal, but Petit didn't finish the game a happy man. A wicked tackle from Everton's Don Hutchison left the Frenchman clutching his leg in agony. He looked in a bad way. 'I thought that was it, my World Cup was over before it had started,' said Petit. 'I feared at first it was broken, but fortunately it was just a bad bruise, but I was scared.'

Wenger left no one in any doubt about the scale of the achievement. 'This is my greatest ever achievement as a manager and I am proud for the Club, my staff, the players and the supporters. We have shown great spirit all season and our last goal typified that as Steve Bould sent Adams through. They have been great players for Arsenal. I am surprised but delighted that we have won the title so soon, but this team can get better.'

Challenging for the Double

There was still, of course, the little matter of the FA Cup final against Newcastle. Arsenal had finished their programme with a heavy defeat at Liverpool, which Wenger appreciated might happen after the celebrations that followed the win against Everton and a 1–0 defeat at Aston Villa. 'The players are physically and mentally exhausted after their efforts in the last two or three months,' said Wenger. 'In a way, after winning the league, that was the reaction, but I am confident that it will be different at Wembley.' And so it was, but final also gave a glimpse of the ruthless streak that Wenger keeps well hidden from the public gaze. The day before the final, Dennis Bergkamp was insistent that he tested a hamstring problem that had bothered him for some weeks. 'Dennis is the kind of player that has to be right, has to feel one hundred per cent fit in his own mind,' said physiotherapist Gary Lewin. 'There are some players like Tony Adams who, like he did in Euro 96, will have six injections just to play in a game. Dennis will not go out on to the field unless he feels he can do himself justice. He felt a twinge during that fitness test and told the gaffer straightaway. Not even the thought of missing an FA Cup final would make him change the way he approaches football.'

It was widely assumed that Ian Wright, who had proved his fitness in the concluding games of the season, would take Bergkamp's place, but Wenger had other ideas. He liked Wright and admired his tenacity and enthusiasm. He knew about the fight that Wright had to break through at the top level and acknowledged that he had a genuine hunger for the game, but he also saw a player who was on the wrong side of 30 and who wasn't going to get fitter as the years went by. With his FA Cup final selection, Wenger looked forward and chose Christopher Wreh and Nicolas Anelka, leaving Wright on the bench. Against a Newcastle team that lacked the fire and passion that had been their hallmark, Arsenal cruised to victory with goals from Overmars and Anelka. 'The title, that was our main aim,' said Wenger afterwards, 'but it would have been an awful feeling to have got this far and then lost the final.' Despite the ease with which Arsenal won, and although it was their cup long before the final whistle, Wright didn't even get asecond on the pitch. Wenger was making a statement and in the close season Wright moved to West Ham, never kicking a ball for Arsenal again.

During the summer came the World Cup and there was a heavy contingent from Arsenal at the finals in France. England qualified for the first knock-out stage, where they went out in such dramatic fashion against Argentina, but it still meant there was extra work for the likes of Tony Adams, David Seaman and Martin Keown. Holland's Marc Overmars and Dennis Bergkamp were beaten semi-finalists and there until almost the end of the tournament, and, of course, Emmanuel Petit and Patrick Vieira would stay right until the last game, playing such a vital part in the defeat of Brazil.

Wenger knew there would be a price to pay and looked to freshen up his squad. He also knew that Manchester United wouldn't take their defeat in the title race lightly and that Sir Alex Ferguson would bring in new players. 'There are several teams in the Premier League with the same financial potential,' said Wenger, 'and then there is Manchester United. They spent £24 million at the start of the 1998/99 season and I can't do that. I have money to spend and I am looking for three players, but I have to be clever and strengthen without spending too much.' In contrast, Ferguson spent freely. He brought in the muscular central defender Jaap Stam and Swedish winger Jesper Blomqvist. Then he added Dwight Yorke to his front line at the start of the season. Arsenal? They signed 17-year-old left-back David Grondin from St Etienne and versatile Argentinian defender Nelson Vivas from Swiss club Lugano. Then in September, after he had excelled against England in a Euro 2000 qualifier, came Fredrik Ljungberg from Swedish club Halmstadt and Nigerian Nwankwo Kanu arrived from Inter Milan in December. Kanu was one of the most gifted players to wear an Arsenal shirt. 'He is not only a good player but a fantastic human being,' said Wenger. 'He had a heart problem and needed surgery, but he came back fit, well and determined. He is a great asset to the Club.' Both Ljungberg and Kanu proved to be sensational signings.

European games to be played at Wembley

Meanwhile, a major decision had been taken to play UEFA home games at Wembley. 'We'd have preferred to play at Highbury,' said chairman Peter Hill-Wood, 'but we couldn't do that and provide normal service for our supporters. That was the deciding factor. UEFA's regulations on the size of perimeter advertising would have meant we lost several rows of seats to make way for the advertising boards. By the time we had complied with that, we would have lost many thousands of seats from our capacity. We would have also lost the disabled enclosure and to us it is very important we provide that facility. All round, there would have been huge disruption.' It was certainly true that 80,000 fans could watch the games at Wembley, but Wembley had none of the intimacy and atmosphere of Highbury and the running track around the old Wembley stadium made it a less than intimidating arena, so the ties weren't really home games for Arsenal or away games for the opposition.

That was to come, though. First Arsenal had to set about defending their league title and although Overmars and Petit were sufficiently recovered from their World Cup exertions to score the goals to beat Nottingham Forest, there followed a worrying sequence of draws against Liverpool, Charlton, Chelsea and Leicester. That was eight points dropped, which, as Wenger knew, was too many. Ljungberg arrived just in time to play against Manchester United at Highbury and scored in a 3–0 win, but Arsenal were starting to fall behind. 'We lost points at home that we shouldn't have done,' he admitted. As for the League Cup, interest ended very early as, after Derby were beaten, Arsenal drew Chelsea at Highbury and what was basically a reserve team was demolished 5–0 by a full-strength line-up from Stamford Bridge.

There were disappointments in personal performances as well. Nicolas Anelka, omitted from the French World Cup-winning squad, started the season in brilliant form and was immediately recruited by the new manager of France, Roger Lemerre, but players such as Christopher Wreh and Luis Boa-Morte, who had looked so promising the previous season, did not improve as Wenger had hoped. 'I just wished we could have signed Kanu earlier,' said Wenger as he reflected on that season. 'We didn't have him fully fit until February and every time he came on he changed the game.'

When it came to Arsenal's European games it would be too simplistic to say that the Wembley factor was to blame, but there is no doubt that Arsenal surrendered a massive advantage by moving away from their home territory. Add to that scenario the absence of Ljungberg, who was signed after the UEFA deadline for the group stages of the Champions League, and Arsenal were up against it from the start. The first game was in Lens. With its massed ranks of 'sang et d'or' (blood and gold – the Lens club colours) banners the Stade Felix Bollaert is arguably one of the most atmospheric in Europe. Vieira, for one, knew what to expect, but he also pledged that he would use common sense when it came to challenges. He was already earning a reputation in the Premier League for his full-blooded approach and accepted that he would have to adjust his thinking in Europe. 'I will use my head,' he said. 'I know what to do.'

So did Arsenal. They showed no fear and attacked Lens from the start. They were so in command that they made light of the challenge from a talented Lens outfit that included strikers Tony Vairelles and the Czech Vladimir Smicer, a future signing for Liverpool. Arsenal dominated and the game should have been beyond killed off. Marc Overmars had scored one, but Arsenal squandered a hatful of others. The main culprit was Anelka and Arsenal duly paid the price in injury-time when Vairelles forced home a corner. The ball appeared to touch Keown last, but Vairelles claimed it. On the face of it, with an away goal that might prove crucial if the teams finished level, the result wasn't too bad, but Overmars didn't agree. 'First, we cannot just blame Nico [Anelka] that we didn't score more than one goal. It is down to the whole team. Between us we should have scored more and we know that. I hope that we don't regret dropping these two points later in the competition.'

Also in the group were Greek champions Panathinaikos and the traditionally tough Dynamo Kiev outfit from Ukraine. When the draw was made, Wenger insisted that the Dynamo team were strong favourites to win the group, because of their massive experience. 'They are good at keeping the ball and in Andrei Shevchenko and Sergei Rebrov they have two class strikers,' he said. The first match at Wembley was against Panathinaikos and Arsenal's aerial power was too much for the Greeks to handle. Tony Adams and Martin Keown headed the goals in a 2-1 win. Dynamo lost away in Athens and drew at home to Lens and after the first round of matches the group had an even look to it. Arsenal were on top, but Wenger knew there were difficult times ahead – and so it proved in the double-header against Dynamo.

The tussle at Wembley was eventful. The Ukrainians didn't seem in the least unnerved by the atmosphere and played with remarkable freedom, with both Rebrov and Shevchenko proving Wenger's judgement to be spot on. However, the match hinged on one dramatic minute in the second half. Bergkamp had headed Arsenal into the lead and it looked as though Overmars would double that advantage as his shot rolled towards an empty net. At 2-0 the tie should have been over, but somehow Oleg Luzhny sprinted back to clear the ball off the line. No sooner had the crowd voiced their disappointment than Rebrov forced home the equalizer. In the second leg in Kiev Arsenal were well and truly put in their place as Kiev hit irresistible form. The cause wasn't helped by Wenger being forced to field a depleted side. Adams was injured, as were Overmars and Anelka, and it was clearly a game in which Bergkamp would not be able to play because of the distance. Dynamo took full advantage, with goals from Rebrov, Olexandr Golovko and Shevchenko giving them an emphatic lead, and although Stephen Hughes pulled one back late on, qualification from the group was now looking in jeopardy.

Arsenal had to win their last home game against Lens at Wembley. Nothing else would do – and they failed. Again Arsenal were hit by injuries that ruled out Vieira and Bergkamp, and Adams only lasted until half-time. Emmanuel Petit was suspended. Lens, playing with the same kind of impressive fluency that Dynamo had shown, won 1-0 with a goal from Mikael Debeve and, to make matters worse, Ray

Parlour was sent off for a wild kick at Cyril Rool. Arsenal were now out and sent what was basically a reserve team to Athens to fulfil their group fixtures against Panathinaikos. Anelka, Mendez and Boa-Morte scored the goals in a 3–1, but essentially meaningless, win.

Giggs scores that goal

The European dream was over, but in the league Arsenal were steadily plugging away, not that the defeat at Sheffield Wednesday will go down as the team's finest hour that season. Wednesday won 1-0 and both Paolo Di Canio and Martin Keown were sent off – Di Canio after he had pushed over referee Paul Alcock and Keown for his part in the build-up to the flashpoint. Arsenal had their chances and Wednesday goalkeeper Kevin Pressman had to save well from Bergkamp, Anelka and Parlour, but it took a speculative shot by Lee Briscoe to beat Manninger and win the match. 'I was disappointed with that result,' said Adams. 'We have to learn to kill off opponents when we are on top. The same thing happened against Lens.'

There was something of a revival, though, as Newcastle were beaten emphatically 3-0 at Highbury, with two goals from Bergkamp and one from Anelka, and a home draw against Southampton and away wins against Blackburn and Coventry looked to have put the season back on track. Everton were beaten 1-0 by a Nicolas Anelka goal in a match that was more one-sided than the scoreline suggests, but Arsenal couldn't find a way past a well-organized and resolute Tottenham side now managed by George Graham. That result seemed to affect confidence within the camp and after a 1-0 defeat against Wimbledon at Selhurst Park there was, as they say, a heated exchange of views in the dressing room. Occasionally such inquests clear the air and produce immediate results. This was not the case with Arsenal. Middlesbrough managed a 1–1 draw, with Anelka scoring for Arsenal, and then came a goalless draw with Derby and a 3–2 defeat at Aston Villa, but that game finally ignited Arsenal and they went on a 19-match unbeaten run.

Fans favourite Freddie Ljungberg announced his arrival at Highbury in September 1998 with a debut goal in a 3-0 win over arch rivals Manchester United. His darting runs from midfield and ability to arrive in the box late brought him 72 goals in 328 appearances, not bad for a midfielder.

◀ **The sight of mercurial Frenchman** Thierry Henry celebrating a goal was a familiar one to Gunners fans during a magnificent career with the Club. Arsenal's record goalscorer hit the net 226 times in 364 appearances. For so long the fulcrum of the team, Henry's main asset, among many, was his speed with ball at his feet.

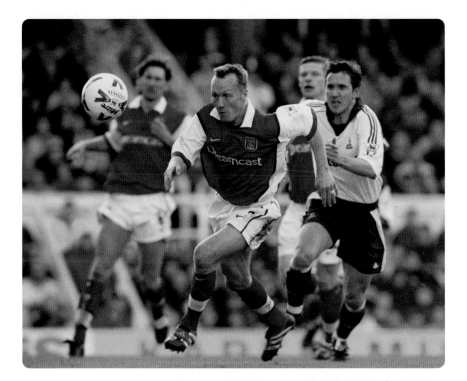

Few players used their experience to greater effect than full-back Lee Dixon. During his 14 years at Arsenal he made over 600 appearances, in every one of which he showed his terrific pace and enthusiasm for the cause.

The other half of a great centre-back pairing with Tony Adams, Martin Keown was also blessed with great pace. Combined with fierce determination and a stern tackle, Keown played a full part in the Doubles in both 1998 and 2002.

Ray Parlour blossomed under Arsène Wenger and put in over 450 appearances in the engine room of Arsenal's midfield. He also specialised in spectacular goals, none more so than this stunning 30-yarder against Chelsea in the 2002 FA Cup Final.

So near and yet so far: Sol Campbell heads the Gunners into the lead against Barcelona during the first half of the 2006 Champions League Final a lead which they held until the 86th minute. Two late goals from the Catalans saw Arsenal's magnificent run to the Final end in heartbreaking fashion.

Another in the line of great French players during Arsène Wenger's reign at the Club was Robert Pires. Voted Footballer of the Year in 2001/02, he scored 13 goals from midfield in that Double-winning season. His six-year stint at the Club ended after the 2005/06 season when once again his goal tally reached double figures including this stunning lob in the 7-0 victory over Middlesbrough.

Highbury's Final Salute ceremony on 7 May 2006 was a superb way to mark the end of 93 glorious years at the famous old ground. Here, streamers fall against the backdrop of the clock, at the south end of the ground, which had witnessed every home game since it was erected in 1935.

One of the brightest stars in the new-look Arsenal is Dutch striker Robin van Persie. His career so far has stuttered through injury but in between times he has scored some spectacular goals. Here he celebrates a truly magnificent volley from the edge of the penalty area against Charlton in September 2006.

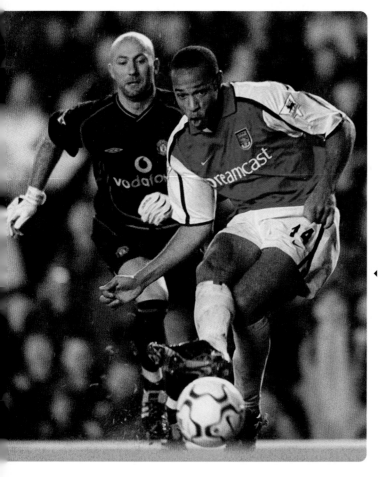

◄ **Arsenal and Manchester United** have served up some cracking matches over the last few years. One of the finest was at Highbury in November 2001 when Thierry Henry profited from two terrible mistakes by his countryman Fabien Barthez in the United goal allowing the striker to score twice in five minutes and seal a 3-1 win.

The other must-see for all Gunners fans is the north London derby. Since the mid-1990s Arsenal have had the upper hand in this famous fixture. One of the finest came at White Hart Lane in November 2004 when Arsenal won a see-saw battle 5-4. Here Patrick Vieira clips the ball over Spurs keeper Paul Robinson to give the Reds a 3-1 lead.

Since his appointment ▶ Arsène Wenger has been a leading figure in the development of the Club's training ground at London Colney in Hertfordshire. The 143-acre site now boasts state-of-the-art facilities suitable for meeting the needs of one of the world's finest football clubs.

The first match played at the Club's new Emirates Stadium on 22 July 2006 was the end of one era and the start of another as Arsenal took on Ajax in Dennis Bergkamp's testimonial match. It was an emotional occasion for many reasons and a fitting tribute to a player who gave the Club 11 years, 423 games, 120 goals and a whole host of wonderful memories.

◄ **Most Gunners fans** believe the future of the Club is in good hands with players of the calibre of Cesc Fabregas now at the heart of the team.

Chairman of the Club Peter ▶
Hill-Wood followed in the
footsteps of his father and
his grandfather when he
was appointed to the post
in 1981. In fact his family's
involvement in the Club
stretches back to 1919.

**Under the guidance of
Arsène Wenger** Theo
Walcott's performances
improved dramatically
during the 2007/08
season and culminated
in a wonderful display
in the Champions League
tie against AC Milan when
he laid on the winning goal
for Emmanuel Adebayor.
▼

Leeds felt the backlash first as they were beaten 3–1 with goals from Bergkamp, Vieira and Petit, and Overmars scored the winner against West Ham at Highbury on Boxing Day. Charlton were the next victims and, although Liverpool held out for a goalless draw, it was a small blip. Between them, Manchester United, Aston Villa and Chelsea still looked to have the title sewn up, but Arsenal were finding form and demonstrating the qualities that all successful teams must have. As Wenger put it, 'It is the ability to draw when maybe you should have lost and the ability to win when maybe all you deserved was a draw.' Arsenal certainly hit an impressive streak of form in the league with successive wins against Nottingham Forest and Chelsea, with Bergkamp snatching the winner in the London derby. Then came the demolition of West Ham at Upton Park. Arsenal were simply irresistible and won 4–0 with goals from Ray Parlour, Marc Overmars, Dennis Bergkamp and Nicolas Anelka.

The feel-good factor that the team derived from their improved results and performances in the league meant that the defence of the FA Cup started with confidence – so much so that even when Arsenal went 2–0 down away to Preston in the third round they came back to win 4–2 with two goals from Petit and one each from Overmars and Boa-Morte. 'Was I worried we would go out? No, not at all,' said Overmars. 'We have our belief in this team and in these players. We did not panic.' The fourth round tie at Wolverhampton Wanderers was to give Arsenal more problems. Dennis Bergkamp left with his nose broken while Emmanuel Petit was sent off for an extravagant, Gallic gesture at a referee's assistant, made because he thought Arsenal were not getting enough protection and that any close decisions were going the way of Wolves. 'Anything I did say was in French so how the linesman could hear me and then understand me, I don't know,' said Petit later. However, Arsenal got through with goals from Overmars and Bergkamp and a fifth round tie against Sheffield United followed.

It wasn't, on the face of it, the most potentially explosive match, but it ended in controversy and even UEFA become involved. The match was at 1–1 when Sheffield United player Lee Morris went down injured. The ball went back to United goalkeeper Alan Kelly, who promptly blasted it out of play, so that Morris could get treatment.

When play resumed Parlour threw the ball down the line to Kanu, whom he thought was going to either kick it out for a United throw or pass the ball back to Kelly. He did neither. As the United defence stood in statuesque fashion, Kanu ran clear, crossed the ball and Overmars put it into the net. United went beserk. It was a legal goal, but totally against accepted etiquette and the spirit of the game. Overmars was surrounded and at one stage United manager Steve Bruce looked as though he was going to call his players off the pitch. 'To be honest,' said Overmars later, 'it was just a huge misunderstanding. I was waiting for the ball to be played out again, but when I looked up I saw Kanu with the ball and ready to cross. I honestly thought that United had been given the ball back and then lost it to Kanu, and I acted instinctively when the cross came in. I just blame Kanu!' The match finished 2-1 to Arsenal, and Wenger and vice-chairman Dein immediately – and it should be said, magnanimously – offered a replay. United agreed and so did the FA, but then UEFA stepped in and attempted to block the decision, although eventually it bowed to public opinion, there was a replay and Arsenal won 2–1 thanks to goals from Bergkamp and, again, Overmars.

Derby were to prove to be no walkover in the sixth round and it took a late goal from Kanu, who had come on as substitute, to put Arsenal into a semi-final with Manchester United. Arsenal and United were emerging as the two main challengers for the league and the head-to-head at Villa Park was a tough, uncompromising affair that finished goalless and with Arsenal down to ten men after Nelson Vivas was sent off for two bookings. However, if that clash was instantly forgettable, then the replay three days later will long live in the memory of anyone who was present. Quite simply, it was a pulsating affair laced with heroes and villains from both sides. United took the lead with little more than a quarter of an hour gone. They had their sights set on a unique Treble of the FA Cup, the Premier League and the Champions League, and Beckham's strike kept them on course for that. The match was played at a frenetic pace and Arsenal equalized after 51 minutes when Bergkamp's shot was deflected in off his compatriot Jaap Stam.

The drama was only just beginning, though. Nicolas Anelka had a goal ruled out and then arch-competitor Roy Keane committed one foul too many and, having already been booked, was shown a red card. It was all pointing to an Arsenal win, but then came the defining moment, possibly in the respective seasons of both clubs. With a minute to go Phil Neville brought down Ray Parlour. Referee David Ellery had no hesitation in pointing to the spot and Dennis Bergkamp stepped up. In such circumstances you would normally put your mortgage on the Ice Man converting, but, perhaps conscious of the crucial penalty he had missed for Holland in the shoot-out against Brazil in the previous summer's World Cup semi-final, his shot, although accurate, lacked venom. Schmeichel in the United goal flung himself to his left and tipped the ball away. Now the psychological advantage was with Manchester United and they capitalized on it with one of the finest goals ever seen in the FA Cup as Ryan Giggs intercepted a wayward pass from Patrick Vieira, went on a mazy run that took him past Vieira, Lee Dixon, Martin Keown and then Dixon again to fire past David Seaman. Arsenal went close to an equalizer from Tony Adams who headed wide at the far post, but United won – and there was no question that the fall-out would be severe.

'I am convinced,' Arsène Wenger subsequently said, 'that the season for us was decided at that match. If we had won the semi-final, we would also have won the league. Of that I am certain.' The dressing room was morgue-like. 'No one said a word,' said Dixon. 'It was eerie. No noise, just a lot of disappointment.' And no one felt it more than Bergkamp. He could not be consoled and Overmars came out afterwards to speak on his behalf. 'Dennis will recover, you can be sure of that,' he said, while standing in the car park at Villa Park waiting to get on the team coach. 'He is a very strong person. I know him and I know he will come through this moment. He did it after he missed against Brazil. Just look – he has had a fantastic season. He will do it again. I know him and I know he has character.' Vieira was also devastated. 'All the hard work we put in and I gave the ball away to Giggs. I feel terrible.' It was Adams the leader who then came to the fore, telling Vieira that he was one of the main reasons Arsenal had done so well in the first place and not to forget that. He similarly encouraged Bergkamp, but the momentum of the season was now with United.

Arsenal were to push them close, responding to the setback by hammering Wimbledon 5-1 at Highbury and then tearing Middlesbrough apart on their own turf by 6-1. It was Nicolas Anelka who struck to see off the challenge of Derby and a memorable exhibition of skill from Kanu was the highlight of a 3-1 win at Tottenham. With United also on a winning streak it was vital that Arsenal won at Leeds, who were by then managed by Arsenal old boy David O'Leary. The Irishman gave notice of what Arsenal could expect when he said, 'This is a big game for us. We are not dreaming about our summer holidays just yet. I would never let the players thinks that way.' And nor did he on the night. Seaman was called on early to save a penalty from Jimmy Floyd Hasselbaink and the omens looked good. 'When he saved that I thought they were going to win,' said Hasselbaink afterwards, but Arsenal could not get past Nigel Martyn and the game was decided by a late and necessary re-shuffle of the Arsenal defence. The combative Winterburn was taken off and replaced by Nelson Vivas. The Argentinian may have been versatile, but left back was not his favoured role and late in the game he was missing as a cross went to the far post and Hasselbaink forced the ball over the line. Now all United had to do was beat Tottenham and the title was theirs, no matter what Arsenal did against Aston Villa at Highbury. For 90 minutes Arsenal fans did the unforgiveable and supported Tottenham. There were even chants of 'Come on you Spurs' from the Clock End when news filtered through of a Les Ferdinand goal, but while Kanu scored the winner for Arsenal, Tottenham wilted as first David Beckham and then Andy Cole scored the goals that gave the Premier League to United, who also went on to win both the FA Cup, the European Cup and the coveted Treble.

Anelka leaves and Henry arrives

In his time at Arsenal Nicolas Anelka was given the nickname 'L'Enfant Terrible' (literally the Terrible Child) and characterized as moody, sulky and a difficult individual to deal with. In reality he was probably just shy, but he was certainly strong-minded. Stories had linked him with the likes of Juventus and Lazio, but there was only one club that Anelka wanted to join. Explaining his reasons for wanting to leave Arsenal, he said, 'When I was a kid growing up in Elancourt [a dormitory town some 15 miles from Paris] I had one dream – to play for Real Madrid. I loved everything about the club. I loved the way they played football, I loved the name and I even loved the all-white kit... I know they want to sign me and there is nowhere else I want to go. It is as simple as that. I have loved my time at Arsenal, but now I know I have this opportunity I want to move.'

For Arsenal it was a smart piece of business in that Real offered substantially more than the £500,000 the Club had paid for him, so Anelka fulfilled his dream and went to Madrid, but Wenger rarely lets anyone leave the Club unless he has a replacement in his sights and he saw Thierry Henry as the perfect man to take over. Henry had not enjoyed a fruitful spell at Juventus, the club he had joined after the World Cup. In fact, his form had been so poor that his place in the French squad had been taken, ironically, by Anelka, but Wenger believed that Henry had more to his game than the ability to play wide, the role he had been assigned by the Italians. He saw a striker in the making.

To further bolster his squad, ahead of the UEFA deadline for the first round of Champions League and UEFA Cup games Wenger moved for Croatian striker Davor Suker and he saw the two captures as a statement of intent. 'We have given ourselves the experience of a player like Suker and the promise of a young man like Henry,' he said. ' Our ambition is there for everyone to see.' There were other new faces, too, as Oleg Luzhny arrived from Dynamo Kiev and Wenger secured long-term cover in the left back role by signing Brazilian full back Silvinho, but it was Henry who was to emerge as the star. So impressive was his form that he regained his place in the French team and was to be the star of the European Championships that were jointly hosted by Belgium and Holland at the end of the season. Indeed, he was named player of the tournament, but that accolade seemed a lifetime away in his early games for Arsenal.

His confidence had been dealt a blow in Italy and it was the supreme man-management skills of Wenger that helped him regain his self-belief and, by the following May, blossom into one of the most feared strikers in the country. 'Arsène Wenger has revolutionized the Club and its structures,' he said. ' I am happy with my life in London and I love Arsenal. Most of all I am happy working with Arsène Wenger. I owe him so much.' Henry proved to be both likeable and intelligent. He arrived with just a smattering of schoolboy English, but was comfortable enough with his adopted language to give interviews in English within six weeks. 'What I love about England is that no matter what your race or colour there is a chance and an opportunity for everyone. I love that,' he stated.

New season, new resolve

The priority for Wenger was to launch a successful start to the season. He had gone on record as saying that the time it took his team to find their form had cost them dearly in the previous campaign and a Dennis Bergkamp strike and an own-goal from Frank Sinclair ensured that the 1999/2000 league programme started with a win against Leicester. The Dutchman, along with Emmanuel Petit, was on the mark again at Derby – 'more resilient than brilliant,' said Wenger – to ensure a maximum return from the first two matches. A goalless draw at Sunderland meant that Arsenal went into their match against Manchester United with both confidence and morale high. Emmanuel Petit, one of the most influential players at the Club, hurt knee ligaments at the Stadium of Light and was sidelined for eight weeks, but all seemed well against United in the first half, which Arsenal dominated, and they were ahead at half-time with a goal from Freddie Ljungberg. Far from being a 'library', because of a reputed lack of atmosphere and passion, Highbury had been a fortress for some 20 months and Arsenal seemed unbeatable on their own patch, but Keane scored twice to end that sequence. The news was no better when, after beating Bradford City, Arsenal went to Liverpool and lost 2–0. Already United were six points clear in a head-to-head contest that would dominate the forthcoming years. 'I don't think it is possible for a team to lose more than four games a season and win the league,' said Wenger.

Two defeats had already been registered and Henry, despite the lethal-looking link-up with Bergkamp, still had to score. 'I have to get fitter and find my best form,' he said. 'I still haven't adjusted to the English Premier League and to a different style of football. That takes time.'

Arsenal had opted to continue with the strategy of playing Champions League group stage games at Wembley, but the stadium could not replicate the buzz and atmosphere of Highbury. As Ken Friar, the managing director at the time, said, 'We had no choice, because of the restrictions we had at Highbury and its reduced capacity, but Wembley was difficult. Yes, we would get 70,000 people coming along, but there were still around 10,000 empty seats and at Wembley those spaces can look vast.' Arsenal built up to their Champions League programme with a home game with Aston Villa. The Croatian Suker scored twice and Kanu completed the scoring. Then came the first European clash with Fiorentina in Italy. Bergkamp had made the trip by a car, a source of immense fascination to the Italian media, who bombarded Wenger with a series of questions about the journey: what sort of car was it, how many times did he stop for petrol, how many miles did he drive and how fast was he going? Arsenal, as they did in Lens the previous year, should have started with an away win. With ten minutes left, Arsenal were awarded a penalty that was taken by Kanu. However, goalkeeper Francesco Toldo pulled off a stunning save and Arsenal came back with one point instead of three. However four days later, there was cause for both celebration and relief as Arsenal went to Southampton in the league. The match was goalless until Henry came on as substitute to score the winning goal.

Europe was back on the agenda during the following midweek and Swedish club AIK Solna came to Wembley. In truth they were never going to be the strongest team Arsenal had ever met in Europe and they were beaten 3–1. Ljungberg opened the scoring for Arsenal only to see Kristir Nordin hit the equalizer. It had all the hallmarks of another night of frustration for Arsenal until Wenger's team delivered two body blows as first Henry and then Suker scored in quick succession. Just like the season before Arsenal had four points from their first two games, but top of the group were Barcelona and it was to Catalunya that Arsenal went next in their European campaign.

Kanu scored the goal at Highbury that brought Watford's stubborn resistance to an end as Arsenal kept up the pressure on Manchester United at the top, but they traveled to Spain without the injured David Seaman and Emmanuel Petit. Again Bergkamp made the journey overland and was in the starting line-up, but the first half didn't go well as Barcelona - 'technically perfect in the first 45 minutes,' according to Wenger - led 1-0. The scoreline was still the same when, with 15 minutes left, Wenger decided to make his change. Off came Ray Parlour and Bergkamp and they were replaced by Thierry Henry and Davor Suker. The Croatian's previous affiliation to Real Madrid prompted fierce barracking from the Nou Camp crowd, but he kept his cool and was, in fact, instrumental in the late equalizer scored by Kanu when his shot after a mazy run was only parried out to the Nigerian. Arsenal finished with ten men, though, after the usually placid Gilles Grimandi was sent off for violent conduct, but Wenger felt confident. 'The two most difficult away games, in Florence and in Barcelona, are out of the way now and we have got draws in both. Now we have Barcelona at Wembley and everything is in our hands.'

Unfortunately, both Barcelona and Fiorentina looked more at home at Wembley than Arsenal. Barcelona won 4-2, benefiting from a highly dubious penalty, awarded when Dutchman Phillip Cocu jumped into Adams. Arsenal were reeling after this setback and worse was to come when Gabriel Batistuta scored to secure a win for Fiorentina a week later. Arsenal finished their group games with a meaningless 3-2 win in Sweden, having already been assured of third place. 'We will never feel as at home at Wembley as we do at Highbury,' admitted Wenger. 'It is a psychological thing.' He was, however, to get his wish and see European football at Highbury as UEFA had introduced a system whereby the teams that finished third in the groups would move into the UEFA Cup and Arsenal decided that, in a competition with a lower profile, they would go back to their home ground.

Vieira was part of the team that convincingly beat Everton 4-1 with strikes from Suker, who scored twice, Dixon and Kanu, but as a result of a spitting incident involving Neil Ruddock at the West Ham game he was suspended for the clash with Chelsea at Stamford Bridge. It was to be an afternoon of high drama. The defeat against Barcelona clearly weighing on their minds, with less than an hour gone Arsenal were two goals down, despite playing impressively. Chelsea, looking very strong under the management of Gianluca Vialli, had yet to concede a goal at home and it looked as though that record would be extended. Then, in 15 mesmeric minutes, Kanu turned the game on its head. His goal in the 75th minute looked to be nothing more than a consolation, but with six minutes left he equalized – and he hadn't finished yet. In added time he found himself chasing a ball to the left-hand corner flag. The ball had held up on the rain-sodden turf and that caused a problem for Chelsea goalkeeper Ed de Goey. He had committed himself, was wrong-footed by Kanu's magnificent footwork and could only watch as the Nigerian curled the ball into the net from an impossible angle. 'I was never going to cross the ball,' said Kanu. 'After I beat the goalkeeper my mind was concentrated on one thing – how to score. It was 2–2 and there were just seconds left. It was what I had to do.'

However, the sequence of results that followed summed up Arsenal's season. The win at Chelsea put Arsenal second in the league behind Leeds, but when Newcastle came to Highbury the match finished goalless. The North London derby was, as ever, a feisty affair and there was plenty of controversy. Tottenham won 2–1 and Arsenal had two players sent off. Ljungberg went after a clash with Justin Edinburgh, referee David Elleray insisting that the Swede had used his head against the Tottenham defender, and Martin Keown later joined him after collecting two yellow cards. Wenger is alert in these situations and before he went to the post-match press conference he checked a video replay of the Ljungberg incident. It revealed that Edinburgh had indeed been hit on the head, but by an object thrown from the crowd and aimed at Ljungberg. 'One hundred per cent I will punish Ljungberg if he did use his head,' said Wenger afterwards, knowing full well that the evidence would support his player.

Arsenal responded with a 5–1 win against Middlesbrough, with two goals from Bergkamp and a hat-trick from Marc Overmars. It was the perfect preparation for the start of the UEFA Cup campaign. Nantes, regarded as one of the leading French clubs, were soundly beaten 3–0 at Highbury. Again Bergkamp and Overmars scored, as did Nigel Winterburn. Two weeks later Gilles Grimandi, Thierry Henry and

Overmars scored in a 3–3 draw in the second leg, which was enough to secure participation in the later rounds of the competition in March.

This year the FA Cup had been moved forward, with the third round taking place in December rather than the usual January, and it was a competition that the holders would miss, because Manchester United had agreed to play in the Club World Championship in Brazil and were exempted. Blackpool were easily beaten 3–1 in a month when Arsenal collected ten points from a possible 12 – a run in which the highlight was a 2–0 win over Leeds at Highbury with goals from Ljungberg and Petit. At the beginning of the month at Leicester Matthew Upson had been given his chance at centre back and, although Arsenal won 3–0, Upson damaged knee ligaments and was out for the season. Leicester was also the venue for heartbreak of a different kind in January. In the fourth round of the FA Cup Arsenal had drawn 0–0 with the Foxes at Highbury. The replay went into extra-time and still there was deadlock, but Martin O'Neill's team emerged as 6–5 winners in the penalty shoot-out. A war of words came afterwards. 'Leicester did not want to come out try to win the game,' said Wenger. 'They played for penalties.' O'Neill was brusque in his reply. 'Rubbish... total complete and utter rubbish.' Whatever the recriminations, Arsenal were out of the FA Cup and following their pre-Christmas League Cup exit to Middlesbrough the targets were now the Premier League and UEFA Cup.

Over December and into January form in the league had given grounds for genuine optimism. A draw against Sheffield Wednesday and a convincing 4–1 win over Sunderland had left Arsenal in third place and at the end of January they went to Old Trafford. It was suggested that they would be able to capitalize on United's weariness after their exertions in Brazil, but Wenger wouldn't hear of it. 'I only think about Arsenal, not any other teams,' he said. 'We have 39 points from 20 games and that is not bad, not bad at all, but we are conceding too many goals and we have to work harder defensively.' In Manchester Ljungberg gave Arsenal an early lead and Henry missed openings that would have added to that lead. The price for those wasted opportunities was paid 15 minutes from time when Teddy Sheringham equalized. Wenger, deprived of several established players, was upbeat rather than despondent. 'I have to give credit to the team,' he said. 'Our target was to show how strong our spirit was and the draw was fair.'

However, a major setback was on the horizon at Valley Parade when Arsenal were muscled out of the match against Bradford City. Henry scored a belter, but Dean Saunders stunned Arsenal with the winner. Now Arsenal had to beat Liverpool at Highbury, but they lost 1-0. The importance of the defeat was not lost on Vieira. 'We have to be careful now, very careful,' he said. 'We have overcome many problems this season and we are still in two trophies, but unless we start winning again we could end up with nothing.' They did beat Southampton and then came the chance to extend their run in the UEFA Cup.

European opposition again

Deportivo La Coruna of Spain were the opposition and they were blown away. Arsenal won 5-1, with goals from Lee Dixon and Thierry Henry before half-time. Deportivo pulled a goal back with a penalty from Djalminha, but any worries that Arsenal would wilt ended when the same player was shown a red card following a clash with Gilles Grimandi, and two more goals from Henry and another from Kanu sealed the win.

A league game at Aston Villa was next on the agenda and it was to be a flashpoint for Emmanuel Petit. The match was an uneventful one, with Lee Dixon scoring for Arsenal in a 1-1 draw. However, as Petit made his way to the bench after he was taken off, he was goaded by some Villa fans sitting behind the dug out. He responded with an obscene gesture and was pilloried for it. He was unrepentant afterwards. 'To be honest, why should I apologise? I am tired of the racism I have to put up with and why weren't the people responsible for it dealt with?' Petit was known for his off-the-wall remarks. In one press conference he said – in a serious manner – that he wished he was a dog! 'Why? Because you get fed, looked after and you have no worries.' He was later fined by the FA for the Villa incident.

A defeat at Middlesbrough now put a huge question mark against Arsenal's title ambitions, but there was always the UEFA Cup – and

Werder Bremen were the opposition. Thierry Henry and Ljungberg gave Arsenal a first-leg lead and the second leg belonged to Parlour. He scored a hat-trick, with Henry also on the mark again in a 4–2 win, but the gloss was taken off by a red card shown to Henry for what seemed to be an innocuous tackle. Henry would miss the first leg of the semi-final against Lens, but despite his absence Arsenal won 1–0 with a Bergkamp goal at Highbury, and a European final place was clinched with a thoroughly professional 2–1 win in the second leg thanks to goals from Kanu and the returning Henry.

The final, however, was as much about affairs off the pitch as it was matters on it. The venue was Copenhagen and the opposition was provided by Galatasaray of Turkey. They had played Leeds earlier in the competition and there had been ugly scenes in Istanbul, which had resulted in the deaths of two Leeds fans. There was talk of Leeds fans going to Denmark for revenge and on the eve of the game there were frequent skirmishes between rival fans. This both alarmed and surprised Arsenal. Their supporters had no reputation for hooliganism in Europe and there was a deep suspicion that outsiders had made their way to Copenhagen just to cause mayhem and confront the Turks. The build-up was distinctly unpleasant and on the day of the game David Dein made visits to hospitals to see supporters who had been victims of stabbings. Arsenal had come to Denmark in a confident frame of mind. They had no problem with the venue. After all, this was the city where Arsenal had won the 1994 Cup-Winners' Cup, although things were slightly different in that instead of being underdogs Arsenal were now favourites against a Galatasaray outfit that were looking to be the first Turkish team to win a major European trophy.

Adopting the same mindset as Arsenal had done six years earlier, the Turks, who weren't short of quality and had the former Tottenham star Gica Popescu in their line-up, played without pressure and looked the more composed outfit, although it was Arsenal who had the best opening when Martin Keown rampaged upfield, only to see his close range shot hit the bar. It went to extra-time and when Romanian star Gheorghe Hagi was sent off the initiative was with Arsenal, but they couldn't force a way through and Galatasaray were more than happy to go to penalties. Patrick Vieira and Davor Suker both hit the woodwork and, although Ray Parlour found the net with his effort, it was former Tottenham man Popescu who, ironically, scored the vital kick. United had steamed away with the league title and even though Arsenal's second place meant qualification for next season's Champions League, the Club had finished 1999/2000 with nothing and Wenger would be active in the transfer market in that summer.

Out with the old, in with the new

There were going to be major changes and that meant the departure of several players who had contributed so much to the Club. After 13 years at Highbury Nigel Winterburn was finding himself an increasingly peripheral figure and he left to go to West Ham. Wenger, though, had Silvinho and a young Ashley Cole in that left back role. Two of the big names to leave were Emmanuel Petit and Marc Overmars. Both wanted a fresh challenge and a deal was agreed with Barcelona for the two of them, but into Arsenal came Cameroon international Lauren from Real Mallorca. He was to prove a huge asset over the years and Wenger once said, 'You know when I look back Lauren has to be one of my best ever signings. I signed three players, not one, when I bought him. A great professional.'

Wenger had three other targets in his sights – two from the French squad that had won Euro 2000 and a Brazilian from Corinthians. The first pair were duly signed when Robert Pires came from Marseille and Sylvain Wiltord, after long and hard negotiations, arrived from Bordeaux, but the Brazilian Edu was delayed until the following January due to a passport problem. Both Pires and Wiltord were to excel, to the surprise of many. Pires, in particular, was regarded as something of a 'butterfly' player, someone who looked great, but had no substance. The Arsenal training routine and the rigours of the English season were to change that. 'Of course, it was hard at first, it really was,' he said. 'There were tackles that didn't even bring a free-kick that would have been a red card in France, but this league toughened me and made me a much better, much more complete player. Initially, everytime I went down I was sworn at and called a 'tricheur', a cheat. That wasn't the case. And Highbury was incredible. The other French players, like Patrick, Thierry and Manu Petit, had told me what a wonderful place it was, but until I saw it I didn't believe it.'

It looked a formidable enough squad, but the start was not a good one. On the season's opening day Vieira was sent off for throwing an arm at Sunderland player Darren Williams. Arsenal were already trailing to a goal from former Gunner Niall Quinn and even Sunderland manager Peter Reid sympathized with Vieira, but if Wenger thought he had problems at Sunderland there was worse to come. Arsenal were at home to Liverpool, and goals from Lauren and Henry should have been a source of relief for Wenger. Instead he was fearful for the future of Patrick Vieira, who had been sent off for the second time in a matter of days. 'Maybe after what happened at Sunderland, this will prove to be too much,' said Wenger and from Barcelona Petit commented, 'I think Patrick may now leave. I saw the second booking and it wasn't even a foul.' Vieira stayed and was outstanding as Arsenal beat Charlton 5–3. Even through Vieira's suspension, Arsenal stayed on the heels of Manchester United and a stunning volley from Thierry Henry was enough to beat United in October. 'I was a bit down because I had not scored for seven weeks,' said the striker. It was an important result, because there was a big gap between us and United last season, but we can't base the whole season on beating Manchester United.'

At home at Highbury

With the redevelopment of Wembley, Highbury was needed to stage Champions League matches and the difference was immediate. 'We just felt at home,' said Bergkamp. 'It was different at Wembley. Now we are where we belong.' Arsenal started their European campaign with a win in the Czech Republic against Sparta Prague, with Silvinho scoring the goal. It was a bloodless victory, but in the first home game, against Shakhtar Donetsk from the Ukraine, there was genuine drama.

The visitors were two up in the first half hour, but Sylvain Wiltord pulled one back just before half-time. Despite incessant pressure, the scoreline stayed the same until the last five minutes, when Martin Keown became an unlikely hero and gave Arsenal victory. 'We always thought Martin would be a threat to them in the air,' said Wenger.

The manager also knew that Arsenal were benefiting from the experience of previous Champions League campaigns. 'These are top, top teams that we are playing,' he said. Next up were Lazio of Rome, who were now managed by Sven Goran Eriksson. He was mightily impressed as a Dennis Bergkamp-inspired Arsenal won 2–0 with two goals from Freddie Ljungberg. 'They could win the Champions League,' declared Eriksson. 'Technically and physically, they are very strong.' Ahead of the return match in Rome Robert Pires was a touch concerned – with good cause it would appear. 'Have I ever played in Rome before? Yes, once. It was with Marseille and we lost 6–1. Let's hope it goes better this time!' It did. Bergkamp didn't travel, but Arsenal still looked accomplished and, thanks to a goal from Pires, secured a 1–1 draw. Another issue dominated the post-match headlines though, as Vieira claimed he had been subjected to horrendous racist abuse from Lazio's Sinisa Mihajlovic, who was later forced to issue a public apology. 'He called me all the names you can imagine and some more,' said Vieira on the return journey, but he got his apology and Arsenal guaranteed their place in the next round.

Indeed, Arsenal clinched the top place in the group with a resounding 4–2 win over Sparta Prague with Dixon, Parlour, Lauren and Pires scoring the goals. Wenger sent a shadow team to Donetsk for the match that completed the programme and those who went could consider they drew the short straw. Travelling media were advised to bring sleeping bags and their own food, while Arsenal took their own chef, Rob Fagg, and their own food. It was 4–1 to the Ukrainians on a windswept, cold night.

However, there was sad news to come from Arsenal at the beginning of November when George Armstrong, a member of the 1971 Double-winning side and reserve team coach, died suddenly of a brain haemorrhage. 'It was a great shock. He always looked so fit,' said Wenger. Clearly the team were affected and they lost 2–1 to Ipswich at Highbury in the League Cup. On such a sad night, the result seemed unimportant.

'It has been a very difficult night, because most of the players had worked with George for many years,' he added.

The League Cup has never been high on Wenger's list of priorities, but the Premier League is and Arsenal were falling behind. They went into December on the back of impressive wins against Southampton away and Newcastle at home, but were hammered 4–0 at Liverpool. Their response was to beat Leicester 6–1, but they then drew at home to Sunderland and Chelsea, and away at Leicester, and lost at Charlton on New Year's Day. Four games without a win was only allowing Manchester United to assert their dominance, but Wenger stressed that the title race was not over. 'Manchester United keep on winning, but we are not going to surrender the title at this stage of the season,' he said.

The FA Cup was to be one potential road to success and it could not have started in more contrasting surroundings than the ones Arsenal were used to in the Premier League and Europe – the Club were drawn away to Carlisle, where Sylvain Wiltord scored the winner. In the fourth round came a resounding 6–0 win at Queens Park Rangers, where two own goals and strikes from Pires, Bergkamp and two from Wiltord saw Arsenal reach the fifth round to play Chelsea. Wiltord was becoming the FA Cup talisman as he scored two more and, with another from Henry, Arsenal reached the quarter-finals to face Blackburn at Highbury. Wiltord was on the scoresheet again, along with Adams and Pires, and Arsenal was set to meet Tottenham in a semi-final at Old Trafford. However, the run-up to the game was overshadowed by the tragic death of former Arsenal player David Rocastle, at the age of 33. His passing was marked by a minute's silence ahead of the league game against Tottenham and the silence was impeccably observed by the fans of both clubs. Arsenal won that game 2–0, but in the FA Cup there was the potential for a different outcome.

There were two talking points going into the cup clash. First, Old Trafford was queried because of the distance that the two sets of London fans had to travel, but the stadium's capacity was the only one that could come close to satisfying the demand for tickets. Secondly, Tottenham had a new manager, as George Graham had been ousted after the FA Cup quarter-final win against West Ham and replaced by Glenn Hoddle. It seemed as though it would be the dream homecoming for Hoddle as

Gary Doherty put Tottenham ahead, but after Vieira equalized Arsenal was the team in the ascendancy and it was Pires who scored the winner in the 79th minute. 'We did it the hard way, because we were creating chance after chance,' said Wenger. 'Unfortunately we also missed chance after chance.' At the Millennium Stadium in Cardiff, the temporary new home of the FA Cup final, Arsenal would meet Liverpool.

In the league Arsenal were 13 points behind Manchester United and the day they went to Old Trafford was the day the title race was over. United won 6–1 and it was 5–1 at half-time. The dressing room talk at the interval was one of the few times that Wenger has ripped into his players. 'Everything went wrong for us today,' said Wenger. Sir Alex Ferguson said, 'We are now 18 points ahead and with our goal difference it will make it impossible for them to catch us.'

There was still Europe, though. The second group stage didn't start especially well as Arsenal travelled to Moscow to take on Spartak. With the time difference, Arsenal trained late at the stadium and looked out of sorts during the game. Even after Silvinho gave Arsenal the lead they still had problems, particularly with the treacherous pitch, and they eventually lost 4–1. 'This is a difficult period for us,' admitted Wenger, but he still believed Arsenal could progress and his optimism seemed well-founded as Arsenal took a 2–0 lead inside an hour at Highbury against Bayern Munich, with goals from Henry and Kanu. It was Bayern, though, who showed the resilience as Tarnat and Scholl scored to give the Germans a draw.

However, against Lyon Henry silenced a passionate French crowd with the winning goals and Bergkamp scored at Highbury in a 1–1 draw, with Edmilson scoring for Lyon. Now Arsenal had to beat Spartak Moscow at Highbury, although they left it late, Henry winning the match in the 82nd minute. It was now down to the last game. Elber scored the only goal of the game for Bayern and then Arsenal were sweating on the result from Moscow where Spartak were playing Lyon. If Lyon failed to win, Arsenal were through. The match in Munich finished four minutes earlier than the one in Moscow and Wenger was left sweating on the result. 'Those four minutes seemed like 90!' he said, but the match was a draw and Arsenal advanced to the quarter-final where they would play Valencia, with the first leg at Highbury.

The Spanish team were ahead a half-time, but Arsenal hit back and after Henry equalized Ray Parlour hit the winner. 'Again we failed to take our chances,' said Wenger, but the task in the Mestalla Stadium would be difficult. 'I have played there with France,' said Robert Pires, 'and the atmosphere is very hot.' So it proved. A 1–0 win would take Valencia through and for 75 minutes Arsenal held out until Norwegian John Carew climbed above Adams to score.

In order to ensure a Champions League place Arsenal now refocused their attention on the league, but a 3–0 home defeat to relegation-threatened Middlesbrough, which included own goals from Silvinho and Edu, didn't bode well. However, wins over Everton and Derby meant that a victory over Leeds at Highbury would ensure Champions League football for the following season. Ljungberg and Wiltord scored the goals and Arsenal won 2–1. Arsenal did need a point from their last two matches to finish runners-up and avoid the inconvenience of the Champions League qualifying rounds, but fortunately that was secured in a goalless draw at Newcastle.

Another cup final and a shock signing

Now there was the excitement and tension of an FA Cup final against Liverpool. With the League Cup already won and the UEFA Cup final to come, Liverpool under Gerard Houllier were evolving into a team of knock-out specialists. On the day the game proved deeply frustrating for Arsenal fans. Henry was denied what he thought was a clear penalty when Stephane Henchoz handled his shot on the line, and chance after chance went begging. After 72 minutes Ljungberg made the breakthrough and it looked as though Arsenal's season would have some tangible reward after all, but Michael Owen drove home a Gary McAllister cross that Arsenal failed to clear and equality was restored. 'The problem was that we seemed to forget we were still level,' said Wenger. 'We reacted like we had gone behind after having so much of the game and we pushed too many men forward to get the second goal.' That approach creates space, which is the last luxury you want to afford a player Owen, who chased a long clearance, outran Lee Dixon and slotted the ball past David Seaman for the winner. 'The match was a little bit like our season,' said Wenger. 'We look like we should win, but we cannot finish.' To remedy that, Henry suggested Arsenal needed an out-and-out predator or, as he put it 'a fox in the box'.

Come summer 2001 Wenger appeared to have solved the 'fox in the box' conundrum by signing Francis Jeffers, a 20-year-old striker with a growing reputation, from Everton. Then from Glasgow Rangers came Giovanni van Bronckhorst, a man equally at home at full back or in midfield. Goalkeeper Richard Wright joined from Ipswich and finally there was the transfer that stunned football when Sol Campbell joined Arsenal from Tottenham. Other players had made the move between the two clubs before, but no one with the profile of Campbell. A string of clubs on the continent had wanted him, as well as Liverpool, but, said the former Tottenham captain, who left White Hart Lane on a Bosman free transfer, 'I chose Arsenal for football reasons. I felt this was the place to be.' Campbell seemed somewhat taken aback by the venomous reaction to his move. His effigy was hung from a lamppost and the hate mail was abundant, but among the letters were some which, while they didn't support the fact that he was now playing for Arsenal, sympathized with his decision.

A regular defensive partner for Campbell would be Ashley Cole. He had already been penciled in by England manager Sven Goran Eriksson as the England left back of the future and had established himself at Arsenal. He was quick, dynamic and had an eye for a goal from his upbringing as a left winger. Defensively he was occasionally found wanting, but he was emerging as one the best left backs around. 'I have been here since I was 11,' said Cole. 'It is such a fantastic feeling to be part of the first team.'

The indications were that 2001/02 would indeed be a season for Arsenal to remember when they started with a 4–0 win at Middlesbrough with Henry, Pires and Bergkamp scoring, the latter twice. Not so impressive was the first midweek game against Leeds at Highbury, when Arsenal lost 2–1. 'We have to learn to be consistent,' said Wenger. 'If we are going to achieve anything this season, we have got to get that right.' The response was immediate as Leicester were beaten 4–0 and then the team went into an international break which featured England's 5–1 triumph against Germany in Munich. The return to the domestic programme brought a 1-1 draw at Chelsea with Henry scoring and then came the start of the European campaign, away to Real Mallorca.

The date of the game was 11 September, the day when terrorists flew planes into the Twin Towers in New York and the Pentagon in Washington. The horror had unfolded live on television and there was talk of UEFA cancelling all matches as a remark of respect to the thousands who had lost their lives in the atrocity. There was also the possibility that all flights in and out of London would be blocked as Britain could be the next target for the terrorists. However, after discussions with UEFA it was decided that the game should go ahead, but the atmosphere that night was unreal. The events of the day had affected everyone and the teams didn't do much more than go through the motions. Ashley Cole was sent off after giving away a penalty, but when asked about the incident afterwards he didn't rant or rave, aware that across the Atlantic there were hundreds of families who had genuine causes for grievance. Arsenal lost 1-0, but it didn't seem at all important. It was a more normal atmosphere eight days later, though, when Arsenal beat German team Schalke 3-2 with two goals from Henry and another from Ljungberg.

In the league Arsenal were to remain unbeaten until October, when Charlton won 4-2 at Highbury, but they kept their sights on the title, even though they had a frustrating European night in Athens, losing 1-0 to Panathinaikos. It was a reasonably open game until the Greeks scored, but then they rolled over injured and stopped play at regular intervals, much to Arsenal's frustration. Henry was particularly incensed with the tactics. 'Be there for the second leg,' he said afterwards. 'Just be there. That is all I am saying.' In that return match Henry took revenge with two goals and a 3-1 win over Mallorca at Highbury was enough to put Arsenal through to the second group stage, even though they lost their final game to Schalke.

Despite flurries of the inconsistency that concerned Wenger, Arsenal were able to maintain their challenge on three fronts. The League Cup run ended at Blackburn in December, but Arsenal were still within touching distance of the top of the league and there was the FA Cup to come. Campbell had to be at most dignified and focused when he went back to White Hart Lane for the first time since his controversial move and was outstanding in a 1–1 draw. 'His best performance yet for us,' said Wenger, who had even more reason to be optimistic at the end of November when Manchester United were beaten 3–1 at Highbury, with Henry capitalizing on mistakes by Fabien Barthez. The demanding matches now came thick and fast, and against Juventus in the Champions League Arsenal made up the ground they lost in defeat in Spain against Deportivo La Coruna. It was superb stuff, with Stuart Taylor in goal taking over from the injured Seaman. 'A great night, a great, great night,' said Taylor afterwards. Two goals from Ljungberg and another from Henry put Arsenal back on course for Europe.

A surprise home defeat by Newcastle in late December provoked a heated exchange between Sir Bobby Robson and Wenger. The Arsenal manager was unhappy with several decisions, including the one that gave Alan Shearer the chance to score from the penalty spot. 'There are people at this Club who have got to learn how to lose,' said Sir Bobby in response to Wenger's complaints. The Arsenal manager's reply? 'I don't want to learn how to lose' – and his team promptly went on an incredible run that would see them unbeaten until the end of the season. Nowhere did Arsenal show more guts and guile than in a 2–1 win at championship-challenging Liverpool. The odds were against Arsenal, especially from the moment that Van Bronckhorst slipped and fell in the Liverpool area. He did not appeal for a penalty and neither did his team-mates. 'It was a fall, as simple as that,' said the Dutchman afterwards. 'I didn't even look round at the referee. When I did, he had a yellow card in his hand.' As it was the second one van Bronckhorst had been shown, he was off. When Arsenal did appeal, they were given a penalty when Jerzy Dudek brought down Freddie Ljungberg and Henry converted from the spot. Into the second half and Ljungberg scored a second. Liverpool pulled one back, but Arsenal held on and went second in the table. Liverpool inflicted some damage on the Arsenal title challenge with a 1–1 draw at Highbury in January, but they hurt Manchester United even more by winning at Old Trafford.

In the FA Cup, those who felt there might be an upset at Watford were to be proved wrong as Arsenal won 4–2 in the third round. In the fourth round Liverpool were beaten 1–0 with a goal from Bergkamp and then Gillingham were brushed aside 5–2. In the sixth round Arsenal drew 1–1 at St James' Park and comfortably won the replay with goals from Campbell, Pires and Bergkamp. However, there was to be a dreadful price to play, because Pires fell badly, twisted his knee ligaments and missed not only the rest of Arsenal's season but also the World Cup in the summer of 2002. The semi-final took Arsenal back to Old Trafford and an own goal secured an FA Cup final place against Chelsea. 'We did enough to win,' said Wenger. 'We deserved it.'

In Europe the fates conspired against Arsenal. A draw away to Bayer Leverkusen in mid-February courtesy of a Pires goal had illustrated just how much the Frenchman would be missed when he was struck down by the injury against Newcastle in late March. In the return fixture Arsenal won easily with Vieira, Pires, Bergkamp and Henry on the mark in a 4–1 win. A fortnight later, though, Arsenal failed to reproduce that form against Deportivo at Highbury and lost 2–0. The win ensured the Spanish club would progress and they made it clear they would not be doing Arsenal any favours in the last group game. For Arsenal to go through Arsenal had to win in Turin against a Juventus team that had already been eliminated, but Deportivo also had to beat Leverkusen. Deportivo striker Roy Makaay, though, gave a statement of intent. 'No, we won't play our strongest team,' he said. 'Why should we? We are already through.' In Turin the atmosphere was created by the few thousand Arsenal fans who had bothered to make the trip and Israeli fans who were in the city to see their team play a UEFA Cup match the following night. Wenger knew what would happen. 'As soon as the Deportivo team sheet came in,' he said. 'I knew we were out. It was a reserve team that they put out while Leverkusen were at their strongest.' He was proved right, but at least his team were still challenging for the Double.

On for the Double

In the league Sunderland were decisively beaten at Highbury with goals from Wiltord, Bergkamp and Henry. 'We needed to get over the disappointment of Europe very quickly,' said Wenger. 'The players responded exactly how I expected.' Vieira was outstanding and clearly the players were motivated by the cruel injury to the ever-popular Pires. 'I will be back next season and I will be as good as ever,' said Pires. 'It is disappointing to miss so many important games for Arsenal and, of course, the World Cup for France, but I just have to accept it.' In fact, including the result against the Wearsiders, Arsenal were to win their last seven league games of the season. A win at Charlton put them top of the table. Liverpool and Manchester United were hoping for a slip-up, but it never happened. Even when Tottenham equalized late on at Highbury in the North London derby, Arsenal responded. Ljungberg had put Arsenal ahead, but with nine minutes left David Seaman was adjudged to have fouled Gus Poyet. Teddy Sheringham duly scored from the spot. However, when Henry was brought down, up stepped Lauren to stroke home the winner.

Arsenal had a game in hand on the two north-west giants and it was another all-London affair against West Ham, but the Hammers were resolute and it was not until 13 minutes from the end that Ljungberg – who else? – broke the deadlock. Kanu added a second and now Arsenal really were in the driving seat. And then there were two, because the three-way chase for the title effectively became a two-horse race after Tottenham beat Liverpool at White Hart Lane. Now if Arsenal won at Bolton in a midweek game they would need just one win from their last two matches. Bolton were not their usual combative selves, which was just as well as before the game Arsenal lost Henry before the game to an injury, but it was over as a contest when Ljungberg maintained his incredible run and the much under-rated Wiltord added a second.

However, before Arsenal could contemplate the league there was the small matter of an FA Cup final against Chelsea at Cardiff. Intriguingly it pitted two great friends against each other in Emmanuel Petit and Patrick Vieira. Petit had gone to Stamford Bridge from Barcelona where he had grown weary of being a peripheral figure. Ahead of the clash he said, 'Myself and Patrick had some great years together at Arsenal, but he knows that friendship will be put aside in the FA Cup final. We used to give each other a hug to encourage one another before the kick-off when we played for Arsenal and France, but at Cardiff it will be handshake before and after. He will know we both have a job to do.'

When it came to his team selection for the final, Wenger generated some controversy. Richard Wright had been in goal for every game except the third round tie at Watford when Stuart Taylor had played. He had anticipated playing in the final and there was even a full-page interview with him in the match programme, but Wenger once again showed his ruthless streak. His number one was David Seaman, no question, and the England goalkeeper was duly selected for the clash. 'There is no pact or agreement to play Wright in every FA Cup game no matter what happens,' said the Arsenal manager. 'Every individual has only one agreement with the Club – to win trophies.' Wenger omitted Martin Keown, pairing Campbell and Tony Adams, in his last game in an Arsenal shirt, in central defence. 'My body can't take any more,' said Adams. 'The injuries have taken their toll. That's it.' After a goalless first half it was Ray Parlour who opened the scoring with a surging run and tremendous shot. With ten minutes to go Ljungberg left John Terry gasping with a run and turn, and curled his decisive shot past Carlo Cudicini in the Chelsea goal. The four-year barren spell was over.

However, Wenger had an even bigger prize in view – the Premier League title that Manchester United had monopolized for three years – and where better to clinch it than at Old Trafford. Sir Alex Ferguson's team were fired up and Arsenal's attack wasn't helped by an injury to Henry that kept him out, but just short of the hour Ljungberg proved to be the threat again with a shot that Fabien Barthez could only parry into the path of Wiltord. Arsenal were ahead and it stayed that way. 'The character in this side is unbelieveable,' said Wenger. 'We have not lost away from home and we have scored in every league game this season.' The last game of the season was a formality and Everton were beaten 4–3. The Double was done for the second time in four years.

Chapter Fifteen

THE INVINCIBLES

> We proved that we can battle. We showed that even when we are not at our best, we can get results

The usual suspects would once again dominate the Premier League in 2002/03. Stung by the defeat to Arsenal, both at Old Trafford and in the title race, Sir Alex Ferguson bought Rio Ferdinand from Leeds for more than £26 million, a world record for a defender, but Wenger wasn't idle either. He had watched Brazilian Gilberto Silva in action during the World Cup and decided that, with his competitive edge, he would be perfect for the English game. With the retirement of Adams, he needed defensive re-enforcements and bought Pascal Cygan from Lille. 'I want to maintain this success now,' said Wenger. 'We cannot afford to celebrate too much, because while you do that everyone else catches up.' There was one item missing from the Wenger CV at this stage in his career – a major European trophy – and ahead of the season he was uncharacteristically bullish. 'I believe we have the quality in our squad to win it one day,' he said.

The battle lines for the season were drawn during the curtain raiser to the season, the FA Community Shield at Cardiff. 'There is no such thing as a friendly game between Arsenal and Liverpool,' said Wenger, who wanted a win to give his men a psychological edge for the coming season. There was certainly an edge. The challenges were feisty to say the least, but it was Gilberto Silva who was to be the match-winner. He started the game on the bench, but came on in the second half to drive home an inch-perfect pass from Dennis Bergkamp. Wenger was thrilled by the goal from Gilberto. 'Maybe he has been surprised by the physical side of the game in England, but I am sure he will adapt.' He did, although it has to be said that Arsenal fans haven't always appreciated his contribution and only later, when he was out of action for a long spell with a persistent back problem, was Gilberto truly missed. 'What does he do?' was a frequent question ahead of that enforced break. When he was missing, the question was answered, because the midfield looked fragile without him.

Also on the field in the Community Shield was Kolo Toure, a young player from the Ivory Coast who was to establish himself as a first-team regular and future captain. He had been turned down by other European clubs, but the previous February Wenger had decided to purchase him from Ivorian club Aztec Mimosas and he made his debut for the reserves on a bitter night at Barnet's Underhill ground. On that occasion he seemed to lack direction, but he had talent and a tremendous physical presence, and he proved to be another inspired buy.

A predictable two-goal win over Birmingham launched the defence of the league title with Wiltord and Henry scoring, but there was a much sterner test a week later at Upton Park. West Ham had grown heartily sick of defeats against Arsenal and set upon Wenger's men in a vengeful mood. Joe Cole put West Ham ahead, and ten minutes into the second half the lead had been doubled. An unusually animated Wenger appeared on the touchline and urged his men to double their efforts. Henry responded with a rasping shot on the turn, but it looked to be a token effort when West Ham were awarded a penalty. However, David Seaman, in his last season at the Club, saved it, Arsenal were revived and Wiltord scored an equalizer. 'It is only a draw, but it feels like a win,' said Wenger. 'Thierry's goal was like a missile. I am sure it will be one of the goals of the season.'

Wenger makes strong claims

Arsenal built on that comeback and were to be unbeaten until 10 October and a clash with Everton at Goodison Park. Wenger had tempted fate in the pre-season by declaring that he believed his men would go through the campaign unbeaten. Those words would come back to haunt him as a 16-year-old by the name of Wayne Rooney hit the headlines. Goodison Park has traditionally been a happy hunting ground for Arsenal and there was no reason to change that view after Freddie Ljungberg gave them the lead. Under David Moyes, though, Everton were exhibiting more backbone than they had in recent seasons and they deserved the equalizer from Tomasz Radzinski. Enter Rooney – a man-boy who had the build of a boxer, the attitude of a street fighter and the skill of a truly talented player. In injury time Rooney produced a stunning 30-yard volley that dipped over a despairing Seaman. Come the post-match inquest and Wenger gave another example of how he can manipulate even the most disappointing of moments to his advantage. The media expected a tetchy Arsenal manager, who had been forced to retract his assertion that his team was unbeatable. Instead he walked into the press room and immediately said, 'I have seen today the best young footballer in the country. Wayne Rooney is exceptional.' Job done. Not a word about the pre-season boast. Brilliant. However, the aftertaste of the defeat lingered and the next game, at home to Blackburn, ended with the same scoreline.

The hunt for the Champions League title that Wenger felt would one day be Arsenal's began with a home game against Borussia Dortmund, and Ljungberg and Bergkamp scored the goals in a 2-0 win. Even better was the performance in Holland against PSV Eindhoven as

Arsenal won 4–0 with Gilberto scoring a goal inside the first minute. The Brazilian was on the mark again in Auxerre where a 1–0 win meant that Arsenal had a maximum return of points from the first three games. Champion stuff, but the French team reversed the result at Highbury with a surprise 2–1 win, although the match marked the comeback for Pires after his terrible injury. 'I can't tell you how great it was to come back,' he said. 'It was like a chill in me when I went out on to the pitch. I can't tell you how happy I am.' However, that setback was followed by another 2–1 defeat, this time in Dortmund. The winning goal, though, was a controversial one as giant Czech striker Jan Koller went down as if he'd been hit by a sniper after the slightest of touches – if any – by Seaman. 'I didn't touch him,' protested Seaman after the game and there was another setback when PSV frustrated Arsenal with a 0–0 draw at Highbury. Other results were kind, though, and Arsenal qualified for the last 16.

Back on the domestic front Arsenal chiseled out a 1–0 win at Fulham and Wenger was pleased with the resolve of his men after a difficult patch that had brought four successive defeats. 'This team will fight for its future, there is no question of that,' said the manager. The confidence was back, as Tottenham found out when they were on the wrong end of a 3–0 defeat. During the match Thierry Henry ran from the edge of his own area, brushed aside three challenges and scored past Kasey Keller. 'World class,' was the Wenger reaction. 'You need special powers and strength at this level and he has both those qualities.' The strike was later voted Goal of the Season.

A week later there was disappointment, though, when a limited Southampton side won 3–2 and the problems did not stop with the result. Sol Campbell was sent off for a professional foul and Ashley Cole was hit with a disrepute charge after he verbally blasted referee Paul Durkin at the final whistle. That meant he would be suspended for the clash with Manchester United at Old Trafford in early December. Aston Villa were beaten 3–1 and that was the score as Arsenal started the second phase of the Champions League against Roma in Italy. Henry was unstoppable that night and scored a hat-trick. Patrick Vieira said, 'He should be world footballer of the year,' but at Old Trafford Arsenal were to suffer a massive blow. The goals were debatable as Arsenal claimed that Ruud van Nistelrooy handled before opening the scoring and United's second came courtesy of a deflection off Martin Keown. There were also mutterings of an over-physical approach from United, which brought a sarcastic comment from Phil Neville. 'I think the Arsenal players have it in their contracts that you can't tackle them,' he commented. Arsenal stayed at the top of the table, but Wenger admitted, 'The title race is now open again for Manchester United, but we are still in front and it depends on us.' In December there was one more European game to come before the Champions League took a winter break and it finished goalless against Valencia at Highbury.

The setback at United did not seem to affect Arsenal's confidence, however, and they crowned an impressive sequence of results with a 3–2 win over Chelsea on New Year's Day. Oxford were easily beaten 2–0 in the FA Cup third round, but controversy came in the fourth round when Arsenal were drawn away against non-league Farnborough Town. For safety, rather than monetary reasons, both clubs wanted the game switched to Highbury, but the FA were sceptical. They suspected that Farnborough were trying to make a financial killing and Arsenal wanted to avoid the experience of a small ground, bumpy pitch and facilities that were not quite as comfortable as they were used to. However, sensing that to reject the plan would leave them open to litigation if there was a crowd safety problem, the FA relented, but they introduced a ruling that would prevent a repeat. In future, if a ground wasn't capable of staging a high-profile cup tie, then that club would be barred from the competition. Arsenal won 5–1 and the reward was a trip to Old Trafford in the fifth round.

Wenger opted to leave Thierry Henry and Dennis Bergkamp out of his starting line-up and went with Sylvain Wiltord and Francis Jeffers. It was to be an Arsenal triumph – and a day that Ryan Giggs would rather forget. With the game goalless Giggs was left with an open goal, but somehow he put the ball over the bar. Arsenal's response was a free-kick from Edu that was deflected into the net. Wiltord added a second and Arsenal had some recompense for their league defeat earlier in the season. 'It will give us confidence for the rest of the season,' insisted Wenger. Henry and Bergkamp returned for the Champions League game against Ajax, but after Wiltord put Arsenal ahead, Nigel de Jong equalized. In the return fixture in Amsterdam Arsenal were held to a goalless draw which gave the advantage to Ajax. A further European hiccup was to prove costly. Roma came to Highbury and, despite the dismissal of Francesco Totti, held on for a 1-1 draw with Vieira scoring for Arsenal. Now Arsenal needed to win in Valencia to progress and they went to the Mestalla on the back of a disappointing 2-0 defeat to Blackburn in which Martin Keown suffered a hamstring injury. It was starting to go wrong in the league and in Europe. In Valencia Arsenal's nemesis John Carew scored twice and, despite a goal from Henry, Arsenal were eliminated.

The FA Cup offers fresh hope

The FA Cup was providing salvation for the season, however, and after a 2-2 home draw with Chelsea in the sixth round Arsenal won the replay 3-1 at Stamford Bridge thanks to an own goal from John Terry and strikes from Lauren and Wiltord. The semi-final was to be against Sheffield United at Old Trafford and, not for the first time in his career, Blades' manager Neil Warnock was not a happy man. He protested that referee Graham Poll had missed a clear free-kick to his team in the build-up to the Arsenal goal scored by Ljungberg. Seaman made an incredible save to foil Paul Peschisolido, which was described by the legendary Gordon Banks as 'in the class of mine against Pele in the 1970 World Cup'.

The much-anticipated clash with Manchester United at Highbury produced, as usual, a full quota of incidents. Arsenal were 1-0 down and then 2-1 up before Ryan Giggs headed the equalizer, but it was the dismissal of Sol Campbell that was to cause the lasting debate. He would now miss the FA Cup final against Southampton after he was judged to have elbowed Ole Gunnar Solksjaer. 'It is still an open title race,' said Wenger. Not after the visit to Bolton it wasn't. Arsenal felt they were bullied out of the game. They were 2-0 up through Wiltord and Pires, and three points were there for the taking, but Bolton were fighting for their lives and refused to capitulate. Youri Djorkaeff pulled one back and then an own goal from Keown deprived Arsenal of two points. The frustration was evident on the touchline as Wenger loosened his tie and could not hide his dejection. 'It is not in our hands now,' he admitted and it was virtually beyond them a week later when Leeds won 3-2 at Highbury. That gave the title to United.

Morale was restored ahead of the FA Cup final when Cardiff opponents Southampton were thrashed 6-1 at Highbury, while Sunderland were outclassed at the Stadium of Light in a 4-0 defeat. After Pires' win the previous year, Henry picked up the Footballer of the Year trophy and the award remained at Highbury. In the FA Cup final Southampton manager Gordon Strachan adopted a more cautious policy and a drab affair finished 1-0 to Arsenal with Pires crowning his comeback with the winning goal. David Seaman said afterwards, 'We were determined to win the game after our disappointment in the league. It may not have been a great final, but we are lifting the trophy and that is all that matters.'

Fabregas comes to Highbury

Wenger needed to regroup in the summer. Seaman had gone and so had Oleg Luzhny, but the scouting system so diligently constructed by Steve Rowley paid massive dividends with the arrival of a 16-year-old called Francesc Fabregas from Barcelona. 'I had a call from my Spanish scout,' recalls Rowley. 'He told me he was at a game and there was a midfield player who was sensational, and I had to come over and see him. I had never known him so excited. The kid was Cesc.' Fabregas was not the only arrival, though, as Gael Clichy arrived from Cannes and Arsenal beat off interest from Real Madrid and Barcelona to sign Philippe Senderos from Swiss club Servette. The goalkeeping dilemma was solved with the arrival of Jens Lehmann from Borussia Dortmund. Within weeks he was settled at

Arsenal. 'The spirit is remarkable, there is such togetherness,' said Lehmann. 'It is more relaxed than Dortmund.' In another example of Wenger's spot-on judgement, during the pre-season tour of Austria he had tried Kolo Toure at centre back. Toure had the physique and the power, and if he could develop his tactical nous Wenger was convinced that he would be a huge asset to Arsenal, which is exactly what he proved to be.

At the start of the 2003/04 season the FA Community Shield at Cardiff pitted the great rivals Arsenal and Manchester United against each other – and there was no love lost between the two teams. United won it 4–3 on penalties but the talking point was the dismissal of striker Francis Jeffers after a skirmish with Phil Neville. However, this was not to be the shape of things to come and over the coming season Wenger's team would show themselves to be well nigh invincible. It started with a 2–1 win against Everton and continued with a 4–0 hammering of Middlesbrough on Teeside. Aston Villa were the next victims and Wenger, who knew that inconsistency had blighted Arsenal's title chances in previous seasons, was impressed. 'The side have shown maturity,' he said. After winning at Manchester City, Arsenal were given an early-season scare by newly promoted Portsmouth, but although Teddy Sheringham scored for Pompey, Henry equalized with a penalty. 'We proved that we can battle, ' said Wenger. 'We showed that even when we are not at our best, we can get results.'

A wake-up call was on its way, however, when the Champions League campaign was launched against Inter Milan at Highbury. Quite simply, Arsenal were torn apart by the speed of Obefemi Martins and lost 3–0, which wasn't exactly the right preparation for the next match, at Old Trafford against Manchester United. 'We will just have to stick together,' said Wenger. They did, but it was controversial game in which, certainly as far as Arsenal were concerned, Ruud van Nistelrooy was the villain of the piece. The match was goalless deep into the second half when the Dutchman seemed to engineer a sending off for Patrick Vieira. The Arsenal players were incensed – even more so in the last minute when Martin Keown was adjudged to have fouled van Nistelrooy in the area. Van Nistelrooy took the spot-kick and hammered it against the bar. At the final whistle there were ugly scenes as he was surrounded by jeering Arsenal players. It was an unedifying sight and the FA acted with fines and suspensions for players from both clubs.

Arsenal had recovered their composure by the time Newcastle came to Highbury and they won 3–2. That was followed by the second Champions League game in Russia against Lokomotiv Moscow, where the match finished 0–0. Wins at Liverpool and at home to Chelsea kept Arsenal at the top of the Premier League – the only unbeaten team in the top flight. In Europe, however, it was a different story. Once again, travel to Eastern Europe was to prove a problem as Arsenal went down 2–1 to Dynamo Kiev in the Ukraine, with the second Dynamo goal coming from a slack piece of goalkeeping by Jens Lehmann. Now they were bottom of their group. Hope of a revival came at Highbury on Guy Fawkes night. Dynamo were pushed back, but were holding out until Ashley Cole scored two minutes from time. 'That could be our most vital European goal of the season,' said Thierry Henry afterwards. It was to set up what is still regarded by many as the finest night Arsenal have enjoyed in Europe.

A famous victory in the San Siro

Arsenal had, at the very least, to win in the San Siro against Inter Milan. To match the three-goal margin that the Italians had secured at Highbury seemed beyond the realms of possibility, but Arsenal, with Henry close to unplayable, won 5–1. Vieira was missing, but strikes from Ljungberg, Edu, Pires and two from Henry clinched a remarkable win. At the end of the game Lehmann stood in the Arsenal dressing room and declared, 'I have played in Germany and I have played in Italy, but I have never come across a team spirit like there is at this Club. Never.' A 2–0 win against Lokomotiv meant that Arsenal finished top of their group.

A glimpse of the future was evident in the League Cup. Wenger's ploy of blooding youngsters was proving successful and the run this season took them to the semi-finals. In the match against Rotherham in late October, which Arsenal won 9–8 on penalties, at 16 years and 117 days Cesc Fabregas became the youngest player in the Club's history to play in a first-class game. In the next round, against Wolves, he became the youngest ever scorer. With Europe now on hold until February, Arsenal continued their impressive league form. No one could beat them. If a 1–0 was needed, that's what they got, as the results against Blackburn and Southampton showed. Draws were chiseled out at Leicester and Charlton, and when the mood took them the likes of Leeds, Middlesbrough and Wolves were beaten impressively.

Come the FA Cup and there was no sign of the successful run ending. Leeds were destroyed 4–1 at Elland Road, Middlesbrough by the same score at Highbury and Chelsea were overcome 2–1. In the sixth round Portsmouth were thrashed 5–1 at Fratton Park and Henry was in such majestic form that he was applauded off the pitch by the most passionate fans in the country. At the end of January Jose Antonio Reyes arrived from Sevilla. His time at the Club didn't exactly start in the way he would have liked, as he scored an own goal in the second leg of the League Cup semi-final at Middlesbrough, 'but he showed character to play,' said Wenger, who revealed that the Spaniard had insisted on turning out despite suffering from a virus. Reyes later came good, scoring one crucial goal in particular.

By the end of February Arsenal were nine points clear of Chelsea and Manchester United in the league, and in Europe it was also looking good. The second group stage of the Champions League had been scrapped and Arsenal were now drawn against Celta Vigo of Spain. The team line-ups had a strange look, with both sides featuring an Edu and both scoring! The Arsenal one scored early and then it was the turn of Celta's Edu to get on the scoresheet. Then, not to be outdone, Arsenal's Edu put Wenger's men back in front and, although Igancio scored a second equalizer for Celta, Robert Pires hit the winner. Off the pitch, plans for a new stadium at Ashburton Grove, a stone's throw from Highbury, had been announced and Arsenal celebrated by beating Celta 2–0 with two goals from Henry in the second leg of the tie. In the first leg of the quarter-final Arsenal secured a respectable result with a

1–1 draw at Stamford Bridge against Chelsea, but then came a difficult sequence of matches.

Arsène Wenger criticized the domestic programme that allowed an FA Cup semi-final to be played just four days before a European week. Arsenal had already drawn 1–1 with Manchester United in the league, but the timetable ahead meant they had to play United again at Villa Park on the Saturday, the second leg of a Champions League quarter-final against Chelsea in midweek and then go into the hectic Easter schedule, which started with a home game with Liverpool. At Villa Park United had already acknowledged that the title would be Arsenal's and they were in a 'no-quarter given' mood. They were highly combative, refused to let Arsenal settle and dug in for a 1–0 win with a Paul Scholes goal. Then came Chelsea and all seemed to be going well when Reyes scored just before half-time. However, Frank Lampard equalized for Chelsea five minutes into the second half and, with extra-time looming, Wayne Bridge hit Chelsea's second. The Treble had gone in a matter of a few days.

The 'Invincibles' take the prize

But the disappointment of defeat was quickly put aside as the team returned to league action. Then came a match when Henry came into his own. 'He won it for us, no question,' said Wenger. 'That was Thierry at his best.' Arsenal were 1–2 down against Liverpool at half-time and the alarmists wondered if the season was going into freefall. Henry had other ideas. Single-handedly he inspired an Arsenal come-back and they won 4–2. Suddenly the league title was Arsenal's for the taking, and it was clinched at White Hart Lane. Arsenal needed just a point, but a full haul seemed likely as Vieira and Pires scored before half-time. Even though Jamie Redknapp and Robbie Keane – from the penalty spot after a skirmish with Lehmann – rescued a draw the title was Arsenal's. Wenger said, 'We have won the title and not lost a single game in the process. That is a tremendous achievement.' The unbeaten league run, however, looked in jeopardy in the last game of the season at Highbury when Leicester led 1-0, but Henry and Vieira scored second-half goals to clinch the win. 'This is my biggest moment since I came here,' said Wenger.'

Arsenal's historic unbeaten season, the first by any top-flight club since Preston North End in 1888/89 was a magnificent achievement. 'To win the Championship is tremendous,' said Wenger, 'But to do it without losing a match... is almost beyond belief'. The league table made impressive reading as Arsenal finished 11 points clear of second-placed Chelsea. The full record was: played 38, won 26, drawn 12, lost 0. 'You win some, you draw some' said the slogans on fans' T-shirts. The 'Invincibles' tag was born.

The challenge facing Wenger now was to ensure the success continued in 2004/05 and there were changes in personnel. Out went two men who had been so much a part of the Club's glorious achievements under Wenger as Martin Keown joined Leicester and Ray Parlour went to Middlesbrough. Also gone were Giovanni van Bronckhorst, who moved to Barcelona on a permanent basis, and Francis Jeffers, who went to Charlton on loan. In came Robin van Persie, a highly individual young player from Feyenoord, and Mathieu Flamini, a hard-working central midfield player from Marseille who had helped his club to the UEFA Cup final. Manuel Almunia arrived as goalkeeping cover from Celta Vigo and there was heartening news about Patrick Vieira. He was being courted by Real Madrid and history shows that what the Spanish giants want, they usually get, but Vieira repulsed their advances. Wenger said, 'This is one of the few occasions in sport where money has played no part. We did not put any pressure on him. It was Patrick's decision alone.' There was a problem at the back, though, as Sol Campbell had returned from his break following England's Euro 2004 campaign in Portugal with an injury and he was to be absent until the end of December. There was also a new face on the Premier League scene as down at Stamford Bridge the 'Special One' had taken over at Chelsea. Jose Mourinho was to live up to his label.

However, the changes in playing staff seemed to be working in Arsenal's favour. They started the season where they had left off and won their first five league matches, including a remarkable 5–3 win over Middlesbrough, a game in which they trailed 3–1 at one stage. Up against them was Parlour who was wary of celebrating too early. 'Even when we were two goals ahead I warned the players not to take it easy for a minute,' said Parlour. 'I knew the Arsenal team, I knew how they thought and how they played. I knew they wouldn't give up.' A home draw with Bolton was regarded as a mere blip – 'frustrating because we were ahead twice,' said Arsène Wenger – but an English league record was set against Blackburn when Arsenal went 43 games unbeaten. They reached 49 with a home win against Aston Villa and the quality of the football had former Arsenal star David O'Leary, then in charge of Villa, purring with appreciation. 'For me, this is the best team there has been at Highbury,' he said. 'They are big, they are strong, they are fit and they are quick.' The magic half-century was on offer if Arsenal could avoid defeat at Old Trafford and Arsenal were not without hope.

Fabregas was emerging as one of the talents of the year and the Arsenal fans had their own song for him. To the 'Volare' tune already appropriated for Vieira they sang, 'He's only 17, he's better than Roy Keane.' The late John Lyall, rated as one of the best judges of a player, described Fabregas as, 'The most exciting young player I have seen in years. He always has time, always has space.' It had the makings of a monumental showdown at Old Trafford and so it was. The record went, but Arsenal appeared to have a genuine case for grievance. First, Ljungberg appeared to have been fouled by Rio Ferdinand when he was clear through on goal, but nothing was given and as the game looked to he heading towards a goalless draw, with just 17 minutes left United were awarded a penalty. Wayne Rooney seemed to make no contact with Sol Campbell, but he went down almost as though he had anticipated the challenge. This was also revenge time for Van Nistelrooy. Just as he had been swamped by Arsenal players celebrating his penalty miss the previous season, this time he wheeled away in a victory run as he put the ball past Jens Lehmann. In injury time Alan Smith set up Rooney for a close-range finish and the run had ended. Afterwards came the infamous Pizzagate affair when Sir Alex Ferguson was hit by a slice of pizza that apparently came from the Arsenal changing room.

Wenger could not afford to look back now. Interest in the Carling Cup had ended with a 1–0 defeat at Manchester United, and after two draws against Southampton and Crystal Palace a second successive title was looking a difficult proposition, but there was still Europe and the FA Cup. The Champions League had started with a 1-0 home win against PSV Eindhoven with an own goal from Alex, and that was followed by a 1-1 draw in Norway against Rosenberg. In Athens a 2-2 draw with Panathinaikos maintained a strong position for Arsenal, but they were disappointed to draw 1-1 at home with the Greeks in early November and achieved the same result in Holland against PSV – a match in which there were two red cards for Arsenal when Lauren and Patrick Vieira were both sent off. Any doubts that Arsenal would qualify, however, were erased when Reyes, Fabregas, Henry, Pires and van Persie were on target as Rosenberg were hammered 5-1. That secured a place in the knock-out rounds, which would come after the winter break.

The league, though, was a concern for Wenger. After the two draws, Arsenal won a pulsating North London derby 5-4 at Tottenham, but if Wenger was hoping this would herald another unbeaten run he was wrong, because Liverpool won 2-1 at Anfield in the next game. It was a defeat that would prompt Wenger to make a major change to the team and he left out Lehmann and drafted in Manuel Almunia, who would be first-choice goalkeeper until early February when he had a traumatic match against Manchester United.

Another FA Cup run

The FA Cup was kind in giving third and fourth round home draws against modest opposition in Stoke and Wolves, and when Sheffield United became the fifth-round opponents, again at Highbury, it was assumed that a quarter-final place was waiting. However, the Yorkshire team drew 1-1 at Highbury and then forced extra-time in the goalless draw replay at Bramall Lane. Arsenal went through on penalties and faced Bolton away in the last eight, where Ljungberg ensured Arsenal made it to the last four with a strike that settled the tie. At Cardiff in the semi-final Blackburn adopted a physical approach, but Arsenal stood up to the intimidation and won 3-0 with a goal from Pires and two from van Persie.

The definitive moment in the league campaign came in early February when Manchester United came to Highbury. Chelsea were emerging as favourites for the title and Arsenal needed to win to keep alive any hopes they had of catching Mourinho's team. Almunia didn't have the best of nights, though, and after United won 4–2 Lehmann regained his place in the Arsenal goal, in time, in fact, for the first leg of the European clash with Bayern Munich in Germany. Lehmann and Bayern's Oliver Kahn were competing for the number one spot in the German national team and the German media saw it as a showdown. It was Kahn who drew blood in the first leg as Bayern won 3–1. At one stage it was 3–0 to the Germans, but a late strike from Kolo Toure gave Arsenal hope. In reality, although a Thierry Henry goal in the second leg allowed the Frenchman to close in on Ian Wright's goal-scoring record for the Club, it wasn't enough to keep Arsenal in Europe.

It was down to the FA Cup and waiting for them in the final were Manchester United. Arsenal had finished their league programme with a 7–0 win over Everton in their last but one match. The last match was lost 2–1 at Birmingham, but by then all the relevant league positions had been decided – Chelsea were champions, Arsenal runners-up, Manchester United third and Everton fourth. The focus was now on Cardiff and Wenger sprung a surprise in his selection for the final. He was already without the injured Thierry Henry and it was assumed he would go for as much experience as possible, but on the eve of the game he announced to Sol Campbell that he was dropped and that the young Swiss defender Philippe Senderos would play. The manager also changed his format into a 4–5–1, although he admitted afterwards that he hated seeing his team play that way and said, 'I don't think I will be doing that again.' United had the best of the game but squandered their chances, and so it went to penalties. Lehmann heroically saved the effort from Paul Scholes and it was down to Vieira, who scored to claim another FA Cup for his team. However, it was to be his last kick of the ball in an Arsenal shirt, because he was to leave the Club that summer.

Wenger's best ever signing

When asked who his best ever signing for the Club was, Arsène Wenger answered without hesitation. 'Patrick Vieira was the best,' he said. 'As a man and as a player he contributed so much to this Club. Yes, Patrick was my best signing.' That is some accolade, especially for someone whose origins can truly be described as humble. Patrick Vieira was born in Dakar, the sprawling capital of Senegal, in a very poor area where unemployment was high, but the ethos of helping one another was strong. His mother, an ebullient woman by the name of Rose, was a single parent and their day-to-day existence was tough, but, said Vieira, 'We went short of nothing. I can never remember being hungry, ever.' However, Rose Vieira wanted a better life for Patrick and his half-brother Nikoro, so she decided to move to France to find work. Rose was soon employed and sent for her sons. Patrick was then only five. It was to be a life-changing move for Vieira, who would go on to captain Arsenal and France. 'My story shows what can be possible,' said Vieira. 'It doesn't matter if you start your life in hard surroundings. If you are brought up with the right values and if you are taught to respect other people, then you can still succeed. Everything is possible.'

Life was not a great deal easier in the dormitory town of Trappes, some 15 miles west of Paris, although the community spirit that Vieira had experienced in Dakar survived. However, chances were available for people who excelled and Vieira excelled in sport. Indeed, at the age of 16 he went to the South of France to play for Cannes. It was a move which would test his character to the limit. He was suddenly in a new environment with no family to call on for help, but the natural grit that would serve him so well in the years to come emerged. Not only did he blossom at Cannes, he was in the first team before he had reached the age of 17 – and his development caught the eye of scouts from Italy. He duly joined AC Milan, but after three years there Vieira was becoming frustrated at his lack of first-team football and the manager, one Fabio Capello, decided that he could be sold.

Favourites to sign him were Ajax and indeed he went to Holland, was shown round the club and was very close to joining them. However, his visit to Amsterdam was noted by Arsène Wenger, who was about to leave Japan and take over at Arsenal. Wenger acted immediately, managed to contact Vieira in Holland and persuaded him to come to England for talks. 'He told me that Arsenal would be perfect for me,' said Vieira, 'and that English football would suit my style of play. I also had enormous respect for him because of his reputation in France. He was known to give young players their chance, so I decided on Arsenal. It was the best decision I ever made.' So in the autumn of 1996 Arsenal signed Vieira.

Wenger knew that it would be difficult for the 20-year-old Vieira, but he was confident that Vieira had the strength of character to adjust to a new country, a new language and a new culture both on and off the field. 'Of course, it was hard at first,' Vieira recalled. 'I mean, I didn't speak any English at all, but I wanted so much to be successful. Arsène was great. I have always had trust and faith in him.' His arrival caused quite a stir. After the first training session Vieira had with his new team-mates, Adams turned round and said, 'We have a new manager and we have just signed a giant spider! He's all arms and legs.' Training has never been Vieira's forte, but the real man emerged during competitive action and he made an immediate impact. 'A great competitor, that came over straightaway,' said Adams. 'You could see in the matches just how much he wanted to be a winner and he had ability to go with his attitude. He won the players over immediately with his determination. It can't have been easy for him, not at all, but he knew he had our respect and he was very quick to pick up the language. His presence made him a natural leader in midfield.'

Not that it was all plain sailing. Vieira had what he amusingly calls 'difficult moments,' when he found out about Wenger the man manager. 'There were occasions when he would call me into his office and told me, quite strongly, that I had been out of line. He would tell me face to face what he felt and what I needed to do to make things right, but the great thing about Arsène is that what was said in his office stayed in the office. Nothing was ever repeated in public. Nothing. He would never say to the media what we had talked about. I understand there were times when he could not defend what a player had done, but he would never criticize them in front of the press, radio or television.'

The natural competitive streak in Vieira made him immensely popular with the crowd, who regaled him their version of 'Volare' – 'Vieira, oh oh. Vieira, oh oh oh oh. He comes from Senegal, he plays for Arsenal...' With Emmanuel Petit he formed, for Club and for country, one of the most formidable central midfield partnerships in Europe. One was right-footed, one was left-footed and, as Sir Alex Ferguson once said, 'For all the great football Arsenal play, those two, they don't mind a scrap, do they?' In many ways, it was the ultimate compliment.

Vieira also took it on himself to act as minder for some the less physically imposing members of the team, players such as Robert Pires. On one occasion, during a clash with Aston Villa at Highbury, Pires had an on-pitch disagreement with defender Olof Mellberg and as he walked off at half-time he was subjected to a barracking by a group of Villa players. 'My English was never good, but I did know there was a lot of shouting and it was directed at me. I also knew enough English to realize that what they were saying was not very nice!' says Pires. 'I just tried to ignore them and just walked as quick as I could up the tunnel to get to the dressing room. I didn't want to know. Suddenly it went quiet. I looked round and there was Patrick. He had seen there was a problem and had come to my assistance. Basically, he said, "That is my friend. If you take on him, you take on me." Funnily, no one among the Villa players fancied their chances, but that was Patrick. He was always there if you needed him. He would always stand up for you if he felt you were in trouble.'

That was Vieira, captain material if ever there was, so when Tony Adams decided to call it a day, Vieira was his natural successor. 'I was so, so proud when Arsène Wenger asked me to be captain of the team,' said Vieira. 'Look at the legends who have had that honour. Look at the men I have followed. I could not have even allowed myself to dream while I was growing up in Senegal that one day I would not only play for one of the most famous clubs in the world, but that I would lead them out as captain.'

However, there are other sides to the character of Vieira and behind the facade of an aggressive, powerful midfield player there is a man who cares about important issues such as racism. He had the infamous row with Sinisa Mihajlovic of Lazio during a Champions League game in Rome when the Serbian made disrespectful comments. Some black players would have turned the other cheek. Vieira is not one of those players. He spoke eloquently about the incident afterwards and Mihajlovic was forced to make a public apology for his remarks.

The other cause that is close to Vieira's heart is the academy he has set up in his homeland of Senegal, which he created because, 'I wanted to give something back to the country that gave me life.' Called the 'Instituit Diambars', which translates as the Institute of Champions, it is located in the coastal town of Saly, about 40 miles south of Dakar, and the pupils receive an academic education as well as honing their football skills. 'To me that is very important,' said Vieira. 'Senegal is not a rich country and education is not easy to get. I wanted to make sure that even if the pupils do not make the grade as footballers, the very least they would have is a good academic education. That is priceless.' The academy has been an inspiration to hundreds of youngsters in Senegal and is beginning to produce some excellent graduates.

Three empty but eventful seasons

So the 2005/06 season – and it was to be Arsenal's last at Highbury – began without Viera, who was a difficult player to replace, they also lost Edu, who had moved to Valencia on a Bosman transfer. In the league, Arsenal always seemed to be playing catch-up behind Chelsea and Manchester United and eventually finished third, while the FA Cup campaign ended in the fourth round when they lost at Bolton. In the League Cup, the youngsters did the Club proud and reached the semi-final, before losing on the away goals rule to a battle-hardened Wigan outfit.

However, in Europe Arsenal were tantalizingly close to the supreme honour in European club football. The route to Paris started at Highbury with a 2-1 win over FC Thun, but it was close. The Swiss were at 1-1 against ten men when Robin van Persie was sent off, but Dennis Bergkamp scored a late winner. A more impressive performance came against Ajax in Amsterdam when Ljungberg and Pires scored in a 2–1 victory. Then came a moment to savour in Prague. Thierry Henry was on the bench after returning from injury and was not expected to play. Jose Antonio Reyes started, but was injured after just 15 minutes. Cue Henry, who started the night one short of Ian Wright's record of 185 goals. Six minutes after coming on he was level with a stunning individual goal and then he went ahead after a mazy run that took him past a breathless Sparta defence. In the return match he scored again. 'Ian Wright is a legend – to beat his record was tremendous,' said Henry. A 1–0 win in Berne against FC Thun – 'It was so cold not even the coffee I had at half-time could warm me up!' said Robert Pires – followed by a goalless draw at home with Ajax and Arsenal were through the group stage to meet Real Madrid in the first knock-out round.

Meanwhile, Wenger had used the transfer window to sign Abou Diaby from Auxerre and Emmanuel Adebayor from Monaco, as well as teenage sensation Theo Walcott from Southampton. By the time the clash with Real came around it was clear to everyone but the most optimistic of fans that the Champions League was the one legitimate target left for the season. The Bernabeu had not been the happiest of hunting grounds for English clubs over the years, but Henry was at his magnificent best as he scored to give Arsenal a 1–0 lead from the away leg and a goalless draw at Highbury took Arsenal through to play Juventus – and Vieira – in the quarter-finals. In the first leg at Highbury Fabregas was stunning in central midfield and eclipsed Vieira by putting Arsenal ahead. Henry, who had left Juventus as a disaffected winger to blossom at Arsenal, scored the second and Arsenal were comfortable enough in the goalless second leg in Turin.

The last four beckoned and Arsenal faced the tournament's surprise team, Villarreal. Kolo Toure got the goal that gave Arsenal a first-leg lead and in the Madrigal, Villarreal's compact ground in Spain, Arsenal were comfortable enough at 0–0 until the last five minutes. The Spanish were given a penalty and up stepped Argentinian international Juan Riquelme, but Lehmann proved that not only are Germans good at taking penalties, they can also save them. He went the right way and Paris beckoned. 'Congratulations? Why congratulations?' said Lehmann afterwards. 'We are in the final, but we have won nothing yet.' However, Henry sounded a more human note, when he said, 'Just thank God for Jens!'

Before the final in Paris there was the little matter of the last game at Highbury and the emotional celebrations which closed the stadium that had been Arsenal's home since 1913. The listed Art Deco facades of the East and West Stands would remain, but the building itself would soon be demolished, to rise again as the Highbury Square residential development. Wigan, ironically on their first visit to the ground, were the opposition and it was a game on which much was resting, not least a Champions League place which Arsenal were contesting with Tottenham, who were at West Ham. Pires started the party, but Paul Scharner and David Thompson put Wigan 2-1 up. Then Henry hit a marvellous hat-trick and the joy from a 4-2 win was matched by the delight at hearing West Ham had beaten Tottenham. There was a cruel blow to Arsenal before the end of the league programme, however, as in the last minute of a 4-0 win against Sunderland at the Stadium of Light Diaby was the victim of a particularly nasty tackle that would put him out for almost a year.

And so to Paris. The omens were good. Henry, who had done so much to get Arsenal to the final, was born there and had enjoyed his greatest moment in international football there when France won the World Cup in 1998. But Barcelona ignored the omens. The problems for Arsenal started in the first half when Lehmann was sent off for bringing down Samuel Eto'o. Arsenal re-grouped and showed their character. Pires was taken off so that Almunia could take over in goal and the resolve that had brought Arsenal to the final became evident as Campbell headed them into the lead before half-time. It was still that score with 15 minutes to go – until Henrik Larsson came on as substitute for the Catalans. He laid on the equalizer for Eto'o – Wenger swears to this day it was offside – and then Juliano Belletti scored the winner with ten minutes left. 'We can be proud,' said Henry, 'but some of the refereeing decisions were horrendous.' He then opted to stay at Arsenal for four more years by signing a new contract.

A new home

As 2006/07 dawned Wenger decided that more change was necessary. He had refused to bow to requests from Pires for a longer contract than the one-year deal he was offering and the Frenchman left to join Villarreal on a Bosman. Also on his way was Sol Campbell, who, suffering from personal problems, had not returned for the second half of the match against West Ham at Highbury in February. Wenger gave him time to re-focus and he was back in the first-team squad in April, but ultimately left to join Portsmouth. With Bergkamp also retiring Wenger lost an awful lot of experience in one fell swoop. There was another high-profile departure when Ashley Cole joined Chelsea, but Arsenal were able to sign French international William Gallas from Stamford Bridge to take his place. Another new man was Czech international Tomas Rosicky who came from Borussia Dortmund, while Julio Baptista arrived at Arsenal from Real Madrid, swapping with Jose Antonio Reyes in a season-long loan deal.

This was also a season of adjustment not just in terms of personnel, but in terms of location, too, as Arsenal moved into their new Emirates Stadium, a state-of-the-art football arena with a capacity of over 60,000 at Ashburton Grove. The first game played there was Dennis Bergkamp's testimonial. Of course, the stadium was as new to the Arsenal players as it was to the opposition and some have argued that the unfamiliar stage contributed significantly to the team's disappointing season. However, it is certainly true that too many matches were drawn, including the first two, against Aston Villa and Middlesbrough. Only one team won there that season – West Ham survived a siege – and, yes, Arsenal did the double over eventual champions Manchester United, but they finished only fourth and were again faced with qualifying for the Champions League for the coming season.

The youngsters excelled in the League Cup and took a full-strength Chelsea team all the way in the final, in which Walcott scored a magnificent goal, but they were beaten 2–1 and the match was also infamous for a mass brawl which ended with Arsenal's Emmanuel Adebayor and Kolo Toure being sent off, along with John Obi Mikel.

The FA Cup run included a stunning 3-1 win at Liverpool and victory in a replay at Bolton, but Mark Hughes's well-organized battlers from Blackburn frustrated Arsenal at Emirates and then won the replay.

Again Europe looked the best bet, but Arsenal were to fall victim to the oldest mistake in the book – an attacking player who tries to be a defender. Croatia Zagreb were beaten in the qualifying round and group wins in Hamburg and at home to Porto put Arsenal in good shape to reach the knock-out rounds, but a defeat in Moscow against CSKA and a draw at home, despite pummeling the opposition, proved to be setbacks. A comfortable 2-1 win against Hamburg at Emirates meant a draw in Porto in the last game would put both teams through. It ended goalless and the well-organized PSV Eindhoven were the next opposition. The away leg was tight and the Dutch won 1-0. However, in the second leg Arsenal believed they would go through and they were content to settle for extra-time after Brazilian defender Alex scored an own-goal to level the tie. However, with two minutes left Alexander Hleb gave away a needless free-kick and Alex made amends to PSV by heading the equalizer.

The start of the 2007/08 season brought the news that fans had been dreading – Thierry Henry had gone to Barcelona – but Wenger wasted no time in bringing in re-enforcements, signing Eduardo from Zagreb and bringing in the accomplished right back Bacary Sagna from Auxerre. In fact, the season could not have got off to a better start. Sparta Prague were easily defeated in the Champions League qualifier and it was late November before Arsenal tasted defeat for the first time in Europe when they lost 3-1 in Seville, but by that time in the group stage they had already seen off not only the challenge of Seville, but also Slavia Prague and Steau Bucharest. In the first knockout round AC Milan forced a goalless draw at Emirates, but Arsenal produced arguably their best performance of the season when they won 2-0 in the San Siro to earn the right to play Liverpool in the quarter-finals. This was the kind of game to which Wenger was referring when he said, 'Big decisions did not go our way.' Arsenal drew 1-1 at home and were denied a clear penalty when Alexander Hleb was brought down by Dirk Kuyt. At Anfield no sooner had a stunning run by Walcott helped to make it 2-2, which would put Arsenal through, but then Kolo Toure was adjudged to have brought down Ryan Babel. Liverpool went ahead and then clinched a 4–2 win.

There were other season-defining moments, too. In the Carling Cup Arsenal lost 5–1 at Tottenham in the second leg of the semi-final and that did nothing for the confidence of reserve goalkeeper Lukas Fabianski. In the FA Cup Arsenal were hammered 4–0 at Manchester United and Emmanuel Eboue was sent off, but in the league, the prize that Wenger wants above all others, the match at St Andrews against Birmingham was without question a watershed in Arsenal's season. Eduardo was the victim of a poor challenge by Birmingham's Martin Taylor and suffered a horrendous injury. This clearly upset Arsenal and even though Taylor was sent off and they were playing against ten men, they never imposed themselves on the game. However, they were 2–1 ahead with a minute left when Gael Clichy was harshly judged to have given away a penalty. The match should have been beyond recall by then, but Birmingham equalized and Arsenal never recovered. They dropped valuable home points against the likes of Aston Villa and Middlesbrough, and in April lost 2–1 at Old Trafford. Emmanuel Adebayor had given them the lead, yet within minutes William Gallas was penalized for handball, Cristiano Ronaldo equalized from the spot and Owen Hargreaves clinched the points with a free-kick. 'We were so, so close,' said Wenger. 'No, I am not depressed. I believe in the potential of this group and I am certain we will have success with them.'

The harsh truth, of course, is that in the seasons 2005/06, 2006/07 and 2007/08 Arsenal won no silverware, yet those seasons have also reflected just why Arsenal remain one of the most stable clubs in the country. The rest of the Premier League may look on with envy at the success rate of Arsenal and Manchester United, but if they want to emulate that success they would do well to follow the blueprint laid down by those clubs. Directors, managing directors, chairmen and vice-chairmen may come and go, but at Emirates and Old Trafford there has been one constant – the manager. Can you, for example, imagine the managers at Juventus, AC Milan, Real Madrid or Barcelona enduring a similar dry spell and still being in a job? Indeed, at Real Fabio Capello won the Primera Liga and was immediately out of work, while Roberto Mancini won three successive Scudettos with Inter Milan and was rewarded with his P45. Arsène Wenger? He was offered a new contract, which will keep him at Emirates for another three years. 'Why would we want Arsène to go?' chairman Peter Hill-Wood has said. 'He has been a fantastic manager for this Club and we play tremendous football. We have a huge waiting list for tickets, huge. We sell out every game and look at the players Arsène has brought to the Club. World class, really world class. No, we want to keep him here as long as we can. As far as we are concerned, he can stay for as long as he likes.'

Chapter Sixteen

THE FUTURE'S BRIGHT

THE FUTURE'S BRIGHT

The move to Emirates represents a new and exciting phase in Arsenal's history

Ken Friar started out making the tea and opening the mail as a 15-year-old office boy at Highbury. Danny Fiszman first stood at the Clock End and marveled at the skills of Danny Clapton when he was just ten. Both have a deep bond with Arsenal, and in particular with Highbury, so it is appropriate that the pair were the masterminds behind the Club's move from its historic home to the new £350,000 million Emirates Stadium.

Arsenal had always known that, ultimately, Highbury couldn't satisfy the Club's needs. 'Back in 1970 there was talk of us going in with Tottenham to build a new ground,' says Friar, 'but the discussions about this relocation began back in 1998.' Those discussions were prompted by Arsenal's participation in the Champions League and the fact that the restrictions imposed by UEFA's advertising obligations meant the ground's capacity was reduced to 35,000 for European matches. A decision was taken to move to Wembley for the home games, but, concedes Friar, 'You can't really say that was successful for us. There were 70,000 people there, but the stadium held many more than that. It was not conducive to the atmosphere. It meant every match was like an away match.'

The search for a site began. At one stage Arsenal considered buying Wembley, although pressure from within the FA prompted a rethink, and there was the possibility of developing Hendon aerodrome, an area at Finsbury Park and another at Kings Cross. Finally, the Club found Ashburton Grove, less than a mile from Highbury. 'We were shown the triangle of land where we are now and we decided to have a go at it, although it turned out to be a much bigger scheme than anybody visualized and, with hindsight, I'm not sure we would have done it if we'd known what we were going to face,' says Friar.

An ambitious project

Just to give an idea of what Arsenal had to accomplish before they could even start work on developing the 60-acre site at Ashburton Grove, although some of it had lain derelict for 25 years, the area also featured a light industrial estate with 120 small businesses, a waste transfer station, 2,500 apartments and a health centre. Talks had to be held with Islington Council, the owners and tenants of the properties, Network Rail and even Sainsbury's, who had an interest in the land. There was inevitably opposition to the planned move and objectors made their feelings clear at public meetings, but their concerns were addressed and Friar is convinced that the vast majority of Arsenal fans backed the move. 'We had no letters saying that what we were doing was ridiculous and that we should stay at Highbury – not one,' he says.

Logistically, the building of the new stadium and the evacuation from Highbury was a demanding project. For example, the Club discovered it had to deal with Japanese knot weed, the incredibly invasive plant that can destroy the foundations of buildings. 'I'd never even heard of the stuff, but apparently all builders know about it,' says Friar, 'and it was growing at Ashburton Grove. Someone called the local authority and development work had to stop for a while. One man had kept a horse down there for 12 years, so he had squatters' rights. Network Rail owned the land and they didn't even know he was there! Apparently there was also a wild kestrel nesting in one of the stands at Highbury and the work there had to cease. I asked if they were certain about this and they said they were, but then I asked if this kestrel had a bell round its foot. It was the bird that we used to keep the pigeons away!' In fact, the building programme was scheduled to take 30 months, but it was completed in 29 and the new stadium opened for Dennis Bergkamp's testimonial match in July 2006. That was, as Friar says, 'a fantastic achievement'.

Friar admits that the move from the Highbury stadium that had been so much part of his life was an emotional one. 'I had a few difficult moments over at Highbury on the last day. You can imagine how I felt, because my whole life had been wrapped up in that one building, but the last match there was special. We even had fireworks that were let off from Emirates – it was symbolic, if you like.' Also symbolic was the relocation of the famous bust of Herbert Chapman, that used to have pride of place in the Marble Halls at Highbury and which now sits in the Club's offices at Highbury House, emphasizing its long history and respect for tradition.

A state-of-the-art stadium

Emirates is without doubt one of the most amazing modern football stadiums in Europe. It has comfortable seats, stylish dressing rooms, elegant restaurants and bars, and an impressive media centre. The playing surface at Emirates is 113 x 76 metres, compared to 105 x 70 metres at Highbury, but the new pitch is as perfect as the old one. Indeed, the swooping lines of the stadium's top edge were specifically designed to ensure the grass receives as much light and air as possible, to keep it in tip-top condition. As well as being a football stadium, Emirates is used as a conference centre – in March 2008 it hosted an important, and, given the Club's French connections, rather fitting, meeting between British prime minister Gordon Brown and French president Nicolas Sarkozy – and a concert venue – in May 2008 Bruce Springsteen and the E Street Band were the first act to perform there.

However, above all Emirates is an exhilarating place to watch football. The dates emblazoned on the boards at the front of the upper tier proudly remind spectators and players alike of the years in which Arsenal has won titles and trophies – the empty spaces wait for future successes to be added. Well over a century of history has come together in Emirates Stadium and although it's probably fair to say that David Danskin and the workmates who gathered at the Royal Oak in Woolwich in 1886 would be astounded by Emirates and what Arsenal is today, they would undoubtedly recognize the ethos of the Club, its love of football and its desire to continue challenging for new honours.

Index

K

Kanu, Nwankwo **274, 276, 279, 280, 281, 283, 284, 289, 295**
  signing of **268–9, 270**
Kelly, Eddie **140, 142, 143, 144, 150, 154, 164–5**
Kelsey, Jack **108, 109, 112, 118, 123**
Kelso, Phil **29, 30**
Kennedy, Ray **140, 141, 142, 143, 147, 148, 151, 152, 158, 159, 160, 161, 164**
Kent Junior and Senior Cups **24**
Keown, Martin **219, 223, 225, 250, 264–5, 268, 270, 272, 275, 281, 284, 296, 301, 302, 303, 304**
  emergence of **183, 230**
  goals **271, 287**
  re-signing of **210, 214, 215, 231**
  transferred to Leicester **308**
Keyser, Gerard **68**
Kidd, Brian **164, 168**
Kirchen, Alf **83, 86, 88**
Kiwomya, Chris **220**
Knighton, Leslie **31, 37–8, 48–9, 51, 60**

L

Lack, Leslie **87**
Lambert, Jack **61, 62, 69, 72, 78**
Larsson, Sebastian **21**
Lauren **285, 286, 287, 295, 302, 310**
Lawton, Tommy **111–12**
Lazio, Champions League game against **314–15**
League Championship wins, Arsenal
  1930/31 season **69**
  1932/33 season **71–2**
  1933/34 season **76–7**
  1934/35 season **78**
  1937/38 season **83–4**
  1947/48 season **94–8**
  1952/53 season **107–10**
  1970/71 Double-winning season **143–55, 162, 179**
  1988/89 season **194–200**
  1990/91 season **201–6**
  1997/98 Double-winning season **251, 259–68**
  2001/02 Double-winning season **291–6**
  2003/04 season **304–8**

League Cup final
  defeats **136–7, 139, 192–3, 318**
  victories **190–1, 210–11**
League Cup upsets **139, 142, 173, 182–3, 184**
Leeds City Scandal **45–7**
Leeds United
  1968 League Cup final victory over Arsenal **136–7**
  1970/71 battle with Arsenal for title **144, 146–52**
  1972 FA Cup final victory over Arsenal **158–60, 162–3**
Lehmann, Jens **303–4, 305, 307, 309, 310, 311, 316, 317**
Lewin, Gary **188–9, 228, 239, 267**
Lewis, Albert **44**
Lewis, Dan **53–4, 60, 61**
Lewis, Reg **83, 88, 89, 93, 95, 96, 97, 98, 99, 100, 101, 102, 103**
Limpar, Anders **201, 202, 205, 207, 216, 217, 231**
Linighan, Andy **201, 207, 210, 213, 214**
Lishman, Doug **98, 101–2, 103, 104, 110, 111**
Liverpool
  1950 FA Cup victory over **100**
  1971 FA Cup final victory over **153–5**
  1987 League Cup final victory over **190–1**
  1989 victory over to win League title **198–9, 218**
  2001 FA Cup final defeat to **288, 290–1**
  2002 Community Shield match against **298**
  2008 Champions League defeat by **253, 319–20**
Ljungberg, Freddie **268–9, 270, 281, 309**
  goals **278, 279, 282, 284, 287, 289–90, 292, 293, 295, 296, 299, 302, 305, 310, 315**
Lloyd-Davies, Edwin **44**
Logie, Jimmy **94–5, 96, 98, 100, 104, 108, 109, 110, 112**
London Charity Cup **24**
London Colney **9, 17, 18, 19, 189, 249**
London Senior Cup **24, 26**
Loughborough Town, 12–0 record win against **16**
'Lucky' Arsenal tag **27, 35, 63, 64**

Picture credits